THE LIFE OF
ST. ANTHONY MARY CLARET

"At all times I am thinking of remedies for these great evils [attacks by anti-Catholics]. After much consideration, I see clearly that the best antidote for such poisonous attacks is the formation of good priests, priests who are learned, virtuous, zealous, given to prayer. Not less necessary is the need of catechizing and preaching to the youth of all classes and the propagating of good books and leaflets. There is still faith in Israel if we get to work. Courage, then, do not be dismayed. At the sight of the virtue and strength of good priests, the impious lose their audacity and boldness."

Sursum Corda

—*St. Anthony Mary Claret*
Autobiography, Ch. 4, Part 4

St. Anthony Mary Claret
1807-1870   63
Missionary, Archbishop, Founder
(This photograph was taken in 1857.)

Feast Day Aug 23

THE LIFE OF
ST. ANTHONY MARY CLARET

~~Modern~~ Apostle *of Catalonia*

(Former Title: *Saint Anthony Claret—Modern Prophet and Healer*)

by

FANCHÓN ROYER

"I will teach the unjust thy ways: and the wicked shall be converted to thee."
—*Psalm 1:15*

TAN BOOKS AND PUBLISHERS, INC.
Rockford, Illinois 61105

Copyright © 1957 by Fanchón Royer.

Previously published in 1957 by Farrar, Straus and Cudahy, New York, and Ambassador Books, Ltd., Toronto. Reprinted by arrangement with Farrar, Straus and Giroux.

Library of Congress Catalog Card No.: 85-52248

ISBN: 0-89555-288-4

Printed and bound in the United States of America.

TAN BOOKS AND PUBLISHERS, INC.
P.O. Box 424
Rockford, Illinois 61105

1985

To

The Missionary Sons of the Immaculate Heart of Mary
whose devotion and generosity have renewed
in our country
Spain's priceless gift to America

Summer 2011

CONTENTS

FOREWORD

When our Holy Father, Pope Pius XII, on May 7, 1950, raised Anthony Maria Claret to the ranks of the saints, the world witnessed once again the triumph in the court of heaven of one who had experienced disappointment and frustration in his response here on earth to the impulses of divine grace. As we review the extraordinary succession of events which culminated in the canonization of this completely dedicated servant of God, there can be no doubt that from his earliest days Divine Providence had marked him out for a career of outstanding achievement in the service of the Church. What impresses us most strikingly is that his growth in personal holiness and his heroic struggles for the sanctification of his fellow men seemed to follow pathways which human prudence might have avoided. Nor can we overlook, in retrospect, the indications which Anthony Claret's life affords of the heavenly reward which is always consequent upon generous and unfailing self-sacrifice. Those who give themselves entirely to God can conquer reverses of fortune which too often lead only to discouragement and failure when they afflict those whose devotion to heavenly ideals is divided and calculating.

In the early years of his life, Anthony Claret might well have been regarded as vacillating and emotionally unstable. He became successively a specialist in the trade of his father, a volunteer in the army, a student of languages and of engrav-

ing. When he decided to follow the higher life, he received
ordination as a diocesan priest, thought for a time of becoming a Carthusian priest, became a novice in the Society of
Jesus and finally returned to the status of a diocesan priest.
His widely diversified interests might have been reproved, in
one of less consuming energy and zeal, as desultory and
superficial.

The fruits of his efforts were, however, abundant and un-
mistakable. Gradually he became known as a man of God
from whom unusual success might be expected even in assignments which ordinary people could not be asked to undertake. In 1851 the post of Archbishop of Santiago in Cuba was
offered to him after its responsibilities had proved too heavy
for his predecessors to bear. To accept it meant to withdraw
his active support from the Congregation of the Missionary
Sons of the Immaculate Heart of Mary, which he had founded
only two years before, and which was to prove to be so important in the diffusion of his apostolic zeal. Yielding to the
will of God, he found himself once more in a new environ-
ment, with new problems and disappointments, and new
sources of suffering. Only the power of God's grace, of which
he was the obedient instrument, can explain the amazing
transformation which he was able to bring about in Santiago
within the short span of nine years.

Again, however, it became evident that God had destined
him not for the rewards that provide the incentive for natural striving, but for the painful tribulations which test the
faith of those who lift their eyes to the eternal rewards of
heaven. The people who owed so much to him repudiated
him. No less than fifteen attempts were made on his life and
he was saved only by miraculous intervention from the consequences of a brutally inflicted wound. Recalled to his native
land by what may have been meant as a merciful intervention

on his behalf, he continued his self-immolating priestly ministry until shortly before his death in 1870.

Anthony Claret was a century ahead of his time. His forward-looking plans lacked only the material advantages of our own age to bring them to fruitful realization. Priests of today can find in him not only an inspiring example, but a pioneer worker in the fields of the apostolate which they must cultivate. Teaching, writing, preaching missions, the direction of souls—all these works of the ministry were raised to unprecedented levels of perfection in the priestly life of Anthony Claret. His life was not that of a man who became a priest; it was the life of Christ our Lord, renewing itself in one who accepted, without reservation, the immolation of human nature which the priesthood demands.

The Claretians, spiritual sons of an eminently zealous and saintly founder, will become better known and esteemed throughout the English-speaking world with the publication of this book. May they multiply their beneficent works as they extend in space and time the divinely inspired apostolate of St. Anthony Claret. May this great saint of God remain for them and for all of us a powerful intercessor in heaven as we strive to uphold the ideals of virtue to which he dedicated his life.

RICHARD J. CUSHING
Archbishop of Boston

PREFACE

FANCHÓN ROYER, who has won a distinguished place in hagiological literature, has presented to the American people a modern saint and a friend in her latest book, *St. Anthony Claret*.

Mrs. Fanchón Royer came to know Claret by her contact with the Claretians in California on the occasion of producing moving pictures of the Missions and of seminary activities. She discovered the founder of the Congregation of Sons of the Immaculate Heart of the Blessed Virgin (Claretian Fathers) and loved him. Her work is the fruit of this knowledge and love.

St. Anthony Mary Claret is a modern saint. We give him this title not particularly because he was canonized in modern times, in the jubilee year 1950, but because his spirit, aspirations and methods were as modern as they could be if he were living today. The right of Claret's title to modernity is evident as the following points show. He was an expert and successful craftsman. In his business, as well as in his educational ministries, he made extensive use of his artistic draftsmanship. Thus he established the visual educational method particularly in the teaching of catechism. Pope Pius XI called him "the precursor of Catholic Action." The present Pope Pius XII enumerates several undertakings and declares that they were "a prelude of modern Catholic Action." These undertakings are: the establishment of committees to succor those confined to their homes, of orphanages for abandoned children, of lending libraries for the underprivileged, of various kinds of workshops, of saving associations and of lay societies for the defense of religion, chief among which was the Academy of St. Michael for Artists and Writers. Claret's modern spirit is revealed also in his foundations, since among them we see a secular institute, the Daughters of the Most Holy Heart of Mary or Religious in Their Homes. These institutes have been recently counted among the States of Perfection. Another outstanding feature of Claret's modernity is described by the same Pope Pius XII in his bull of canonization in these terms: "This varied and extraordinary form of apostolate . . . presaged in a certain manner the important reforms introduced in the pontificate of Our Predecessor Pius X. In this respect, suffice it here to mention the division of the catechism into three parts which were so deftly explained by him that they were accepted by nearly all the dioceses of Spain; the restoring of *decorum* in liturgical ceremonies; the propagating of Gregorian chant and establishing of boys' choirs; finally, the reorganization of the seminary of Santiago, Cuba, and later of the Escorial in Spain, which became a center of piety and learning and an example worthy of imitation." We may consider as a modern trend the fond interest in the welfare of children and powerful endeavors to raise to higher level the condition of the poor, the ignorant, and the worker. Claret distinguished himself in this interest and endeavor in a remarkable manner. This is also a point emphasized in the bull of canonization: ". . . he spent himself . . . never tiring of hearing confessions, seeking out small children and catechizing them so that they might learn their faith as they began their schooling, visiting the sick, assisting the dying, and on occasions curing purulent ulcers, defending the downtrodden, rendering help and solace to the needy and afflicted." Finally, Claret's modern spirit is shown by the gigantic use he made of the press as a means of religious instruction.

How the workers would delight in watching Claret managing his weaving factory and giving a helpful hand to the employees! He won over the hearts of the farmers by organizing a model farm as a school of agriculture when he was archbishop of Santiago, Cuba. The common people avidly read Claret's numerous books dealing with their daily problems. The workers of today will look at the humble laborer in the weaving industry with hearty approval, and will feel a sort of class pride seeing Claret rise though reluctantly to the dignity of archbishop and become the adviser of the royal family. They will love Claret particularly because in the midst of all this glamour he looked forward with a longing heart at the glory of dying without money, without debt and without sins.

Claret was a true friend of America. During the Vatican Council that he attended, he met Bishop Amat of Los Angeles, California. When Claret found out that the bishop needed expert sisters to teach young girls in his diocese, Claret heartily recommended the Sisters of the Immaculate Heart of Mary for this purpose. The bishop gladly accepted the recommendation. Claret predicted a glorious future for the Church in America. His love for America was with him to his last day. Just a little before his death, noticing that one of the co-founders of his Congregation had come to visit him, he made an effort to rise from the bed and in this position he whispered, "America." Then he paused for awhile and pathetically he pleaded: "You will go to the United States!" When the visitor assured the dying man that he would comply with his wishes, the archbishop relaxed happily.

Claret's spirit was fashioned so much after the pattern of the American spirit that any American who knows him will love him.

MANUEL MILAGRO, C.M.F.

THE LIFE OF
ST. ANTHONY MARY CLARET

"O my God, I should not like Thee to say of me what Thou didst say of the priests of Israel: 'You have not gone up to face the enemy, nor have you set up a wall for the house of Israel, to stand in battle in the day of the Lord.' (*Ezechiel* 13:5). Thou dost say, O my God: 'I sought among them for a man that might set up a hedge, and stand in the gap before me in favor of the land, that I might not destroy it: and I found none.'(*Ezechiel* 22:30)."

—St. Anthony Mary Claret
Autobiography, Ch. 16, Part 3

I

THE SON

HAD THE FORTHRIGHT Catalonian inhabitants of Sallent been asked to name their model boy, the unhesitant reply would have been: "Juan Claret's third, young Anthony." And they might have added that the weaver's son was also the smallest lad of his age in the whole town, though any day now his slight frame would probably begin to shoot up and fill out, justifying the promise of his well-developed head and wide, heavy-featured face. Then someone might have mentioned the fact that this little Toñín with the large dark eyes had been born on Christmas Eve—a most excellent omen! How they had all felicitated Josefa Clará and her good husband because Heaven had sent their new offspring precisely on *La Noche Buena* so that the most joyous of all the great feasts could be his baptismal day! It was indeed on the Miracle Birthday itself, Christmas 1807, that his name was inscribed in St. Mary's parish record: Antonio Juan Adjutor Claret y Clará.

When, almost at once, this Christmas babe escaped a fatal accident, the people of Sallent had naturally interpreted such a blessing as the confirmation of Heaven's special favor. The difficulty arose because of Josefa's poor health. Unable to nurse this fifth of the eleven children her love was to welcome into the Claret home, she was forced to turn him over to a wet nurse and see him installed in a rented cottage occupied by the nurse and her children. At the time the woman's landlord was making an excavation to extend the cellar of the little dwelling; a project which, owing to a miscalculation or some other carelessness, caused the catastrophe. In the middle of the night the cottage suddenly collapsed, killing the nurse and her four sons! How did the Claret baby miss the same grievous end? An act of God surely! Josefa had carried him home to spend just that one fatal night!

Was the story of his seemingly miraculous rescue partially responsible for Anthony's surprisingly early preoccupation with the subject of eternity? We have his statement that, at no more than five years of age, *siempre*—the Spanish word for "forever"—fascinated and terrified him. He would lie awake for hours in the nights whispering *siempre* over and over, listening with foreboding to the threat in its soft syllables, while his imagination conjured up vistas of endless reaches of time. If only one year of his young life seemed so long, a light punishment so appalling, what of the interminable hereafter which he already knew must be punishment "forever and ever" for all who failed to love and obey Our Lord on earth? Toñín also knew that there were many who callously disobeyed God; and when he thought of this, it plunged him into deep depression. His natural compassion was so great that if he imagined the sufferings of others, even people he had never seen, his heart felt scalded by pain. At these times his only consolation was his dream that one day, having grown older and much wiser, he might devise a way to rescue all the careless or ignorant people who appeared impervious to that terrifying concept which haunted his black, wakeful nights—*siempre*. Surely they would heed the warning that he must cry out to them and, reforming their ways, let themselves be saved from the awful eternity in store for sinners!

In spite of this extraordinary anxiety in a five-year-old the precocious Toñín was not a morbid child. Actually, he was bland and good-natured, of a cheerful, if quiet, disposition. The distress he experienced alone at night and which, at the time, he confided to no one, was not initiated by timidity but by that prodigious sense of responsibility for his fellow human beings, itself an outgrowth of his natural generosity and affection. He was quite as unable to think of himself first as most boys are unable to consider the good of others ahead of their selfish interests. Remembering his childhood, Anthony Claret did not credit himself. He wrote with simplicity: "I received from God, solely as the result of His goodness, a good nature and disposition." *

II

His first seven years, spent in the high, narrow house in Cos Street above Juan Claret's cloth-making establishment, saw Spain embroiled in the bitter struggle to throw off the Napoleonic yoke which was known as the War of Independence. Catalonia was repeatedly overrun by the French troops. Among other depredations, they burned the nearby towns of Manresa and Calders. Periodically, before the menace of the advancing enemy, the villagers of Sallent would pour out of their homes and streets to take refuge in the rugged mountains flanking the town their ancestors had strung along the banks of the Llobregat river.

For Toñín, the earlier flights were exciting rides on the shoulders of his father or his cousins. When he was five,

* See the notes in the back of this book for an explanation of the source of this and ensuing quotations.

however, he abruptly put an end to this procedure, not from a wish to appear manly, but simply because he couldn't bear to think of his half-blind old grandfather stumbling along somewhere farther and farther behind the rest, all alone with his anxiety and his handicap. The little boy insisted on accompanying Josefa's father, Juan Clará, in the rear of the refugee column. Clasping the gnarled hand, he would carefully lead his grandfather around the obstacles cluttering their path of flight. His whole attention centered on aiding the old man, this child who shrank at the mere idea of *siempre* thought not at all of immediate and tangible danger. Meanwhile, he developed a love for the aged that he would never lose.

This made it impossible for him, in later years, to join the groups of mocking boys who made sport of the eccentricities and infirmities of the old. And when the parish church was crowded for Mass, he always gave up his seat to the first "old one" he saw standing. As the favorite of Sallent's approving oldsters, young Anthony became the recipient of their confidences and counsel. Perceiving the value of their experiences and enjoying their stories more than play, he made many opportunities to talk with them and listened attentively to the wisdom they had for him. Throughout his lifetime he called this rapport with the aged: "One of the many graces God has given me."

School began for Anthony with his sixth birthday when his parents sent him to study with Maestro Pascual. A good and punctual student, he was never punished or scolded. His teacher placed strong emphasis on the study of catechism, in which Anthony was soon letter-perfect. With three of his classmates he was able to make a faultless recitation for the parish pastor before a churchful of parishioners when their proud instructor presented the boys for this public demonstration. (All his life Anthony Claret would preserve a holy picture, the prize he was awarded on this occasion.) Although he frankly admitted that while he was committing the catechism "parrot-fashion" he had not comprehended its wording, he would always consider this effort his most important primary study. For very soon he began to connect the catechism answers with the religious truths his parents had already taught him in simpler terms. And when he consciously pursued this identification of familiar facts with previously unclear passages from the work he knew to incorporate the sum of Christian doctrine it became a fascinating adventure of which he exclaimed: "Now I understand! This means that, and that. How dull I must have been not to have seen it before!"

grew into it

He would come to believe also that, even while the terminology of the catechism had seemed obscure, much of its meaning was being impressed on his subconscious from the very beginning. But however it happened, Anthony Claret would always maintain that his thorough grounding in catechism proved his greatest asset during the unsure years of youth, particularly those spent away from his family in a strange city. When faced with a new problem, a sudden emergency or, of course, any temptation, he never lacked an undeviating rule for his guidance, a rule so deeply rooted in his mind and conscience that it operated automatically to assure his triumph over the natural confusions and invitations to error that beset the majority of adolescents, not excluding those from devout Catholic households. This infusion of *exact* truth, he said, freed him from interior struggles over matters moral and ethical. He gives us an example. What to do with a coin picked up in the street posed no problem. The idea of pocketing it on the theory that he had no way of positively identifying its rightful owner didn't even occur to him. Reasoning that it had probably been dropped from the balcony of the house above, he unhesitatingly knocked on the door and restored the coin to an amazed householder. He never experienced the usual adolescent dissatisfaction with the parents he knew to have been appointed by Providence to constitute authority for him. It was not even admissible, he felt, to importune them for special privileges. When his devoted mother occasionally asked his preference when she wished to make him a gift, she knew what his reply would be: "I always like whatever you give me."

"But we all prefer some things to others," she would urge gently.

"Well, what I prefer is what you give me."

Are we inclined to label such tractability in the young, "abnormal" or, at the least, "stuffy"? If so, why? If we accept the axiom that "father—or mother—knows best," certainly when father—or mother—is a fine Christian parent intent upon nothing but the child's good, why should we be amazed to find the child agreeing with us? In any case, the atmosphere of harmony which pervaded the unpretentious provincial home that sheltered Toñín Claret's boyhood is not difficult to understand in view of this son's unselfishness and the high respect in which he held his parents.

It was also natural that for a boy of this sort his earliest ambition was for the priesthood. He first spoke of this desire when a visitor to his primary school happened to ask him about his plans for a career. His determined, "I am going to be a priest," was so convincing that it resulted in an invitation to join Dr. Juan Riera's Latin class. When he had completed his elementary studies, he transferred to this class with high hope. Unfortunately, however, before he had progressed beyond the rudiments of Latin grammar Padre Riera's death caused the discontinuance of the course.

III

Sallent was a community of only three hundred families and, although it had the distinction of being a hundred percent literate, it had no higher educational facilities. Juan Claret, in spite of his capability and industry, was not affluent enough to send his son to the seminary at Vich. Under the vacillating rule of Fernando VII, Spain had not yet recovered from the havoc wrought by the long war with Napoleon which had been so injurious to commerce. Moreover, the modest profits of the Claret enterprise (always dependent on the labor of the entire family), had all gone into the purchase of a new, considerably more spacious house in which the small factory could function more efficiently. It seemed that the lad who wanted to become a priest had reached the end of his formal schooling—the end of his dream!

He was now taken into the shop. He did not complain because of the ruin of his personal plans, but applied himself willingly to mastering the weaver's art and trade. While Josefa and her daughters spun the thread and his brother, also Juan, worked beside the hired help at the looms, Anthony was assigned to all manner of jobs with thread and fabric. This experience, supplemented by his characteristic diligence, soon made him an expert craftsman; whereupon he was entrusted with the supervision of his co-workers.

Although his father may have suffered qualms that this best of sons had lost the opportunity of becoming the Claret family's first priest, his sense of the practical recognized that bringing the boy into the shop had been a most advantageous move. The death of the Clarets' second boy, Bartolomé, had left only Juan and Anthony now of an age to fill responsible, full-time positions; and the latter gave every promise of becoming invaluable in the organization. Not only had he learned the techniques in record time, but it was clear that he instinctively _knew_ men! Relations with the laborers had never been as good at the plant. Anthony had a genius for gentleness. Without lessening his firmness in dealing with the errors in the employees' output, he preserved their self-respect and good will. Young as he was, he had already proved himself a capable foreman!

It is unlikely that the senior Claret ever realized that his own gruff, if well-intentioned, reproofs for slipshod workmanship were the source of much embarrassment to sensitive Anthony or that, more than anything else, they had inspired his son's very different tactics with the men. Certainly this obedient youth would never have presumed to criticize his beloved and respected parent, but he couldn't help seeing that these brusque reprimands not only gave rise to resentment but occasionally confused the chagrined workmen so that they scarcely knew how to go about correcting their mistakes.

As his authority increased, Anthony approached the problem of correction in an altogether different manner. "Before pointing out the defects of the faulty work I would commence by praising its good points, saying that it was a creditable job only that a little slip had been made here and another one there, but if these were corrected the work would be perfect. . . . Presented in this way, the workers accepted my corrections with humility and amended their mistakes. . . ."

The modern psychologist is not the original fellow he would have us believe. But neither, Anthony Claret assured us, was he. For, as in all his successes, he traced this insight into the human heart and his gift for evoking willing cooperation to the authentic Source. At first, "I knew not why I did this, but afterward I recognized it to have been from a special grace of gentleness which the good Lord had given me."

IV

His childhood devotion to religion continued. He heard Mass as frequently as possible on week days. On Sundays and feast days he invariably heard both the High and a Low Mass. He had always been especially attracted by devotions honoring the Blessed Sacrament. (During his primary school days he had been so captivated by a book his father gave him, entitled *Finezas de Jesús Sacramentado* [The Goodnesses of Our Sacramental Lord], that he had committed it to memory.) Now it was one of his several devotions. Since making his First Holy Communion at the then extraordinarily early age of ten, he received the Sacrament with great frequency. And each Sunday and Holy Day he would return to church for the afternoon and evening devotions.

His heart was deeply stirred by prayers to, and contemplation of, our Blessed Mother. The presence of the Virgin was very real to him. "Praying in church before Our Lady of the Holy Rosary never tired me, and I addressed her with such confidence that I was firmly convinced the Most Holy Virgin heard me. I used to imagine a sort of wire line proceeding from the image I was praying before to the original in Heaven. At that time I had never seen electric telegraph, but I used to envision some such system between the image and Heaven."

In view of this special love for Our Lady it was natural that he rejoiced and found relaxation in the daily recital of the Rosary in his father's shop. Three times during the working day (which commenced at 8 A.M., and continued until 9 P.M.!), the chatter of the looms gave place to a reverent hum as the crew prayed in unison one of the three sections of the Rosary. There was nothing particularly unusual about this in those times when the people of Spain, and the Catalonians especially, were in general exceedingly pious. "In addition to the entire Rosary that I offered every work day, I also used to say a Hail Mary each time the clock struck the hour. Then too, I knelt to say the Angelus at the proper time."

Such diversion as this serious young man required he enjoyed in his own home. Even as a small boy he had felt no inclination to seek the companionship of children outside. And he never took any satisfaction in aimless social activities.

It would be wrong, however, to assume that Anthony Claret's natural piety was an indication that his eventual sanctity was preordained; that it demanded little, if any, effort on his part. Like all of us, he had to meet and struggle with his personal forms of temptation. That his temptation may have been to a subtler variety of sin than ours, doubtless made it more painful. Anthony was not spared the full agony of contrition, nor the most rigorous self-discipline. Even as a child he had once been struck "as by a bolt from the blue," by a spiritual test which was augmented by its utter inexplicability. In spite of his deep devotion to the Virgin he was, incredibly, tempted to blasphemous thoughts against her; and this, precisely while he was praying to her! And now he found it necessary to confess that he was suddenly and just as mysteriously assailed by a fierce aversion to the earthly mother he so greatly respected and whose tender love for him he had always reciprocated with his whole heart! When his confessor asked what steps he had taken to vanquish this evil, he replied that he had merely increased his prayer and made sure to show Josefa more gentleness and humility than before this fantastic humor had fallen upon him.

"Who advised you to practice these things?" asked the amazed priest.

"No one, Padre."

"Then God Himself is your teacher, my son. *You* have only to go ahead being faithful to His grace."

More prayer, more love and more humility before temptation—it was as simple as that. For the conquest of these drastic and distressing trials, the Divine Wisdom had granted young Anthony Claret the perfect method, a method equally applicable to the most ordinary temptations.

II

THE CRAFTSMAN

SEVENTEEN-YEAR-OLD Anthony had mastered all that his father's factory could teach him. Textile production and, especially, the art and technical execution of design now absorbed all his interest. He walked around the shop and, on holidays, along the familiar streets of Sallent in perpetual excitement, his head filled with ideas for new patterns and the machine adjustments required for their achievement.

Juan Claret recognized that his son had the skill and enthusiasm to reach the very top of their profession. He therefore approved Anthony's proposal that he be sent to Barcelona, Catalonia's great textile center, to complete his training by familiarizing himself with the latest improvements in the cloth-making industry. He would surely return to the family plant so expert a director of weavers that it would be well worth the temporary loss of his services. Moreover, except for the immediate sacrifice, the project would not be a financial drain on the family—which now numbered six children. (Five of the Claret children had died before 1825.) The employment the youth could easily obtain in the city factories would defray his living expenses, books and instruction.

and capital city of Catalonia

12

But to assure himself of his boy's safe establishment in Barcelona, Juan Claret went with him on his journey.

Anthony secured work immediately—with the prominent firm, *Los Vigantes*. He also enrolled in the school conducted by the Board of Trade, where he undertook courses in drawing, Castilian and French. The first he considered essential for his perfection in design, while a command of languages would be advantageous, not only to his study, but in his future business negotiations. (His first tongue was, of course, Catalán.) He also studied geography, mathematics, and astronomy. Every moment of the day and far into the nights over his books, he concentrated furiously to increase his value to the industry which now dominated his imagination to the point of obsession. ". . . all this constant writing, studying and drawing on work days as well as holidays cost me much labor, but I reaped great benefit from it. . . . And afterward when my courses had been successfully completed, I knew a joy and satisfaction that used to make me walk about the house wild with happiness."

At this time he would have declared that nothing short of attaining the stature of Spain's very finest fabric designer could satisfy his ambition! He sent away for all the latest London and Paris patterns. After meticulously studying, he tested them on the looms, with such success that he surprised himself.

"This sort of work came to me without instruction, or rather, instead of teaching me how to analyze and perfect patterns, the past-masters of the art hid it from me." He did not explain this comment. Was the technique he acquired by independent study and experimentation involuntarily withheld by poor teaching, or deliberately, by the envy of the experts? In any case, he recognized his aptitudes for his chosen work as his best assets. ". . . of all the subjects I have ever studied, all the things to which I have directed my attention in life, there is none I have understood so well as factory work."

Señor Ferrer, superintendent of *Los Vigantes*, was soon accepting the suggestions of this eager and ingenious youth on patterns, relying on him to direct the machine adaptations for their proper execution. His admiration for Anthony made him like to be with him and he frequently invited the village boy to go walking with his sons and himself. Anthony profited by the lessons and example given him by his employer, a man of intelligence and integrity. And meanwhile, the other workers came to depend on the newcomer's dexterity both in fixing the new designs on the looms and in repairing the machines when they occasionally broke down. All these abilities very quickly made his name known throughout the city's extensive textile trade. Certain substantial financial interests were already considering a means of exploiting the talents of young Claret.

He was pleased by his rapidly won prestige. A good salary allowed him to dress well and he knew he was cutting quite a figure in his own circle. However, all his real joy lay in the work itself, which grew more fascinating by the day. True, there were certain decidedly uncomfortable moments in the realization that, under the impact of this "delirium," his religious fervor was steadily cooling. He heard Mass regularly and said the Rosary daily, but he realized that his devotions had come to be almost mechanical. He had abandoned the childhood dream of the priesthood, but he certainly wished to think of himself as a devout Christian; and the difficulty he now encountered in following Mass and saying his prayers with attention was most disturbing. Actually, Maestro Pascual's prize catechism pupil was still very much alive somewhere below the surface to stir the conscience of Barcelona's most promising young weaver and designer. No matter how overpowering his interest in the

fine work that had already set him apart, he could not escape
the implications of his earliest lessons. He felt that life could
not be justified by any degree of skill at the tracing board,
or before the most fascinating of machines! Memory nudged
him with the old, deeply impressed lines: *"Why did God
make you?"* *"To know Him, to love Him and to serve Him
in this world; and to be happy with Him forever in Heaven."*

He repeatedly resolved to banish the distractions that were
devitalizing his prayer. But it was a heartbreaking struggle.
"My efforts were useless, for crowds of thoughts came rushing upon me like a wheel that revolves so rapidly it cannot
stop. Besides, there came to me during Mass new ideas, new
discoveries, etc. There were more machines in my head than
saints on the altar, and all this only contributed to my un-
easiness." In this contest between his rightly-disposed will
and his compelling inclination, we find Anthony Claret's
strongest, most stubborn temptation. That it was for nothing worse than perfection in his work—an ambition generally
conceded to be a virtue—did not lessen its inherent danger
to his soul.

II

There now came another reversal of direction for his great
gift of dedication, although the crises that, together, were to
achieve spiritual victory arose from circumstances outside
his control. The first of these was a concrete offer from a
financier wishing to back a company to utilize Anthony's
outstanding skill in the work to which he had been fully ex-
pecting to devote his whole future. That the proposition was
first submitted to Juan Claret for approval may have been
owing to Anthony's extreme youth; but care had also been
taken to include provisions well calculated to be most attractive to the father himself. The plan was to form a new
organization which would absorb the Claret establishment

and Juan would figure prominently. The whole family would benefit by this expansion; while the clever son, as director of the factory, would be afforded a splendid personal opportunity.

Juan Claret was delighted. After his lifetime battle to survive war-induced depression and repeated political upheavals, the unanticipated availability of big capital in a steadily improving market looked like the fulfillment of all his effort. He was proud of the son whose success had made possible this welcome advance in their material prospects. And now, too, in his own old age he would have the comforting assurance that he had at last brought his loved ones through to prosperity!

Confident that his son would share his enthusiasm, he hastened to tell Anthony the great news and to explain the various favorable ramifications of the proposition. The manufacture of excellent and lovely fabric was the central interest of them both. Now at last they would command undreamed-of facilities for the achievement of ever-better results!

It must have been a deep disappointment to be met by hesitation and, finally, to understand from Anthony's almost inarticulate temporizing that his son was definitely opposed. "While I loved factory work so much and had made progress in it . . . I could not bring myself to resolve to embrace this fair business opening. On the contrary, I recoiled before the idea of accepting these opportunities so welcomed by my father. I told him that this did not seem to be the right time for it as I was very young and, moreover, so small that the workers would resent being ordered about by me. My father replied that this should cause me no anxiety, because any other foremen could handle the help, while I devoted myself wholly to the factory direction. But my only answer was that later we would see since, at the moment, I was not inclined to take such a step."

Juan Claret found this reaction inexplicably vague and confusing. He knew just how well his weavers always had taken his son's direction. But the indications were clear. Anthony wanted no part of the proposition that had been so heartening to himself! It was a double blow. It not only meant the loss of a material opportunity which might never come again, but it was the first open opposition his son had ever offered him. However, Juan Claret proved himself a forbearing, rather than an outraged, parent.

At that time Anthony was almost as surprised by his strong aversion to this development as was his father. Later, however, he would remember that he had just been undergoing a very trying experience. For days a warning had been beating in his head—incessantly: *"What doth it profit a man if he gain the whole world and suffer the loss of his soul?"* Why had these long-familiar words come to distract and, finally, overwhelm him just now, when the fulfillment of his ambition, the reward of all his study and labor, was at hand? He longed to be able to forget the disappointment and mystification on the honest face of his good father while he had been quibbling and dodging without knowing why. Well, thank God, parental love had won the fight in the heart of Juan Claret. The subject of the new factory had been dropped and life had gone on as before in Sallent, sustained only by the little plant which had always absorbed the labor of the hard-working Clarets!

III

THE SEMINARIAN

IT WAS in Barcelona that things began to change, at first almost imperceptibly. The work proceeded and Anthony continued to enjoy it and the esteem it brought him. Nevertheless, a sense of unreality was settling over his activities. What was the origin of this growing doubt that the manufacture of anything, even the finest cloth in all Spain, was justification for the absorption it demanded at the expense of the complete man, who has a soul to save and grave responsibilities to his neighbors, as well as an intelligence and a body to train? The ideal, of course, had been excellence in the execution of useful labor. But the proof of that excellence would inevitably be manifested in prestige and material benefits, would it not? How could he be sure the rewards might not become ends in themselves? And so it would commence again, that relentless refrain: "*What doth it profit a man...?*"

And now, two melodramatic experiences shocked him into a realization that the worldly life is, indeed, beset by most dangerous pitfalls. The first involved an unanticipated incitement to carnal sin by a determined young woman whose intentions he had not remotely suspected. Only his automatic

18

also, ends do not justify the means (total absorption)

appeal to the Virgin for aid, he was ever-afterward convinced, vouchsafed his escape from the trap set for him by a female so malicious that, seeing her desire frustrated by his precipitous flight, she had run out onto a balcony to scream scandalously that she had just been insulted by the youth who was fleeing down the street!

The second disillusionment came from the perfidy of an acquaintance by whom he had been persuaded that they should pool their savings for investment purposes. All transactions were to be handled by the young promoter, whose idea of "investment" was the purchase of lottery tickets! However, a run of incredibly good luck had soon netted a substantial profit, deposited with Anthony for safe-keeping. Then one day when they had again made a large winning, his partner appeared to declare that he had "lost" the money, as he certainly had—in a card game. Soon thereafter, Anthony discovered that their entire capital was missing, along with his more valuable personal possessions. In a desperate attempt to retrieve the original loss, the gambler had sent good money after bad! Nor did he stop with this, but proceeded to steal some jewels from another house to which he had access. The proceeds from their sale was dissipated in the same way; and now, on the complaint of the lady he had robbed, the man was arrested, convicted, and sentenced to prison.

Although he was not greatly concerned over his monetary loss, Anthony suffered intensely before what he considered the cloud on his own good name. Many were aware of his association with the criminal. Would they be likely to believe in his innocence? For days, supposing himself an object of public contempt, he could hardly bear to step into the street. However, he soon saw with relief that it had occurred to no one to blame him for any part in his partner's defection.

Nevertheless, he began to lose his appetite, and then his health. It was the summer of 1828 and the heat aggravated his debility. Whenever he could manage it, he would join a group of acquaintances on little excursions to the shore. Wading in the cool surf of the "Old Sea" behind Barceloneta, he found relief and refreshment; and, during one such outing, the second definite crisis in his struggle toward spiritual certainty. This time the circumstances were more impressive than had been his reluctance to commit his future to a big new factory.

He had wandered off alone and was enjoying the surge of the water over his feet and ankles when, without the least warning, a gigantic wave lashed the shore and in a breathless flash swept him into the sea on its powerful back-roll! Before his stunned companions could make a move, he was far beyond reach of aid, and then entirely lost to view. Since his inability to swim was well known, he was soon given up for lost by his friends, who hastened away to notify his relatives.

We can only imagine what his first reaction was to this shocking occurrence, for surely no man has ever looked death in the face and reported his emotions in a manner more laconic. "I was struck by surprise to notice that, though unable to swim, I was floating on top of the waves, and, after invoking the Holy Mother of God, to find myself on shore [again] without even a drop of water having entered my mouth. During the time I was floating, I had remained as serene as could be, but afterward, when I had regained my feet on the shore, I trembled with fright at the thought of the danger I had escaped through the Most Blessed Virgin's intercession."

These brief, almost brusquely underwritten lines do, however, communicate the fact that the favored youth comprehended the magnitude of the miracle, and its meaning for him. His life has been saved in spectacular circumstances by the Virgin—to whose protective love he would now forever owe a very special debt. As a matter of fact, she had twice preserved his life within a few short months. He now marveled at his obtuseness in having failed to recognize what she had been requiring of him since that earlier, only slightly less dramatic escape. It had happened during his little vacation in Sallent the preceding January when, following a baptism, he had looked in on the dance given by the baby's parents. But since parties were little to his taste and dancing especially abhorrent, he had merely paid his respects to the hosts and then left. Hardly had he attained the street when the house had collapsed, causing the deaths of twenty-eight of the merrymakers![1] Aware, as he was, that twice in his life he had missed death beneath the ruins of a fallen edifice, why had he not instantly recognized the significance of the coincidence? Was he so insensitive that it had taken this last and much more direct look into the face of eternity to show him the point?

Well at least now he knew. Now the great riddle which had always lain at the center of his living was solved. Inasmuch as he owed his physical, as well as his moral preservation, and yes, even his good name, to Our Lady, he must now give it all back to her. It remained only to discover the best means for discharging so incalculable an obligation. Within a very few days he had convinced himself that the answer lay in a lifetime dedicated to prayer and praise as a Carthusian!

II

The first step would not be easy. He must tell his father, which he did during one of the latter's regular business trips to Barcelona. Juan Claret was as dismayed as Anthony had anticipated. After all, his son was twenty-one years old, a somewhat advanced age, according to the standards of the time, for beginning to prepare for a life in religion. And moreover, he was already a master in a field where his ex-

1829

ceptional gifts and aptitudes promised great things! At the very least, his father had looked forward to an expansion of his own factory when Anthony returned to Sallent. This new development meant the end of all the fine hopes of future achievement together. It was a kind of abandonment. And, of all things, why must the boy become a contemplative? Weren't secular priests for the vital work of the parishes always greatly needed?

A good Christian, however, Juan Claret recognized that the last word in so serious a matter could not be his. So, though not without real sorrow, he said: "God forbid that I might wish to deprive you of your vocation. But think well over it, commend it to Him, and consult with your spiritual director. If he says it is Our Lord's will, I shall submit and praise it, even though I shall feel it from the bottom of my heart. If it were possible for you to become a secular priest rather than a monk I should be pleased but, in any case, do His holy will!"

Greatly relieved by his father's kindness, Anthony immediately confided in the Oratorian Padre Amigó, who heard him out with attention. Then he counseled this earnest youth whose heart was already yearning for the quiet of the cloister to keep on with his factory work for the present, but meanwhile to resume his study of Latin. Although not quite as stimulating a prospect as Anthony might have desired, he realized that he should be grateful for even this much encouragement; and forthwith arranged to pick up his long-abandoned study of Latin under a Father Tomás, described as "a holy priest and a classical scholar." And then, for a second time, death robbed him of a Latin professor! But this time he transferred at once to the classes conducted by a still more famed Latinist, Padre Más y Artiga, where his enthusiasm, capacity for concentration and never-failing industry insured his rapid advance. In a few short months he was an able translator and could also converse readily.

His older brother Juan had married a daughter of Don Mauricio Casajuana, who was steward for certain Sallent properties belonging to the bishop of Vich. As these two were on intimate terms, Don Mauricio made a point of speaking to the bishop about his young relative-in-law whose dream it was to become a Carthusian. This resulted in the bishop's suggestion that Anthony be sent to him for an interview. Notified that the prelate wished to see him, Anthony felt only consternation. If he took advantage of this privilege would the bishop not attempt to influence him against the monastic life he coveted in favor of the secular priesthood? Perhaps his family had even hinted through Juan's father-in-law that this was their own hope. On the other hand, a mere student could hardly ignore a summons from the ecclesiastical authority!

He confided his worries to his professor who suggested seeking the advice of a St. Philip Neri priest named Cantí who was widely esteemed for his wisdom, prudence and experience. Padre Cantí listened sympathetically while Anthony painstakingly reviewed all his reasons for believing it inadvisable to present himself in Vich at this time. Though impressed by his manner, the priest could not agree with his logic. His tactful advice: "Go to Vich in the certainty that, if it is God's will that you join the Carthusians, his excellency will be the very last one to oppose it, and will even support you in it."

"This was enough for me; I was silent and obeyed him," wrote Anthony Claret many years later, observing his habitual brevity in reporting his purely personal reactions. Thus, at the beginning of September 1829, bringing to a close his four years of labor and professional success, he left Barcelona and, in accordance with his parents' desire to accompany him to Vich, proceeded to Sallent. There he passed some days with all his family before setting out—on St. Michael's Day, following an early Mass—in a steady drizzle which made a melancholy business of the long trudge over slippery mountain trails to the see city.

His brief comment, "We arrived in Vich that night soaked through to the skin" throws little light upon his general state of mind. Certainly neither it nor the succeeding observation suggests that he was aware of much elation: "Next day we went to see Bishop Pablo de Jesús Corcuera who gave us a cordial welcome." But, as it turned out, Anthony might have spared himself his anxiety on the score of the prelate's attitude regarding his future. Bishop Corcuera did not utter a word against the Carthusian plan when offering him a place in the diocesan seminary and a home with the palace chaplain, Padre Fortunato Bres.

III

So Anthony relaxed and turned his attention to the episcopal city which was to be his home for longer than he now imagined. And what he saw did inspire enthusiasm. Four times larger than Sallent, Vich was no bustling industrial community, but a cultural center, a very old Catalonian town whose three-mile extension was encircled by historic walls penetrated by nine gateways. Its twelve hundred houses were largely three-story stone structures whose massive façades followed the capricious curves of its narrow, cobbled streets. Above the homes jutted the steeples of the twenty-four churches which formed the spirit and focussed the life of the Vicenses, a citizenry quite indifferent to the fact that their single theater remained dark most of the year. (Even when some company did occupy it briefly, it was dismayed to find itself playing to an almost deserted house.)

Centered upon a high, mountain-girded plateau, Vich commanded magnificent vistas of snow-blanketed peaks and the nearer fruit orchards that were the boast of Catalonia. Its climate followed a cycle of contrasting heat and cold whose rigors "formed hardy bodies and stern souls." Home of generations of martyrs, religious founders, distinguished prelates and poets, its moral tone could hardly have been improved as an auspicious atmosphere for the training of seminarians. And so numerous were the candidates who presented themselves each term at the venerable seminary that, although it was spacious, it was inadequate to house them. Thus, at the time of Anthony's arrival, by far the majority were day students.[2] From the private lodgings it managed somehow to provide they overflowed all the town, filling the streets with their picturesque, full-swinging mantles that, rather than the soutane, were regulation garb. In conformance with seminary requirements, all these youths were the legitimate sons of "old Christians" whose grandfathers, as well as fathers, were known to have led exemplary lives. (Recent converts, usually Jews, were suspected of motives of convenience.)

Conversos

The less prosperous seminarians frequently obtained their livings in return for tutoring children, acting as secretaries, or lending their services in such other capacities as might be required by the families with which they resided. Naturally, these could not interfere with their duties as students. It seems possible that Padre Bres had anticipated using Anthony as secretary but, if so, he quickly changed his mind, for he immediately became aware of his young guest's outstanding intellectual gifts, spiritual attainment and industry, and was convinced that the time and energy of one so promising should all be devoted to the development of his potentialities.

The priest, his protégé, and one servant occupied plain comfortable quarters on the second floor of an old mansion facing on Dos Solas street in the higher and most desirable section of Vich. In his private chamber, a room thirteen by twenty-six feet, Anthony settled down beneath a portrait of St. Bruno, the Carthusian founder, to intensive study.

IV

Presently he again came into close touch with a St. Philip Neri Oratorian when Padre Bach was appointed his confessor. Padre Bach was greatly esteemed. Anthony made a general confession of his whole life to this wise and holy priest and then entered upon a schedule of weekly, and finally, semi-weekly confessions. In an epoch when it was not customary for seminarians to be conceded Communion oftener than twice monthly at fifteen-day intervals, he was permitted this privilege four times weekly. Daily, he served Padre Bres's Mass, devoted a half hour to mental prayer, visited the Blessed Sacrament and also the altar of Our Lady of the Holy Rosary in the Dominican church ("no matter how much it rained"). Even when the snow drifted high in the streets, he never missed these attentions to the Blessed Mother who had brought him to Vich!

"We read the lives of the saints every day at table; and with my director's consent I took the discipline three days a week, Mondays, Wednesdays and Fridays; and on Tuesdays and Saturdays I wore the hair shirt. With these devotional practices I regained my fervor without, however, relaxing in my application to study. . . ." In fact, he studied so un-remittingly that he contracted a chest disorder, though this does not seem to have been serious enough to have interrupted his work as a first year philosophy student.

While he did not conceal his monastic goal from Padres Bres and Bach, Anthony was careful not to divulge it to his classmates. Why? Did some premonition warn him that his own hold on his dream was, at best, precarious? Certainly he seems to have been <u>overconscious</u>, from the beginning, of some need to protect his determination from challenge; to be alert at all times to impending opposition. But Bishop Corcuera had not argued with him and Padre Bach had long since concluded that this young man doubtless had been destined by God to the Carthusians. The conscientious confessor had even gone so far as to write a prior of that order in Anthony's behalf.

As a result, less than a year after his arrival at Vich, everything was suddenly arranged for his transfer to the Carthusian monastery at Montealegre. At first Anthony could scarcely believe the good news. With hardly a regret for his new friends at the seminary, he said a quick farewell and, armed with other letters which Padre Bach had prepared for the prior and another religious of the establishment, he set out on his journey. It was midsummer of 1830.

V

His <u>long tramp</u> lay through Barcelona, the city of other dreams and aspirations. In retrospect, how futile his former life now appeared! But not all of it. It was, after all, among Barcelona's clacking looms and disillusionments that he had finally discovered his true vocation. He would walk its <u>noisome streets</u> for a last time today with a heart full of gratitude. He pushed on eagerly, watching for its rooftops to appear against the thunderheads that were beginning to boil across the sky.

Just before he reached the suburbs a bolt of lightning cracked the heavens open and disgorged a pounding rainstorm beneath a spectacular bombardment of thunder. He was running for shelter even before the water had laid the road's thick <u>overlay of dust</u>. It rose about him in a suffocating cloud, protesting the first <u>pelting</u> and his <u>flying feet</u>. His weakened chest pained dreadfully under the strain of his effort to escape this devilish combination of swirling soil and downpour. He felt he was really ill, and to this was added the sudden assault of a strange terror. Something seemed to be suggesting: "Perhaps God doesn't want you to go to the Carthusian monastery!"

How long may an inner warning have been preparing him for such a climax? Anthony Claret never explained it—and probably could not have explained it. But the alarm he experienced at this moment convinced him that he was being called upon to sacrifice the personal preference for the contemplative life which had first turned him to religion; to abandon all self-determination for the total obedience of the priesthood! Now in the simplicity that was henceforth to beautify his entire life, he faced away from Barcelona and commenced the long walk back to Vich.

If he was embarrassed to present himself before those he had so recently bid good-by forever, he did not show it. Nor did Padre Bach show surprise at his quick return. "I recounted all that had happened to my director, but he answered me never a word, neither a good one nor a bad one, and so the matter was dropped."

Anthony, subdued, settled down to the years of laborious study that extended ahead, but that he could now take tranquilly, one by one, free of intruding anxieties for personal ends or affections. The details were in God's hands, and his sole responsibility was to become as fine and finely instructed a priest as he possibly could. New devotions were added to those long faithfully practiced. Besides the eight days of spiritual exercises every Lent, Bishop Corcuera required the enrollment of all his seminarians in the Congregations of the Immaculate Conception and of St. Aloysius Gonzaga, devotions the bishop personally supervised. It was his conviction that time allotted to the cultivation of pious practices was

even better spent than in the classroom. He often assured his
students: "It is preferable to know a bit less and be pious, *devout*
than to know much and have little or no piety, for in the
latter case, it is easy to become puffed up by the winds of
vanity."

Anthony Claret was not one whom the "winds of vanity"
could "puff up," but he was grateful that the pious practices,
henceforth to be as constant and regular as breathing, in his
case imposed no diminution of study. Since earliest childhood
he had required surprisingly little sleep, and now he could
work or pray through the nights, relying upon intermittent
catnaps to refresh him for a return to his books. His scholastic
record was always satisfactory in spite of his late start, and it
improved as he progressed from philosophy into theology.
He found great profit, as well as pleasure, in the lives and
works of the saints. From St. Peter and the *Acts of the* *Avila*
Apostles to Santa Teresa de Jesús' *Interior Castle*, all the
magnificent literature and records of the Faith contained, for
him, endless fascination and inspiration to ever-greater zeal.

Early in February, 1831, he was appointed to Sallent's va- *office*
cant benefice, a privilege to which he was entitled by reason *of*
of having been born there. The bishop now gave him the *good*
tonsure and, from that time forward, he wore the robes of
the Church and recited the breviary. However, except for
the Christmas season, Holy Week, and certain feast days
which positively demanded his ministrations in Sallent, and
the summer vacations, he stayed at Vich attending his classes,
studying, and pursuing his personal devotions in the Dos Solas
Street room.

There he was surrounded by cherished symbols which
never failed to stimulate him toward the realization of his
vocation. His crucifix stood upon the table with the reminding
skull at its foot. There was the likeness of St. Bruno; a large
canvas depicting the descent into hell of a condemned sinner;

and, where he had hung it behind the door, the ingenious synoptic picture of four verses, respectively entitled: *Death, Judgment, Hell, Heaven.* Each verse ended with the line: *Por toda la eternidad*—For all eternity. Meditating on the warnings and promises here set forth, he now well understood the reason for the five-year-old Toñín's obsessive preoccupation with: *siempre!*

During his second year of philosophy he caught a severe cold which assumed such threatening proportions that his superiors ordered him to bed. One morning as he lay, feverish and perhaps somewhat fretful, fighting off pneumonia, he was suddenly assailed by what he described as a "terrible temptation." Appalled, he invoked the protection of the Virgin, his guardian angel and his name saints. He made the Sign of the Cross and resolutely forced himself to think of indifferent subjects, but the temptation did not withdraw. And then, he was amazed to see Our Lady standing before him! "Her dress was bright red, her mantle blue, and in her arms I saw a garland of exquisitely beautiful roses. . . . Myself I saw as a beautiful child on bended knees with hands joined in prayer. . . . The Blessed Mother addressed me with these words: 'Anthony, this crown is yours if you conquer.'

"I was so absorbed that I couldn't utter one word. Mary Immaculate then placed on my head the crown of roses she carried in her right hand. . . . At my right side, there was a group of saints, all in an attitude of prayer. I recognized only the one who resembled St. Stephen. It was my opinion then, and indeed it still is, that these were my patron saints praying and interceding for me, so that I might not succumb to temptation. To my left I saw a great multitude of demons drawn up in order like soldiers who fall back to form lines after a battle has been fought. . . . I murmured, 'What a multitude there is! And how strong they look!'

"While all this was going on . . . I did not know what

was happening to me. As soon as it was over, I found myself free from temptation and with a joy so deep that I scarcely knew whence it came. I am positive that I was not sleeping, nor was I suffering from dizziness in the head, or from any other infirmity that could cause such an illusion. What made me believe that this was a reality and a special grace from the Blessed Virgin was that, for many years afterward, I was not assailed by any temptations against chastity. If later on an impure temptation came to me, it was so insignificant as not even to merit the name. All praise to Mary! Another victory to Mary!" Every year of his life was drawing him closer, deepening his tremendous debt of love to the Mother of God, whose lovely name he added to his: *Antonio María*.

After this experience, Anthony's ardor could only be satisfied by an ever more intense study of the saints. Alongside his friend Jaime Balmes, a particularly brilliant seminarian destined for a lustrous career in philosophy, he sat for hours in the library, steeping his mind and filling his heart with the record of the works and methods of the martyrs and spiritual titans who had always prevailed to preserve Christendom against the forces of evil.

VI

He had little time to worry over the growing political tension that the same forces were now building up to an inevitable climax in Spain—the nation which could count its saints by the score! Or did he foresee that his trials with the troublemakers would materialize soon enough and that he must concentrate on those considerations which would fortify his spirit against the day when he would have to go forth to meet them head-on, as a Padre of the Church?

That day came unexpectedly soon! The death of Fernando VII in 1833 precipitated a bloody civil war. The monarch's brother, Don Carlos, attempted to seize the throne from Fernando's infant daughter, Isabel II. Although the army and treasury upheld her rights, the most powerful nobles were *Carlistas;* and their cause was also extremely popular in the staunchly Catholic north. Isabel's margin for victory was therefore uncomfortably slim and, in the hope of strengthening her position, María Cristina—her mother and regent—now accepted the support of the small but aggressive anticlerical party. The opponents of religion eagerly seized this opportunity to decree a sweeping confiscation of Church properties. Hundreds of convents and monasteries were suppressed, relations with Rome were severed and, finally, the *Cristinas* launched a persecution during which in Madrid alone no less than a hundred priests were massacred!

It seems likely that it was the spreading terror combined with Bishop Corcuera's recognition of Anthony Claret's notable progress toward spiritual perfection that influenced the prelate's decision to hasten the young student's ordination. A firm exponent of late ordination, the bishop of Vich ordinarily withheld minor orders until the end of the fourth year of theological studies, the subdiaconate until the fifth year, the diaconate until the sixth. And only upon the completion of the seventh year, following a forty-day retreat did he ordain his priests. Each of these honors was advanced for Anthony who was finally ordained June 13, 1835, the feast day of his patron, St. Anthony of Padua, only five and a half years after his arrival at Vich. Meanwhile, the bishop, already gravely ill of the affliction which was to prove fatal, arranged for the bishop of Solsona to administer this Sacrament. Perhaps partly owing to the prospect of losing the superior to whom he owed so much, Anthony found his long preparatory retreat unforgettably painful: "Never in my life have I made spiritual exercises so full of temptation and trial, yet perhaps from no others have I drawn so many and great graces as I came to know on the day I sang my first Mass, June twenty-first, feast of St. Aloysius Gonzaga. . . . This occasion, celebrated in my home town, gave great satisfaction to my parents and all the *Sallentinos.* . . ." And well it might. For, beyond their pride in being able to receive Our Lord from the hands of one born among them, the townsmen had been given ample evidence of his exceptional virtues and love. As *beneficiado* he had taught catechism to their little ones, been the finest of examples to their young folk. Always one of them, he had still been clearly set apart—and above them— by his unquestionable holiness. This, they assured one another sagely, was the sort of padre a town needed in these dismaying times!

As for the ardent young celebrant—who had once accepted the logic of a future in the textile mills of his own town, and then been fired by the belief that he was called to the life of a contemplative—that which he now saw fulfilled was the earliest dream of all. Truly it had been no empty observation, that prompt affirmation of the schoolboy Toñín Claret: "I am going to be a priest!"

IV

PRIEST, PASTOR, JESUIT

After his theology examination Anthony was granted the faculties of confessor and preacher. These ministries, too, he commenced in Sallent. His initial six-hour session in the confessional opened at five A.M., August 2, Day of the Portiuncula Indulgence. His first sermon, a panegyric on the patroness of his home town, was delivered September 12, the Holy Name of Mary.

There was still before him a three-year course in moral theology and he now reported back to Vich. There had been a lamentable acceleration of the *Isabelino* suppression and, in the opinion of Vicar General Luciano Casadevall, diocesan governor since Bishop Corcuera's death in July, the dispersion of his seminarians was imminent. For this reason, Padre Anthony was directed to pursue his studies privately. At appropriate intervals he must present himself for the examinations; and meanwhile, continue his ministries. Don Luciano was in dire need of priests to hold the diocese together in a period so turbulent and this may have been his primary motive in ordering the program of private study. He was deeply concerned over the situation in Sallent which, owing to its strong Carlist sympathies, was regarded with suspicious animosity by the government. Young Padre Claret's knowledge of the *Sallentino* temper should make him an invaluable agent of concord in his native place.

His reappearance there to undertake his difficult double assignment greatly delighted his fellow townsmen, who descended upon his confessional and attended his sermons in droves. Though he was not to receive the title of *vicario* (assistant pastor) until more than a year later,[1] he busied himself from the start with all manner of parochial duties and, on feast days, preached to the faithful. Meanwhile his study progressed so well that he could declare: "I applied myself [to my books] . . . until I knew the authors of moral theology as I knew the catechism."

The justly proud parishoners saw nothing for comment in the face or figure of the young Padre who hastened about the church and town in their service, or who, in an emergency, could be found bent over the books he would patiently push aside to attend their solicitations. They had known him all his life. But how did he appear to strangers? The existing portraits made not long after this period [2]—a crude pen sketch by Dr. Solá y Abadal of Manresa which depicts a heavy, peasant-type physiognomy further weighted by a rather dour expression, and Paciano Ros's painting of an alert, almost sophisticated and conventionally handsome young cleric—are so dissimilar as to automatically render each other very questionable likenesses. They agree only in establishing the fact mentioned by various biographers: that Padre Claret possessed a large, round head!

From a passport dated June 8, 1835, we may read a doubtless hastily jotted description: "Age, 27 years; regular stature; hair brown, eyes dark; heavy chin; good color." (Probably meaning light-complexioned.) But Padre Fernández throws doubt on two of even these meager notations. Noting that

Claret's less than five foot-one-inch stature in his shoes could hardly have been called "regular," the official Claretian biographer goes on to correct another inaccuracy: ". . . the yellowish tint of the bilious constitution colored his face all his life. . . ." [3] But if these characteristics, as well as his heavy, irregular features, gave him a somewhat unprepossessing appearance, his large dark eyes, customarily veiled by modestly downcast lids, "shone like stars when, from the pulpit, gazing into the distance across the multitudes, they opened wide, animated by the impetuous spirit of an apostle." It was apparent to all that however physically unimposing, there lived in the body of this Padre Claret the fire of an utterly dedicated man of God. Already he was being called "*el santito*— the little saint—of Sallent."

II

During the first two years of his labors the political situation steadily deteriorated. The *Carlistas*, representing the old, more realistically democratic party, were strongly entrenched in the northern mountain section of Spain where they received wholehearted support from the populace. The *Isabelinos*, retaining, if but precariously, the reins of government, although calling themselves "the Liberals," were proving anything but that by their decidedly totalitarian practices. Actually, the original issues of the succession had gradually been submerged as the contending factions began to consolidate their stands on ideological lines. In short, the fight was now primarily a struggle-to-the-death between the Catholic interests and the Freemasons who dominated María Cristina's regency. The scandalous suppression of the orders, looting of religious houses, and the murders of priests merely suspected of Carlist sympathies (which did not, we may be sure, fail to incite reprisals) had produced a blacker chapter than Spanish history had yet recorded.

Nevertheless, there was an overlapping in factional adherence. Not all the Catholics were Carlists; nor all the *Isabelinos* enemies of the faith. It was thus possible for Padre Claret, no matter what his secret inclinations may have been, to steer a neutral course—and this he regarded as his priestly obligation. "How," he asked, "can this eagle of state rise in flight unless its two wings, religion and politics, are in harmonious balance?" This vitally needed balance could only be achieved in an atmosphere of Christian peace and good will stemming from virtues which a priest was bound to cultivate in *all* hearts. His consistent refusal to be drawn into the general controversy quickly won the approbation of his superiors, who decided that his discretion might prove even more useful in the more important post of regent of Copons.

For some undisclosed reason Padre Anthony did not welcome the proposed promotion and, in the hope of having it set aside, he departed for Vich to confer with the authorities. He had judged it prudent not to reveal the motive of his trip, nor that he had chosen the roundabout route through Olost (where his brother José was now operating his own successful textile factory).

By an unlucky coincidence his pastor, Padre Domenech, also left Sallent only two days later in protest against the Liberals' unjustified meddling in parish procedure. The discovery that both priests were simultaneously missing caused a hue and cry. It was assumed by the civil authorities that this meant they had gone over to "the Faction," as the government called the *Carlistas*. Since the "deserters" could not be reached, vengeance was promptly wreaked on the assistant's innocent father. Juan Claret was seized and, had it not been for the energetic interposal of the mayor, Don Francisco Riera, he would have been summarily ejected from Sallent.

Padre Anthony received the outrageous news at Olost. He immediately dispatched a letter to the mayor:

Olost, 16th October of 1837.

To Señor Francisco Riera

My very dear sir: I was astounded by two lines from my beloved father which informed me, without citing the reason, that they wished to throw him out of town. I instantly sent him an *expreso* to ask what might have caused such a thing, saying that, if it could have been because I was imputed to have fled to the Faction, this is false, and I would immediately obtain a certificate to prove it. From his reply, I see that, owing to the impression I had formed of the malice of certain *Sallentinos* of ill will, I had hit upon the point. But thanks to the All Powerful, there are, in the midst of such knaves, fine and worthy persons like yourself. I tell you, Señor, with all the frankness and ingenuousness of a friend, that I have always believed in the benevolence of the house of Riera y Trabal toward me, but now, with this act of which they have written me, you have given such great and evident proofs of your sincerity, rectitude and kindness as I shall never be able to forget.

That you may know the reason for my absence and my situation, I wish to explain that, on the evening of the *fiesta* for the Holy Patron, I received a dispatch from the Sr. Vicar General ordering me to the *Parroquia de Copons* to become its regent. Considering the immense extent of that parish, my poor health —for at times I expectorate blood—and, above all, since I hold the benefice [at Sallent], I resolved to go to Vich to try to alter the vicar general's determination, and so I set out. But upon my arrival at Olost I was told that the rebels were close to Roda and Vich. In view of this, I didn't care to expose myself on the roads [he would certainly have been accused of being en route to the Carlists] and, understanding they tarried in that vicinity, I also delayed here, to the satisfaction of the rector, who is disabled, and of all the faithful, since I am doing all the work I can. Until I receive a reply from the vicar general assigning me to a reasonable post, I shall be here, where I am at the service of all, but especially of yourself—to whom I proffer infinite thanks and upon whom I shall ever look as one of my truest friends. And I kiss your hand.

Antonio Claret, Pbro.

Casadevall revoked the assignment to Copons but now the vacancy in Sallent resolved him to place Padre Claret at the head of his native parish, a charge which his modesty also wished to reject. When other objections were overruled, he cited his insignificant stature as a handicap to the pastoral dignity. It was of no avail. His superior replied with a smile: "Señor Claret, a man is measured by his head."

Anthony Claret was installed as *cura* of Sallent, October 29, 1837, to the gratification of the community. Although the responsibilities he faced would be heavier than any he had yet carried, the difficulties many, it was heartening to know that his flock was composed of lifelong friends and acquaintances.

III

The household he now set up in the enormous old rectory included only his tertiary sister María [4] and an aged servant named Jaime. His program of private devotions continued unchanged. He observed the disciplines adopted at the seminary; he confessed weekly; commenced each day with mental prayer. In the evenings María and the manservant joined him in meditation and the Rosary.

María had been ordered to substitute the straw mat upon which he slept no more than two hours nightly for the meager mattress he had found on his bed. But for his doctor's orders that he rest six hours *on a bed* (which he obeyed save on Saturdays when, in the Virgin's honor, he sacrificed all rest), the mat would have been put on the floor. As it was, he devoted four hours of the prescribed "rest" to prayer. His Mass was at dawn, following which he heard confessions so long as a penitent remained. Afternoons he walked about the town or into the surrounding countryside, dropping in at any houses where there was illness; repeated his calls daily until the afflicted either recovered or required the last Sacraments.

Were his proud parents and numerous relatives living in the vicinity disappointed that theirs were homes he did not visit? He denied himself this pleasure, offering up one more of the sacrifices he considered so necessary to spiritual attainment.

He taught catechism the year around and, during Lent, every day, with the enthusiasm and thoroughness to be expected from one who had always regarded it his own most profitable elementary study. His spacious but sparsely furnished rectory presented few objects for his small pupils to fall over as they surged in for their classes.

His love went out in equal measure to the rich and to the poor; to the established populace and to Sallent's summer vacationists. His charities were constant even when, as frequently happened, he failed to receive the funds apportioned to his parish by the disentailment committees—which had so blithely and speedily liquidated the Church holdings! He was incessantly bringing the dirtiest and most miserable tramps into the rectory that they might be bathed, fed and decently clothed. María never forgot one with a nauseating eruption on his head, whom her brother attended with the utmost tenderness; nor the beggar who, calling at the door while he was taking a late dinner alone, was courteously invited to share the pastor's meal—*at the table!*

In accordance with the Council of Trent edict, he preached each Sunday and feast day, although in the afternoons. (Spanish sermons of that time or, for that matter, today are too lengthy usually to be interpolated during Mass.) He took care to adhere strictly to spiritual themes, avoiding all references or inferences touching upon political issues. The gov-

ernment would have no occasion to complain that Sallent's
new pastor was undermining its jealously cherished authority.
In any case, he knew his obligation to proclaim the Gospel
for the benefit of all; that "a *sacerdote*, in order not to im-
pede anyone's salvation, must never align himself with any
faction." political party

With impartial amiability, he met the partisans of both
the forces now moving back and forth across the land steeped
in violence and the most bitter recrimination. For the questions of the military he happened to encounter on his trips to
Olost and Vich, he had discreet replies. When the quizzers
were *Carlistas*, he said he was from the diocese of Vich, territory preponderantly Carlist; if Liberals, that he came from
Sallent, which they controlled. Thus did he justify Casadevall's judgment that he would make an ideal pastor who
would never create fresh problems for his superiors. But this
was not all. He utilized his good relations with the authorities
(Baron de Meer and General Pavía) to secure their aid in
eliminating the objectionable behavior of their constituents
and camp followers. His complaints of the insults occasionally
heaped upon him in public and the disturbances fomented in
the church environs by the ribald and malicious anticlericals
were not made on his own behalf, but because they scandalized and alienated the people and sometimes even caused un-
seemly and dangerous altercations. His protests were heeded,
the riffraff disciplined. He achieved the expulsion from Sallent
of the objectionable women who had come in with the army.

He had come to regard his former Carthusian aspirations
as an important element in God's plan to detach him from
the world—and to be grateful for it. But he was equally grateful that he had not been permitted to seek his own sanctification outside a life of activity on earth. His earliest anxiety
for the salvation of all his fellow men had reasserted itself
more powerfully than ever; and he saw that, in his case,

prayer and discipline must be combined with strong action
in behalf of others. The form this action should take had
become the subject of his constant meditation. After fervent
petitions to Jesus and Mary, he turned first to the Bible for
enlightenment and then, with renewed animation, to the saints
who had commanded so much of his attention during seminary days. What had Isaias and Jeremias to say to him? That
the unfaithful and the backsliding must be sternly repri-
manded and warned of God's chastisements? That escape
from eternal doom lay only in penance? Yes, but also that
he must temper his reproaches, as did they, with pity for
human weaknesses, both spiritual and natural, extending the
most tender love to all.

Daniel's harrowing experience taught that he must not expect to elude the envy and resentment that might throw one
to the lions, but that even these could not prevail against
God's delivery. Elias' ascent in the chariot of fire after persecution was another illustration of zeal rewarded! According
to Ecclesiasticus, it was the minor prophets who, by faith and
virtue, restored Jacob and redeemed the people.

Example, therefore, must be made the foundation for great
preaching. Every act of Anthony's must proclaim his complete devotion to Our Lord and his love for souls. Only thus
could he follow through in the steps of these and, passing on
to the New Testament, of St. Peter, St. Paul, St. John—who
had ever hastened from place to place snatching their brothers
in Christ from the world's hand into eternal joy. They had
been men of the same order, apostles, or, in a homelier word,
missionaries, who knew no reservations in sacrifice for the
salvation of the peoples of all nations. From them one could
trace the line of selfless abnegation down the ages in the
brilliant and moving records of St. Francis, St. Anthony of
Padua, St. Ignatius, St. Vincent de Paul and unnumbered
more. The labors, pains, genius and overwhelming love of

such spiritual titans and their followers had sent the good news ringing round the earth! But the Gospel must be reproclaimed to each generation of men. How resoundingly it must *now* be reproclaimed in traditionally devout Spain which was straying ever farther from holiness under a persecution that had robbed it of its strongest preaching and teaching orders: the Dominicans, the Jesuits, the Franciscans; that had set up materialism as the ideal!

The answer was clear enough to one long devoted to the records of the saints, to one like Anthony Claret, the little pastor who soon recognized that Sallent would never suffice to fulfill his gigantic zeal. He, too, must be an apostle, a missionary. Had not this destiny been virtually written into the sensitive heart of a five-year-old with that awesome word: *siempre?* It remained but to see how the fulfillment was to be effected!

Since the very term, missionary, was tabu in governing circles, he knew he must probably commence such labors outside his homeland. From an obscure little town in revolution-torn Spain, how could it be arranged? As always, the most direct approach seemed best to him. "So it was I determined to leave my parish and go to Rome, there to offer myself to the Congregation of the Propagation of the Faith to be sent to any part of the world."

When his plans became known, all the foreseeable difficulties and obstructions materialized. His parishoners protested; his superiors objected. His flock could not bear to lose him; and, his value to the Church having been demonstrated in this, his first pastorate, it is easy to appreciate his harassed superiors' reluctance to release him to the mission field, particularly since, in such uncertain times, it was far from clear just how he might achieve his ends. But this time God was with him—and he knew it. "It was only by His aid that I succeeded" [in securing his liberty to set out for Rome].

IV

In 1839 he proceeded to Barcelona where he proposed to board ship for Italy. However, the officials of a quibbling regime refused him a passport. It was disappointing to be thwarted at the very outset but, on this occasion, opposition gave rise to no doubt of the soundness of his project. It was merely a test. Pondering his next step, he visited his brother José and, while at Olost, he remembered Padre Matavera, another Oratorian, who from wide experience might suggest a solution to his dilemma. Journeying on to Tria de Perafita where this priest was stationed (St. Philip Neri's followers, being a more loosely organized group, had not fallen under the ban applied to the regular orders by the liberals), he found Padre Matavera as convinced as himself that he was called to the missions. It was agreed that he should employ his permit for interior travel to gain the French border. If he could manage to cross the international line via a Pyrenees' port of entry, he could book passage from Marseilles.

The first day's walk was through an uninhabited barren terrain to bleak, high-perched Castellar de Nuch, where he arrived at nightfall and was kindly welcomed by the parish priest. The second day should have brought him to the frontier town of Puerto, but, at Tosas, he was warned that robbers were operating in the Puerto district. So he delayed in Tosas until word arrived that the bandits had cleared out. The report was inaccurate.

"I began to climb to Puerto and had just reached the Font de Picaso at the top of the hill when a man sprang up in my path, menaced me with a gun, and shouted: 'Halt!' He came close . . . and ordered me to accompany him to the *señor comandante*. The leader of this band of ten gunmen asked me some questions which I answered frankly. Had I a pass? I had and presented it for his inspection. Why hadn't I taken the road through Puigcerdá? I answered that . . . one with the requisite documents may take any route he wishes.

"They had a number of captives who, while the armed men were speaking to me, at a given signal, started marching. It was apparent that I constituted an embarrassment [but] finally, the commander declared they would have to take me along with them to see the governor of Puigcerdá. [Outright highwaymen, this band pretended to be patriots, had even adopted the title: *sentinels of the queen*.] I said I had nothing to fear from the governor but, for the detention of a legally authorized traveler, they had.

"The march began in file formation. They walked briskly; I slowly, in the rear. Seeing they were ignoring me, I concluded: 'If they really wished to take you along, they would have put you in front or in the middle of the line. Leaving you at the end means you can go your own way.' Therefore, without a word, I turned back toward France. I had taken but a few steps when my original captor noted what I was doing, called to me, and then hurried after me to say in a low tone: 'Don't report this,' to which I responded, 'Go with God, all of you.'"

His gratitude for this simple delivery from an unpleasant and dangerous episode was to be deepened by the sequel Padre Claret would soon hear from a seminarian who had engaged himself, but failed to accompany him on this journey. Crossing these same mountains a few days later, the student was also captured, forced to disrobe for searching, and robbed of all he possessed, and by the identical gang!

Padre Anthony's escape from the bandits marked the end of his immediate obstructions. That afternoon he crossed the border and entered the French town of Auseja. Here his Spanish travel permit was examined and the officials granted him a similar pass. Thus protected, he continued on through Prades to Perpignan—where his papers were exchanged for those required for embarkation—and then, via Montpellier, to Nîmes. Although alone in a strange country and without recommendations, he met the kindest of welcomes in each place, almost, he noted, as though the people had been awaiting him. And in this way he came, at last, to Marseilles.

He had hardly set foot in the streets of the bustling waterfront city when he encountered a man who courteously offered to conduct him to a house where he lodged the five days until the next Italian sailing. And the following day as he set forth to solicit his visa, the same figure again appeared to guide him to the consul and expedite the validation of his documents! Nor did this end the stranger's kindness. Twice daily he called for Padre Claret; took him to visit the city's churches, the cemetery and other spots of interest. And finally, on the day of departure, the gentleman presented himself once more—to carry his friend's luggage to the ship. Apparently Padre Claret never learned his benefactor's identity, contenting himself with the thought: "He seemed more like an angel than a man, for he was so modest, joyful and, at the same time, so grave, religious and devout that, while taking me to the churches, which pleased me greatly, he never suggested entering a café or suchlike place. I never saw him eat or drink, since at meal hours he would leave me, only to return soon to aid me again."

The priest boarded ship in the anticipation of a lonely voyage among citizens of a foreign and often enemy land whose tongue he was unaccustomed to use. And the first words he heard were Spanish! Moreover, the speakers were religious. Joyously, he accosted them. "Are you Spaniards?"

"Yes indeed," came the reply. "We're Benedictines who had to leave Navarra owing to General Maroto. We are going to Rome." And they proceeded to recount the hazards and hardships they had undergone in making their escape from the "attentions" of the anticlericals. Now, quite without resources, they were setting forth in high spirits, depending solely upon Heaven to lead them into a better future. There was also another Spanish cleric aboard, they said. And this proved to be the youth who had planned to accompany Padre Claret and later been robbed by the Puerto bandits! His state, described as "pitiable," aroused the compassion which moved Anthony Claret to devote the rest of the day to his "consolation."

"As my journey was not for diversion, but only that I might labor and suffer for Jesus Christ, I considered I ought to seek the humblest, poorest place that offered opportunities to suffer." He had therefore bought a ticket affording no more than deck space. He took up his station in the prow, the least comfortable section. Sitting on a coil of rope, his head against a cannon, he meditated on Our Lord's example on the disciples' boat. Only He had been able to sleep tranquilly through the raging tempest which had so alarmed the gale-accustomed fishermen.

And now there suddenly rose a violent storm which drove mountainous waves across this deck. Under a merciless assault of wind and water, surrounded by his fellow passengers' terror, the young man who must become a missionary lay back upon the ropes, pulled his coat over his head and, all night long, calmly endured the drenching that was inevitable in his exposed position. Until dawn the sea surged across the deck, then a heavy rain substituted for the salt water which had soaked his shabby garments. Well, they would have to dry on him! His baggage consisted of a spare shirt, a pair of socks, a handkerchief, razor, comb, a breviary and a small Bible. He carried nothing else except a pound of bread and a piece of cheese—his food provision for five days! The bread was as soggy as his coat and extremely salty, but "eat it I did, for I was very hungry."

That day he talked with a congenial Englishman who

proved to be a Catholic and who, doubtless inspired by the priest's obvious poverty, later made an occasion to offer some gold. "I asked myself: 'Shall you accept this money or not? You don't need it for yourself, but those unfortunate Benedictines surely do. You might well take it for them.' "

He therefore gratefully received the coins and promptly distributed them among the religious who, having been fasting of necessity, immediately exchanged this windfall for foodstuffs at the ship's store. Invited to share their feast, their benefactor refused and satisfied his appetite with his still sodden bread, a fact which the Englishman noted with admiration and, perhaps, surprise. As this gentleman prepared to leave the ship at Liorna to continue his trip by land, he insisted on giving Padre Claret his Rome address, expressing the hope that the priest would unhesitatingly apply to a new friend who regarded him highly should he find himself in need of anything whatsoever while in the Holy City.

This compliment by a distinguished individual (so wealthy that he traveled "in Oriental luxury" with his private carriage, servants and domestic pets, and who might have been expected to patronize the rumpled, threadbare figure presented by the poor padre) confirmed the latter's conviction that "the most effective way to edify and move hearts is by giving the example—in poverty, generosity, abstinence, mortification, self-denial." Were not these practices which he, himself, had found so affecting in the saints? Mentioning the respect and even veneration accorded him by the Englishman and other shipmates following this incident, he observed: "Perhaps, had they seen me sitting at table partaking of rich meals, they might have criticized and depreciated me, as I have seen done to others. Virtue, then, is vitally needful to the priest, whom even evil men expect to be good."

When his boat had docked at Civitavecchia, he walked to Rome in the company of the Benedictines and the cleric, arriving in the sun-drenched capital of Christendom as the clocks struck ten. The religious then bid their new friends *adiós* and headed for one of their houses. For the Catalonians things might prove more complicated, as they had no certain destination, nor sure welcome. However, they knocked on the door of the first monastery they saw (the Carmelite Transpontina) and asked the brother porter whether it chanced to house any Spanish religious.

"Padre Comas, our superior, is a Spaniard, that is to say, a Catalonian."

Their spirits soared at this good news; and even higher when they were warmly received by their compatriot. Padre Comas escorted them to the Convento de San Basilio, a good hour's walk from Transpontina. As he had promised, they found several other Catalonians there who ". . . welcomed us with sincere love, despite the fact that they had never seen or even heard of us before."

Anthony Claret had been so sure of the rightness of his procedure that he had set out for Rome with no more recommendation than a letter to his countryman, the recently consecrated Bishop Vilardell of Líbano. And even this small preparation was useless inasmuch as his excellency had already left for the Holy Land. Padre Anthony therefore applied directly to the cardinal protector of the Propagation of the Faith. But his eminence, too, was out of the city. Undiscouraged, ". . . I concluded this was all truly providential since it gave me time for the spiritual exercises I customarily made annually, but which I had missed this year by reason of my journey."

He consulted a Jesuit priest, obtained a copy of St. Ignatius' *Exercises,* and commenced his retreat under the same man who, after hearing his confession, suggested: "As Our Lord has called you to the foreign missions, why don't you join the Society? Then you would go out in the company of a brother in religion, a fine precaution against the dangers inherent in the mission work."

"That I fully recognize," replied Padre Claret, "but how might *I* hope to be acceptable to the Society of Jesus?"

Apparently the retreat master did not agree with his opinion that, neither in virtue nor learning, could he qualify for the Society, because almost immediately arrangements were made for him to enter the Monte Cavallo Novitiate—which he did, November 2, 1839. "Overnight, I found myself a Jesuit! When I saw myself in the holy soutane of the *Compañía*, I could scarcely believe my eyes. I seemed to be dreaming."

V

Padre Anthony now experienced a fervor and humility exceeding any he had known. He was sure that all the other novices were racing along the paths of virtue, while only he dragged behind! Listening to the reading of the list of good works performed by the young Jesuits in preparation for the feast of the Immaculate Conception, ". . . I was confounded and put to shame." The record, of course anonymous that it might not become an occasion of pride, detailed the methods employed by the novices to achieve acts of love and sacrifice in honor of the Virgin. The new brother from Spain, that homeland of throngs of saints including Ignatius himself, was profoundly impressed by the fact that, whereas the rule exacted no stringent mortifications, many were assiduously practiced at the members' election. He noticed that, while their Saturday suppers consisted of eggs and salad, *no one* ever partook of the eggs! Before ample provision, rather than repasts either coarse or sparse, his companions invariably rejected the more palate-enticing dishes.

For exceptional mortifications, permission was requisite. Each Friday evening and on the vigils of the great feasts, cards were distributed upon which those desiring to offer a particular sacrifice (such as to eat on the floor, to kiss the feet of one or more of the brothers, to kneel for protracted periods with arms extended in the form of the Cross, to wash dishes, wait table, etc.) would write these requests. The cards were then submitted to the superior. His will in each case was made known when the father collector later passed from door to door to indicate by a silent motion of his head whether the verdict was "yes," or "no."

Not all acts of self-denial were subject to special permission; others might be less formally solicited. Anthony Claret soon saw that the wisdom of his superiors also frequently supplied wholly uncontemplated mortifications. "I have never had a liking for games, but each Thursday when we went to the recreation field they made me play. Now I asked the father rector to allow me to stay in to study or pray instead of playing. . . ." The diverting of playtime to study or prayer might well have been a sacrifice to many, but hardly to one who had eschewed amusement and the companionship of contemporaries even as a child, a fact the rector doubtless recognized. In any case: "He ordered me '. . . to play and to play well.' In compliance with this command, I took care to play *so well* that I won all the games."

On another occasion: ". . . I noticed that one of the community's priests celebrated Mass very late on feast days. Though he never complained, I thought having to remain so long without breaking fast must cause him discomfort. Feeling for him, I told father superior that, if it were his pleasure and will, I would say the late Mass, since delaying breakfast didn't bother me. The other priest could say his Mass at my assigned hour. Father superior said he would take the matter under consideration. The outcome was that ever after I was ordered to say Mass earlier than before."

He was exceedingly happy with the Jesuits. Catechising, preaching, hearing confessions, he was aware of a steady advance in knowledge under the tutelage of men who were expert instructors. He profited by his first experience in prison work. He preached to the convicts regularly; and, at the St. James Hospital, heard the patients' confessions. Three months after entering the novitiate he commenced, on February 2, 1840, the thirty-day Spiritual Exercises always undertaken at this season.

One morning soon after the opening of the Exercises, he was assailed by a pain in the leg so acute that it prevented walking. When the efforts of the brother infirmarians failed to relieve this affliction (which took the form of paralysis), they feared the Spanish brother might well be crippled for life. What did *this* mean? Anthony Claret was habituated to see God's hand in everything. Thus he accepted the father rector's suggestion: "Let us consult father general. In view of how happy and healthy you have been here, what has occurred isn't natural. To have been overtaken by such a misfortune in precisely these days makes it apparent Our Lord has other plans for you. . . ."

The general, a very holy man, heard their report with attention and then pronounced quietly: "It is the will of God that you go soon, yes soon, to Spain. Do not fear, but have courage and be of good heart." He did not reveal having received inspiration in this matter. But later he wrote in a letter to Padre Anthony: "God brought you to the Society, not to remain in it, but to learn how to win souls for Heaven."

So it was that, in mid-March, Padre Claret sailed back to Catalonia. Vich immediately appointed him regent of Viladrau, a remote mountain town whose aged pastor and inex-

perienced young assistant stood in need of the aid he was
so well qualified to give them. It was May when he reached
his new post—to find himself entirely cured of the mysterious
infirmity which had brought him here!

V

THE PHYSICIAN

WAS PADRE CLARET not right back where he had started—
tied to an obscure provincial post? Now, too, the difficult functions of the regency increased his responsibility,
while its decidedly delicate aspects imposed heretofore unknown restrictions. Charged with the reorganization of a
badly upset parish, where he must utilize all the tact he had
applied to Sallent's political strains merely to maintaining
harmony between a pair of village priests, he had also to
assume the supervision of catechetical instruction, preach and
hear confessions incessantly. For these laborious ministries
he received only food and lodging since, of course, the parish
incomes pertained to the pastor.

These circumstances that might have seemed to mean the
destruction of his mission future did not serve to discourage
Anthony Claret. His confidence that, under any title or
wherever located, he was now a missionary, remained un-
shaken. Actually, though he would prudently label them
"Novenas," he would preach a strong mission here and,
whenever he could be spared for a few days, others in the
surrounding towns.

Aside from its parochial problems, the situation at Viladrau was dolorous. Lying squarely across the path to the Carlists' mountain stronghold, the town was too insignificant to have been fortified; and it had been repeatedly sacked, burned, visited by all manner of violence under the assaults of both sides in the fratricidal conflict which had swept back and forth across this corner of Catalonia. Though the war had officially ended, undisciplined bands still scourged the countryside intermittently, to say nothing of the bandits who improved the general confusion to cover their private depredations. To crown its misfortune, the last of Viladrau's physicians, disgusted by raids on their modest drug supplies and other abuses, had abandoned the place. The sick and dying were thus deprived of all medical attention. This tragedy and waste had created tensions and produced a climate of hysteria especially manifested in the women.

The priest saw that the people's physical sufferings must be alleviated before he could hope to secure their spiritual welfare or leave the village even briefly for the missions he contemplated giving in adjacent communities. "What else could I do but become a doctor of corporal as well as spiritual ailments, especially since I possessed a certain knowledge of medicine which I had studied from books . . . ?"

Perhaps, but it is difficult to believe that until this moment medicine could have claimed much of his attention. Certainly he had not so much as mentioned it in his quite detailed descriptions of his studies. And furthermore, the "prescriptions" with which he now undertook to cure everything from the dangerous ills of infancy to rheumatism and crippling bone disorders were singularly limited and ingenuously simple: oil, herbs and sticking plasters!

His restrained account of this development fails to disclose just how he knew he might now expect to work miracles. They were not occasional miracles but a spectacular series so sustained that they calmed an atmosphere he had found in a nearly hopeless state of agitation. His forthright account of the bare facts leaves no doubt of their true nature.

Calmly shouldering the responsibility for Viladrau's health, he achieved amazing cures of widely varying ailments. A single application of one of the homely agents in every case first vanquished an epidemic which had attacked the babies. A seventeen-year-old cripple, long considered incurable, who hadn't stirred beyond his doorway in years, recovered immediately when he was treated by the regent and was soon able to attend his "doctor's" Masses. A young man so near death that he had lost all physical sensation was restored to full health at the contact of the "remedy."

". . . there was a married woman suffering from rheumatic pains so intense that her nerves had contracted until they had drawn her body into a ball. Despite this lamentable condition, she was with child and in labor the whole nine months preceding the birth." When her time finally arrived, Padre Claret happened to be away conducting one of his already famous "Novenas" in Seva. Relatives of the desperately afflicted woman hastened to Seva to find him.

"They told me the poor invalid was suffering severely with childbirth pains; that there remained no hope of saving her life. The parish priest had administered the Sacraments of Penance, Holy Viaticum and Extreme Unction. In this sad hour awaiting death the woman's friends and she, herself, wished to see me.

". . . I went at once to her house, without even first reporting to the parish rectory. I recognized her critical condition at sight, and *the remedy for it*,[1] but told her husband we ought not apply it at the moment, because it was indispensable to send to the town of Taradell for a surgeon. These good people set out immediately with a letter I gave them for the doctor which explained the nature of the whole case. When he had read it and realized how truly desperate the thing was, he excused himself on the grounds that it would be useless for him to come. Upon the return of the lady's relatives with this news, I therefore set about the case myself, ordering persons around the house to gather certain herbs, boil them, and make the sufferer take deep breaths of the vapor arising from them. As a result, she gave birth to her child without mishap and, not only that, but was cured of her rheumatism so completely that, in a few days, she herself came to Mass."

One can imagine the impact of an event so dramatic on a small community. Although Anthony Claret's narrative of it appears needlessly noncommittal, he knew perfectly well what he was doing! To gain the full effect of this double prodigy, the physician's impotence and fear had to be disclosed. When science had been confounded, a missionary healer could then apply his herbaceous vapors and achieve the victory for God!

He was now assailed by throngs of the afflicted in whom hope had been reborn. And no one who applied to him died! When the sick died during his absences from Viladrau, the bereaved would insist that, had he been there, they would surely have been spared their tragedy. But as "unlike Jesus, I couldn't raise the dead to life again, they remained dead."

In time, he altogether dispensed with his devious "remedies." "As my reputation for curing people spread far and near, I had to contend with all the sick of the towns I visited. ... They were so many and their infirmities of such differing types that, being busy preaching and hearing confessions, I found it inconvenient to prescribe physical remedies. So I told them I would commend their cases to Almighty God and, meanwhile, I made the Sign of the Cross over them, repeating the words: '*Super aegros manus imponent, et bene habebunt*,' [They will place their hands over the sick, and they will be cured] with which they would say they had recovered their health."

These most unusual proceedings and their sensational results he explained in matter-of-fact terms: "My opinion is that they received their cures because of their faith. God Our Lord rewarded it with health of body and soul because they obeyed my exhortation that they confess all their sins contritely. Our Lord did this, not owing to my merits, for I had none, but to lend importance to the preaching of His Word, since for so long they had heard nothing but blasphemies, wickedness and heresy. Our Lord captivated their hearts by these corporal cures."

That he was now beset by numbers whose pleas were for the cure of "another malady, much more troublesome and time-consuming," was not unusual in those days. As he moved about conducting missions at Seva, Espinelvas, and more distant Igualada and Santa Coloma de Queralt, he was constantly solicited by persons seeking his ministrations for friends or relatives declaredly "possessed by devils." Authorized for exorcising by Holy Orders, he could hardly refuse. But Anthony Claret was always realistic and, furthermore, a shrewd judge of character. He was far from convinced by all, or many, of these cases. "Of the thousands I exorcised, I scarcely saw one I was sure was possessed, for I knew their states could come from other causes, either physical or moral. . . . Also, seeing they were losing me too much of the precious time I needed to hear the confessions of those converted by the preaching, I concluded it was more needful to drive the devil from souls in mortal sin than from bodies if, indeed, those bodies did house devils. Persuaded that these 'possessions' could be merely a deception of Satan, I resolved to stop giving exorcisms and take up another plan of action."

He first demanded whether those declaring themselves the victims of possession *really wished* to be cured. When the protestations that they did seemed to ring true, he then insisted on three conditions prior to exorcism. These were: that the subjects accept all his prescriptions with patience and resignation (he had perceived that hysteria is often confused with possession); that they would abstain from all forms of alcohol ("I well knew some of them drank too much and, to conceal the disorders following overindulgence, blamed the Evil One."); that they say seven *Our Fathers* and *Hail Marys* daily. He also advised a good general confession of their whole lives and the reception of Holy Communion "with all possible fervor and devotion."

Padre Claret's medical prescriptions may have been primitive, but he was surely a gifted psychologist. Almost without exception his "possessed" patients soon returned to declare gratefully that they had obtained their cures! His own conclusion: "I don't deny there are people possessed by the devil. There are and I have known some personally. But I do insist they are few. . . . Certain converted ones have frankly admitted to me that their 'possessions' were merely delusions which they encouraged in order to attract attention and compassion for reasons of interest. . . . One lady told me that all she did was with perfect understanding and malice of the will, but that her actions were so extraordinary she surprised herself. No doubt, she said, but that the devil had cooperated with her, not, however, because he was actually in possession, but due to the malice of her heart. . . . [Another] admitted . . . having so long pretended to such possession that she had deceived no less than twenty priests held to be the most learned, virtuous and zealous in [her] city. . . . What wonder that all this made me tread cautiously when dealing with these persons."

A remarkable incident and of quite another sort is credited to the regent. According to the testimony of Don Jaime Bofill y Noguer, a prominent landholder: "While the servant of God was at Viladrau, he put out a fire at my farm, 'Noguer.' It had broken out in the upper story of the house which, used as a storage space for hay, was, at the time, almost full. A north wind of hurricane proportions was blowing and, both the roof and floor being of wood, the natural expectation was that the whole house would be reduced to ashes. I hastened to Viladrau—some twenty minutes' distance— to ask help, while the fire increased in intensity. Among the first to arrive on the scene of the disaster was the servant of God who, while others ineffectively threw water on the flames it was too late to dominate, circled the house blessing it. And these benedictions did extinguish the flames, a fact recognized by everyone. As a result, only a part of the roof and some of the hay were burned, the floor merely singed. All exclaimed, 'A miracle. This man is a saint!' " [2]

The Bofill family raised a chapel on the site of the fire in which may be found an image of the miracle-worker and a plaque commemorating the event.

Following eight months of such notable activities (during which his chest ailment of years' standing seems to have been definitely cured), Father Claret was recalled to Vich. His success in all his undertakings and, doubtless, his growing influence had convinced the diocesan authorities that his scope should be widened. His proven discretion certainly would permit his preaching in more conspicuous centers without attracting the resentment of the missionary-haters that ruled the land.

II

The seeming final defeat of the *Carlistas* had caused the disappearance of their leaders behind the French frontier. But new contention had promptly arisen within the government party itself. After falling out with the queen mother, General Espartero had found himself strong enough to displace her as regent; and to the dismay of many, María Cristina was now an exile in Paris. Catalonia was seething with dissatisfaction, perhaps primarily because Espartero's faction had lowered the tariff on English textiles, which threatened the local industry with bitter competition. In any case, from Paris, María Cristina was doing everything possible to foment a Catalonian revolt. To counter her influence and smother the rising opposition, Espartero now suddenly banned public assembly in that province.

Anthony Claret had just been announced as the distinguished Lenten preacher for the Vich Cathedral! Already the city's hostels were filling with visitors from far and near who coveted the privilege of hearing this thirty-three-year-old padre whose sermons and prodigies had won him renown even while he had been buried in the back country. Excitement was running high in the levitical community which remembered him as a most promising seminarian. But now its *alcalde* received the governor's order specifically prohibiting the scheduled appearance of "that wonder-working priest"! Forced to serve this notice on the popular young apostle, the poor *alcalde* was embarrassed and ashamed. But Padre Claret exhibited no irritation nor discouragement. Quite the contrary. The news that so disappointed the city and the pilgrims was, in his view, actually heartening. Now it was beginning, the persecution that had ever been Our Lord's distinguishing mark upon His true disciple! As he assured the mystified official, this was, indeed, a day of glory!

Now however, his superiors, who had hoped so much from their plans for him, felt it too dangerous to retain in Vich one whom the authorities had singled out for suppression. He was sent to insignificant Pruit to minister to its villagers. Vich was to have been the introduction to an ambitious mission program. In spite of the truth of his expression to the *alcalde*, the setback must have held disappointment. But he solaced himself in faithful adherence to his vow of obedience. In writing of this period, Anthony Claret passed over the Vich fiasco, perhaps because he did not wish to seem to complain; but it may well have motivated his comments on obedience interpolated into the relation of his immediately following work: "Quite frequently bishops of other dioceses requested my missions for their parishes. . . . My unalterable rule was never to preach missions without my bishop's express order, for two important reasons." The first was his respect for obedience. The second: ". . . was for convenience. By saying, 'If my bishop so orders, I shall go willingly,' I satisfied all requests and was left in peace. . . . It has ever been my opinion that a missionary should not meddle in his assignments; but offer himself to his bishop with, '*Ecce ego, mitte me.*' Thus he will be sent by God Himself. All the Old Testament prophets were sent by Him. Jesus Christ was sent by God, and the disciples, by Jesus."

Padre Claret's cool-headed logic was as sound as his virtue. Following Pentecost of 1841 he saw in his superiors' instructions that God was sending *him* from one Catalonian hamlet to another for the fortification of the village faithful and the conversion of neglected rustics in this difficult time of political transition. Into the summer months he preached to growing crowds—in Vidrá, Rivas, Ripoll. Then, resting briefly at Vich, he prepared for the assignments (Aviñó, Calaf, San Martín de Sesgayolas, Prats de Rey, Santa María de Oló, San Feliú de Terrassola, Horta) that would crowd the approaching autumn and winter with labors and victories truly prodigious. If he had seen himself thwarted at Vich, he was nevertheless being led, step by step, from the semiobscurity of his outland ministry toward the prominence inevitably attained by history's great Christian apostles.

VI

THE APOSTLE

THE LETTER from Rome appointing Anthony Claret an apostolic missionary was received in 1842. Espartero fell from power the following year and a somewhat more lenient government succeeded which declared the thirteen-year-old Isabel "of age" and re-established diplomatic relations with the Vatican. Padre Claret was finally able to initiate an open and vigorous apostolate. True, the political picture was still exceedingly touchy, and he rightly anticipated obstruction, perhaps persecution, from certain quarters. But there were heartening signs that the religious spirit of a traditionally devout and stubbornly individualistic people was reawakening, a blessed development he knew he could, with God's aid, hasten.

Tramping doggedly across the face of Catalonia to reach widely separated stations among the thirteen cities and three hundred towns of its four dioceses, he was retracing the routes, repeating the labors of Blessed Juan de Ávila, his Spanish missionary ideal. The incredible hardships of these incessant sojourns to perform the no-less-demanding exertions of the pulpit and the confessional, of the catechist and

1569

healer to a vast "parish" of a million and a half souls, was the privilege he had prayed for. More than a loaf of bread and the minimum essentials for cleanliness he abjured, as also the horse or mule which would have saved much precious time and strength. But, as ever, he was taking account of the value of example.

He knew his "forever Catholic" Spaniards too well to fear the direct proselytizing of the English Protestants who were now appearing everywhere to challenge the Faith, but he did recognize the heretics' danger as purveyors of materialism. Already he perceived the inroads of the cupidity incited in the hearts of his compatriots by the influence of the champions of "progress." How might he better recall his people to their former simplicity and virtue than to reproduce the holy poverty their forbears had so deeply venerated in Spain's old-time apostles? His silent example in self-denial should more than balance the loss of time occasioned by his long foot journeys; while as for comfort, the very thought was unworthy of a servant of Christ.

Through exhausting heat or bitter snows, he drove himself along the lonely, jagged Pyrenees' trails that might be ankle-deep in dust, or precariously iced. He climbed the sides of heart-bursting canyons, crossed torrents, faced cheerfully into the most violent tempests. Nothing mattered but that he arrive at the next station in time for his engagement. And this he always managed somehow. He was a priest, but also a destitute and sometimes famished man to whom another poor wayfarer might confidently, even proudly, offer a bit of bread as they trudged a while together on the wilderness paths which were the sole means of access to most of the mountain communities. The good talk that ensued was sure to win the heroic missionary another friend to extend his fame and increase the mission attendance. Usually his charming simplicity and sympathetic interest sufficed to captivate these rough-and-ready transients but, if not, he possessed other means.

"*Padre cura,*" joked a pack train driver one day, "would you care to confess my jackass?"

"The one who should confess is you, my friend, who haven't done so for seven years and who stand in great need of confession," replied the priest imperturbably.

The driver was overwhelmed by this confident—and entirely accurate—declaration by a strange padre who had not allowed crude gibing to provoke him. He frankly admitted his fault, which was forthwith rectified!

Padre Claret was quite accustomed to the ridicule, slander and obstruction of those who had been misled by the anticlerical propaganda systematically circulated throughout Spain by regimes whose official policy toward the teachers of the Faith had been one of calculated insult and molestation. A whole generation had now grown up under this policy. Oftener than not when he came into a town to open a mission he would be met by the hostility of certain elements in the population. Fortunately, however, he could be confident that the offenses offered him by these people would lessen as, apparently unnoticing, he went calmly about his ministerial duties and that, by the middle of his stay anywhere, they would cease entirely. No matter how unpropitious its start, each mission invariably proceeded to a close that added one more triumph for righteousness to his remarkable record. He could depend on seeing in the throng gathered to hear his final sermon many who, having commenced as antagonists, were now giving their full attention to his every word!

Although this change of heart was sometimes due to the "second sight" which inspired many of his talks, he did not rely on this method. Reason, he felt, was preferable to dramatic effect and, in the long run, would achieve a better understanding of the eternal verities. To make sure his efforts might be recognized for what they were, he started off by reminding his hearers that the ordinary motives for labor are: money, pleasure or honor. But they were not his motives: ". . . not money, for I do not want a cent from anybody. . . . Nor do I preach for pleasure, for what pleasure can I possibly take in spending myself all day, in being fatigued from early morning until late at night? . . . I must be in the confessional most of the morning, the whole of the afternoon; and in the evening, instead of resting, I have to preach. This is not just for a day, but . . . for months and years. . . .

"Perhaps I labor for honor . . . no, not for honor either. . . . A preacher is exposed to many calumnies. If praised by one, he is misunderstood by another, treated as the Jews treated Jesus, Who was calumniated by maligners of His person, of His words and works, before they finally seized, scourged and killed Him by a most painful and shameful means. But like the apostle St. Paul, I fear none of these things, since I value my soul more than my body. At any cost I must discharge the ministry I have received from God Our Lord— which is to preach the Gospel.

". . . I have no worldly end in view, but . . . that God may be known, loved and served by all the world . . . that sins and offenses against Him may be hindered as much as possible. . . .

"Another thing that spurs me on to preach ceaselessly is the thought of the multitude of souls which fall into the depths of hell . . . who die in mortal sin, condemned forever and ever. . . . I see how many live habitually in mortal sin, so that never a day passes without increasing the number of their iniquities. They commit sin as easily as they drink a glass of water, just for diversion, or for a laugh. These unfortunate ones run to hell of their own accord, blind as bats.

. . . If you were to see a blind man about to fall into a pit or over a precipice, would you not warn him? Behold, I do the same, and do it I must, for this is my duty. . . .

"You may tell me that sinners will insult me, that I should leave them alone. . . . Ah no, I can't abandon them. They are my dear brothers. If you had a beloved brother who, sick and in the throes of delirium, were to insult you with all the angry words imaginable, would you abandon him? I am certain you wouldn't. You would have even more compassion for him, do your utmost for his speedy recovery. This is how I feel in regard to sinners. These poor souls are in a delirium and the more in need of our pity. . . .

"You may say the sinner doesn't think of hell, nor even believe in it. So much the worse for him. Do you by chance think he will escape condemnation because of his unbelief? Truth is independent of belief. . . .

"How often I pray, with St. Catherine of Sienna: 'O my God, grant me a place by the gates of hell, that I may stop those who enter there, saying: "Where are you going, unhappy one? Back, go back! Make a good confession. Save your soul. Don't come here to be lost for all eternity!"' "

With such ringing phrases he was expressing the yearning born in Sallent's black nights thirty years before, when a consideration of erring humanity's fate had banished sleep for a small boy! His hearers, who knew nothing of that, had doubtless listened to similar words in their time, but one thing was certain: never had they been animated by such deep concern, such palpable love! The people knew well that when *this* priest declared himself prepared to offer his life for God and their reform, he was declaring the exact truth. Had they not seen him forced to revise his preaching schedule to avoid police molestation?—and never because he involved himself in political issues, but simply because of resentment of his popularity which it was falsely claimed constituted a danger to the ruling power.

Padre Claret wasted no energy denouncing even the most obnoxious behavior toward himself. He knew it to be primarily attributable to ignorance. The sorry fact was that, as life moved farther and faster into the nineteenth century, which had not merely revolutionized industry but introduced all manner of social and educational innovations, the people had been swept off their feet by worldly distractions and competitions. This was perhaps as responsible as the politically inspired religious suppression for the blunting of spiritual awareness in so many, particularly of the younger generation. To repair these breaks in the solidly faithful front that Spain had, until recently, presented to the world, fresh stimulus and improved instructional methods were necessary. These were the aims of the missions and, if their popularity was any indication, they were being realized. Still, he longed for the assurance that his followers might be left more than the *memory* of the messages with which, praise God, he always proved successful in impressing them—for the moment.

"Traveling from one town to another, my mind was continually pondering ways and means by which I could make the fruit of the missions and retreats more lasting. The solution which occurred to me was . . . to have the sermons and instructions printed and given to the people after each mission or retreat." Though he may not have foreseen that this inspiration was leading toward one of the greatest projects of his life, even the immediate results were more than gratifying. His printers could hardly keep up with the demand for his sermons and instructions!

Members of every class of society flocked to hear him, including the clergy and even the prelates, who were made curious by his success and desired to know how he unfailingly obtained it. Bishop Francisco de Asís Aguilar, one of his earliest biographers,[1] described his first youthful impression of the famed preacher's powerful pulpit presence: "One Monday morning in December 1843 a seminarian told several of us students that the day before he had heard, in the church of Roda, a priest who had spoken for an hour without pausing even to clear his throat. . . . Our friend's enthusiasm awoke our own desire to go hear [this man], which, the following Sunday, we did.

"The roads to Roda were glutted with people who, doing the same and with greater devotion than ours, had left the towns and farms of the region practically deserted. Roda's very capacious church was entirely filled and the congregation had overflowed into the adjoining *plazuela* clear across to the wall that runs along the precipice above the Ter River. After the Rosary, Señor Claret commenced his sermon in a full, clear, vibrant voice audible not only throughout the edifice but to everyone outside. There was not a murmur, movement nor cough from the audience to disturb for an instant the torrent of words and doctrine issuing from his lips.

"It was hardly surprising that young folk had never before heard so gifted a speaker; but the same was true for our elders. All eulogized him with equal vehemence. Some marveled: 'How can he speak so long without rest?' Others praised his vast knowledge of doctrine, his excellently drawn illustrations, so tellingly applied. Many declared: 'He's a saint!' and went on to recount miracles worked through him. And truly, if not miraculous, it was nonetheless astounding to see how well he had conserved a robust health while working day and night between the pulpit and the confessional, hardly sleeping and eating so little.

"Roda, a manufacturing town classified as Liberal during and even after the war, is, owing to its industrial relations with the capital and other great market centers, very up-to-date and conversant with the latest intellectual and literary tastes. For this reason, Señor Claret's triumph there was all the more appreciable." [2]

And this was true all across Catalonia. The churchmen, who were certainly qualified to appreciate his gift of oratory, still found themselves at a loss to explain his sensational results. Even Jaime Balmes, than whom no one more greatly admired his old friend's natural endowments, held that they alone failed to account for his influence on a public which was proclaiming him "the greatest preacher of the day." Clearly then, he was the recipient of supernatural graces. His own quiet reply, when pressed to explain his success, admitted as much: "I pray to Our Lady and demand results of her."

"And if she doesn't grant them?"

"Oh, then I take hold of the hem of her robe and refuse to let go until she does."

There were also favors he did not solicit. After Roda, and a resounding mission at Ripoll, he went, on January 14, 1844, to Olost to pass a few days with his old Sallent superior Padre Juan Domenech and, incidentally, to see José. Following his Mass and thanksgiving the next morning, he was heading for the confessional as usual when, moved by some impulse, he hesitated, then turned back to the rectory. It was exactly six forty-five when, through the half-open door to Padre Claret's room, the pastor heard his abrupt announcement, "I'm off for Vich."

Somewhat startled by this sudden change of plan and, perhaps, by his guest's tone, Father Domenech remarked that a four-league walk, roughly thirteen miles, over the ice would be a risky, if not impossible, business. His horse was at Padre Claret's disposal. But even as he spoke, his visitor left the house! Baffled by such conduct on the part of the habitually amiable and courteous young priest, Father Domenech nevertheless directed his servant to saddle the horse and hasten after the padre. The order was obeyed at once, but inexplicably, the *mozo* couldn't find the missionary, though he pushed ahead all the way to San Salvador, a distance of three miles. Stranger still, neither could he locate a single footprint in all that expanse of freshly fallen snow!

According to eight witnesses,[3] it was seven-fifteen on the morning of January 15 when Anthony Claret knocked on the door of his dear friend and protector Fortunato Bres—in Vich! There he was told (perhaps unnecessarily?) of the accident. Starting out to celebrate Mass at the cathedral that morning, Padre Bres had slipped on the ice and broken his leg. Padre Pi and Pablo Parassola, a seminarian, had carried him back into the house and called Dr. José Puigdollers, while the injured man had kept insisting that they get word of his misfortune to Padre Claret at Olost. Ramón Prat was charged with delivering the message; and was on the point of departing when this was forestalled by the missionary's arrival!

There were also times when, knowing the Spirit of God to be upon him, Anthony Claret was impelled to admit as much publicly; and then, to make prophecies which were invariably fulfilled. One such incident took place the following May during his mission at the Church of Santa María del Mar in Barcelona. The future pastor of Sitges testified to this: "I attended one of his sermons. After a lengthy peroration filled with holy unction and vast learning, he paused a few instants and then, hitting the pulpit a blow to rivet his hearers' attention, said: '*Spiritus Domini super me.*' He waited another moment, then repeated these words while all were held in suspense, before he continued, 'What I have been telling you is as sure as that, within the next few days, there will fall over this city a great tempest accompanied by a flood which will cause much damage.' And a very few days later it happened. The shops and warehouses of Rech and other streets adjoining the plaza of Borne were inundated, along with many more." [4]

None of these marvels could have impaired the humility of a saint and they occasioned no pride in Padre Claret. "God has His ways to keep me humble," he observed, thinking doubtless of his many moments of discouragement. Seldom could he feel he was accomplishing the *lasting* good he so longed to obtain; or the elation such assurance would bring. He saw himself as nothing, the owner of nothing except sin. Even so, he went diligently, unremittingly ahead, struggling ever harder to compensate for his "weaknesses" and the "distractions" he blamed for his "lack of attainment."

II

Meanwhile, though his constantly increasing success fascinated his superiors and contemporary clerics, it repelled and frightened the Spanish *políticos*. The years only augmented his fame and influence, while failing to turn up a single instance which might serve as an excuse for laying hands on him. "The people follow him as though bewitched. If he isn't yet a threat to our 'progressive' government, he may well become one over any night at all! The priests and even the prelates we ran out of Spain during the war hadn't all together the power to dominate the public that, in this one, is a gift!" While such things were discussed in Barcelona, the indefatigable subject was on the road again, this time to Olot and another history-making mission.

Keeping abreast of the avalanche of solicitations for the missions of its famed apostle was a real labor for the Vich chancery. Besides its own parishes, those of all the surrounding dioceses were clamoring for Padre Claret. The petitions piled up so fast that the replies were often delayed for weeks;

and when they did arrive the impatient pastors must needs read that, as the missionary was booked ahead for months, there would still be a long wait for their revivals. For seven months communications had been passing between Padre Masmitjá, pastor of Olot, and Canon Soler, Claret's program coordinator, without the verification of a date for the mission the former so urgently needed for his parish. Finally Padre Masmitjá begged an exceedingly holy Carmelite nun for prayers in behalf of this cause; and he always believed it due to this lady's petitions that almost immediately he received the following message from the canon: "My very esteemed señor: Until now it has been impossible for either the Reverend Claret or myself to arrange . . . his apostolic expedition to my beloved Olot. . . . But today he has left here for Pruit, a parish above Grau, and tomorrow, the thirteenth, or certainly the fourteenth at the latest, he will be there [with you], whereupon you can settle the details, face to face. He goes to your house to receive the hospitality of yourself and your good brothers. I ask only that he may be given full liberty regarding his meals, inasmuch as he has sometimes prejudiced his health in order to seem appreciative of the charitable provision of his hosts. He has his individual methods in traveling and eating, and there is nothing for it but to leave it at that. I give you this hint in the confidence of friendship. . . . I follow him in the spirit, and can't tell you how much I would give to accompany him. That you may all benefit by his priceless visit . . ." [5]

Hardly had the pastor glanced over this letter when the long-awaited missionary appeared and explained: "A miracle of the Virgin of Carmen has brought me to you." This remark confirmed Padre Masmitjá in his belief that the Carmelite's prayers had been manifested to Padre Claret. "But the unquestionable miracle," writes Padre Fernández, "was the preaching that followed." [6] After an inspiring clerical retreat, the apostle threw his heart and soul into what would ever after be referred to as "the great mission of Olot." He entered the church each morning at four A.M. where, save for brief intervals, he remained until nine-thirty in the evening, preaching and hearing confessions. Even then, the penitents frequently followed him to the rectory where the confessions might well continue for another hour. Padre Masmitjá, realizing that the missionary must still append the Office and his private prayer to this drastic schedule, was almost alarmed by such extraordinary diligence.

Every day for a month (August-September, 1844) the immense Church of San Esteban de Olot was jammed to the last inch of standing room for his three-hour sermons. The greatly moved throngs demanded the services of twenty-five confessors; and three priests were occupied throughout entire mornings only to distribute Holy Communion. In the evenings, "the sound of the voices [the multitude praying the Rosary] was like the rumble of thunder." Each day and all day, companies of countryfolk from miles about were to be seen making the Stations of the Cross in the chapel. And it was here in Olot that the faithful began resorting to almost any means to acquire fragments of anything pertaining to the apostle, coveted as relics.

The town unanimously pleaded that he remain among them longer than promised, but this was impossible. He was committed to open the Granollers mission September 15. At the hour of departure, however, the *Olotinos* were persuaded that Heaven was with them, for the skies opened to drop a cloudburst. It was unthinkable that he set out afoot in any such tempest. But that is exactly what he did and, in due course, arrived at his destination in a cheerful mood, impervious to the water which was running off his body in veritable rivers.

The Granollers engagement terminated, he pushed on

without a moment's rest to Valles; the coastal towns lying between San Feliú de Guixols and Barcelona; from Monistrol de Montserrat to Masnou, Tejá, Arenys de Mar, and Arenys de Munt. Everywhere the missions achieved enormous benefits in deepened devotion and moral reform, though the incidents varied. At Arenys de Munt the work was blessed by its impact upon a number of youths who, inspired by the preaching, determined to embrace the religious life. Here too, his always thronged confessional was mobbed by penitents who, in order to preserve their places in line, came provided with lunches! They would gladly wait hours, even days, for the privilege of unburdening their consciences to, and receiving absolution from, "*el santito.*"

A less welcome manifestation materialized at Arenys de Munt, in the form of a group of disorderly women who entered the church while he was preaching to raise a commotion with noisy comment and, finally, screams! But this calculated attempt to prevent the people from hearing his words proved a fiasco. Padre Claret counseled his auditors to ignore the disturbers; and as he proceeded with the sermon the women, deprived of attention, suddenly disappeared and were seen no more in the town. Many held that they were demons in disguise, but they could well have been agents of those interests whose annoyance at Anthony Claret's influence increased in proportion to its growth.

On through the year and until Easter, 1845, without a day's break, he preached and walked, walked and preached, brushing aside all suggestions that he should rest. Rest? Those night hours not devoted to prayer were spent writing and in searching out new techniques for the institution of wide-scale reforms. He organized the Society Against Blasphemy; and dedicated it to the Virgin. It was one of many surprisingly successful works which revealed that, while he was a man of his own time and place in matters of devotion, sacrifice and discipline, Anthony Claret was a century ahead of his time in his methods for reform.

Results for God and souls were all that counted and in their pursuit the word "rest" was, for him, meaningless. Even so, he couldn't begin to do all he longed to do for his compatriots' spiritual welfare. If only he had two, three—or twenty!—likeminded, high-hearted young padres to give him the energetic help he needed! But what hope might he entertain for the foundation of a religious order in these intolerant times? It would be suppressed instantly and then perhaps even his personal efforts prohibited! He did not fear prison or exile, but there had already been many martyrs, so many that thousands of Christians were now bereft of spiritual guidance. So, for the time being, he must content himself with merely doing the work of a dozen men!

VII

THE AUTHOR

A NTHONY CLARET had begun his writing career with a small volume of forty-eight pages entitled: *The Righteous Road* [1] (although an earlier pamphlet, *Advice to Nuns*, is sometimes alluded to as his first book). The first edition, published in 1843 at Vich, was soon exhausted. A second Vich printing and others from Barcelona and Manresa, all in Catalán, were followed by Spanish versions. Each edition was larger than the preceding and also the text was amplified until, within seven years, while it ran through eighteen Catalán and seventeen Spanish printings averaging 10,000 copies each, this devotional work so modestly launched had been expanded to 500 pages! Even this was but the beginning of what was to become a most impressive record by the standards of any time. There would be seventy editions in Catalán, 140 in Spanish (one of 300,000 copies); and the author would live to see a half-million copies in the hands of his people. Finally, after its translation into Basque and Portuguese, "there were few homes among Hispanic peoples which were not enriched, as they still are, by the *Camino Recto*." [2]

Other works followed rapidly and met an equally enthu-

77

siastic reception. This immediate success confirmed his opinion that "nothing may be expected to aid the ends of the Christian apostle as effectively as Catholic books." Sometimes he toyed with the idea of founding a religious press for the issuance of his and other Catholic writers' works, old and new. But for the organization and management of so ambitious a venture he knew he would require the help of dedicated associates, as well as the moral support of one or more influential churchmen. The promotion of these vital developments would take time.

In March, during the Mataró mission, he wrote to his friend Padre Cruells: "I am glad the books I sent you were well received. I believe those now on the presses of Barcelona and Vich, which I wrote for parents and young people, will be just as pleasing. I am presently doing one for married ladies. Seeing the extraordinary fruitfulness of the books, I feel a compulsion to work really more than I am able, and so strongly that I assure you I am stealing the hours [to do it] from sleep." [3]

One may well ask, from *what* sleep? Long before adding this labor to his heavy schedule, he had accustomed himself to manage on no more than two hours' sleep nightly. Now, to make room for the writing, he was robbing himself of even this brief respite from his multitudinous activities. Several housekeepers and chambermaids were to testify that, on this sensational tour of 1843-45, the missionary's beds never gave the slightest evidence of use! In any case, he must have foreseen what he would have considered justification for this latest sacrifice. Already his *Salutary Advice to Señoritas* and *Useful Advice to Parents* were enjoying wide distribution. And the latter, according to Padre Fernández, writing in 1941 "is, perhaps, actually in greater demand in our own day, which has seen the circulation of hundreds of thousands of copies, than it was in Claret's. It has had more than fifteen editions, each of approximately 400,000 copies." [4] Other titles published during 1845 were: *The Rich Epicure* and *Rules for Pure Morals.*

In the artistic sense, it may be held that he was not a great writer but he possessed the gift of exact and forceful expression in easily understood terms. This alone might explain the popularity of his work. But, as in the case of the sermons, the impact of his words on the public was too powerful to be accounted for by his natural talent. As always, his results exceeded logic because, quite simply, his least undertaking was always supernaturally blest! Yet he had the most practical reasons for all he did; and these were what he customarily put forward matter-of-factly, sometimes indeed, almost drily. In the *Autobiography* (the one piece of writing he approached with reluctance but under holy obedience) he invariably attempted to make his successes appear no more than reasonable developments—reasonable, of course, to one wholly dependent on God's aid and direction.

He was, himself, quite aware, however, that there were times when, through special graces granted him from Above, he penetrated the souls of his penitents so readily that he knew them better than they knew themselves. "God has conceded me the grace to read them as I might a book; without any study whatever, I see souls with all clarity," he told the nuns of Santa Teresa de Vich during 1847. And later: "He said we must learn to recognize our defects, identify the things through which we are lost. 'I have already told you individually what they are,' he said. 'You may ask how I know. But why should I *not* know if God tells me?' " [5]

This also explains his ability to hear so many in confession during each event-packed mission and retreat. Unnumbered times, he could not bring himself to wait for deluded or confused penitents to stumble through poor or incomplete confessions, but impetuously reminded them of sins they were "forgetting," hastening their recognition of their precarious states of soul. (He was also saving time he needed for the benefit of others.) The astonishment and chagrin of those confronted with proof that their hearts were open books to this holy man emphasized, as nothing else might have done, the stubbornness and subtlety of the sins that hid beneath insensitivity or self-delusion.

In spite of the frequency of such occurrences, Padre Anthony understood that they were exceptional. This gift was not always granted him, though he always recognized the moments when "the Spirit of God *was* upon him." One day he invited a Carmelite nun to make a general confession. She declined on the grounds that she was unprepared. "Look," admonished the missionary, "it is *now* that I have the light." But it did not suit the religious to improve her opportunity— an unfortunate circumstance she would regret all the remaining days of her life.[6]

II

Immediately after Easter (1845), Padre Claret left Mataró for Barcelona to confer with his printers. Pressing along the road toward the metropolis, he overtook a weary man plodding slowly beneath a bulky pack. Taking note that this was "a good man," the missionary reduced his pace so that they might continue on together. Padre Claret was always quite as eager to converse with an individual he happened upon by chance as to address a multitude. This time, however, the talk was interrupted just as it was becoming animated. The man was obviously disturbed by a group of persons they could see in the distance. When Padre Claret asked him to explain he said he feared they might be government cargo inspectors. If so, they would examine his pack, discover it to be filled with tobacco and confiscate it! Being a poor man,

he had apparently risked an infraction of some ordinance prohibiting the sale of tobacco by unlicensed agents in the hope
of a profit to provide for his numerous hungry children. Buy-
ing the tobacco had taken every cent he possessed and were
he to lose it, his family faced ruin!

Padre Anthony's compassion aroused at the thought of the
needy household, he insisted upon carrying the sack himself.
"They won't say anything to me," he said.

"No, but they won't believe the tobacco is yours, and how
will this help me?" the distracted man complained. However,
he relinquished his load to the cheerful priest.

"What have you there?" came the peremptory demand as
the pair approached the inspectors.

"French peas," replied dauntless Padre Anthony, as he un-
concernedly eased the load off his back for examination.

His companion's agonized state of mind while "the law"
stepped up to "discover all" may well be imagined. But, as
one fascinated by his certain doom, he too drew close and
peered into the now open pack. Happily, no one was observing him, so that the transition from paralyzing fright to
grateful joy reflected in the poor chap's eyes passed unnoticed. In an instant, he had been transported from terror into
the high, free air of hope! For, as affirmed by this marvelous
Padre Claret, his sack actually did contain only the permissible
peas!

The inspection concluded, they continued on and soon
entered the relieved man's home village. There he received
his property from the hands of his benefactor, and from his
lips a few parting words of good counsel. He who had escaped
the penalty for his infraction by a miracle was ashamed of the
vagrant wish that such a marvel might have netted something
more valuable than a store of peas. He hastened to return
thanks that they would at least provide a few meals for his
youngsters. What then was his astonishment when he reached

his cottage, opened the pack and found it brimming over with the dry, sweet-smelling tobacco for which he had risked so much! Overcome by gratitude, he forgot caution and spread the story far and near. All Catalonia was soon talking of little else and Claret's friends, both clergy and laymen, began to seek his confirmation of the anecdote. The only response they received was a smile and, "Let it go." [7]

His May and June missions at Villanueva and Geltrú were so widely acclaimed that they brought the anticlericals' resentment to fever pitch. At the former station he was the victim of an outrageous attack, witnessed by Padre Miguel Gironés. "One day while he was hearing confessions beside the Las Nieves door behind the main altar, a bomb exploded close beside him. The reprehensible attack disgusted Sr. Claret who at first resolved not to complete the mission. 'That there is opposition is a good sign,' he told me, 'but this is too much, so I shall go.' . . . I informed the parish pastor who, in company with the *Alcalde* and other notables pleaded with him not to abandon the work he had commenced. He acceded to those supplications with the result that, from there on, eight or ten of us confessors were permitted no rest whatsoever by the penitents. The preaching produced great fruit in this villa." [8]

His impulse to withdraw from Villanueva had not arisen from concern for his own safety. There is abundant evidence that he coveted martyrdom. But he always obeyed the scriptural injunctions to the apostle as literally as was possible in the nineteenth century. He never touched money; ate what was set before him (and usually less); devoted every moment to spreading the news that "the Kingdom of God is at hand." So, when bombs commenced falling upon his confessional, he doubtless considered it time to shake from his feet the dust of a public harboring such determined "nonhearers." There was, besides, need to avoid danger to others. However, he must have seen God's will in the protests registered by the leading citizens; and proceeded to go on to another notable triumph for Him.

"Why do you always refuse money?" Padre Gironés once asked him.

"Because I have no use for it."

"Well, even a foot-traveler must need things en route."

"No. I lodge in the rectories."

"But you won't invariably find rectories along the way."

"Then I stop at an inn."

"Where you must pay!"

"They've never charged me anything."

"But in the event that one should, *quid faciendum?*"

"When that occurs, we shall manage however we are able." [9]

The series of missions that had occupied him for nearly two years terminated in June, and he returned to Vich and a summer of writing. As a result, in the ensuing year ten new subjects flowed off Catalonia's presses. Though several of these were directed to children, others treated some decidedly "touchy" customs of their elders. For, if piety has ever been characteristic of the Spanish race, so has its love of gaiety, diversion and fine dress. The futile and morally dangerous aspects of these addictions he handled sternly in *Gallery of Disillusion* and *Spanish Women as Seen by the French.* The latter "invaluable work," writes Fernández, "could be read, if not with pleasure since it opposes their preferences, to great advantage by feminine fashion slaves of any time or place. It can never lose its pertinence because its doctrine is based on the eternal Christian canons relating to moderation in dress and adornment." [10]

It seems sure that his published messages varied little from the lengthy sermons delivered day-in and -out during the missions. They were filled with the same truths, Biblical illustrations, and references to the lives and works of the saints which, though probably familiar to his readers, may not always have been properly comprehended. Certainly he never resorted to novelty or cleverness to enhance the appeal of his topics. To understand the immense popularity of those which uncompromisingly denounced contemporary practices and their favorite foibles, it is necessary to know something of the sentimental heart of the Spanish woman. For this he unerringly selected phrases not only appropriate but irresistible.

"Now observe, my daughter, the contrast between the luxurious dress of many women and the raiment and adornments of Jesus. . . . Tell me: what relation do their fine shoes bear to the spikes in Jesus' feet? The rings on their hands to the nails which perforated His? The fashionable coiffure to the crown of thorns? The painted face to That covered with bruises? Shoulders exposed by the low-cut gown to His, all striped with blood? Ah, but there is a marked likeness between these worldly women and the Jews who, incited by the devil, scourged Our Lord!

"At the hour of such a woman's death I think Jesus will be heard asking: '*Cujus est imago haec et circumscripto*—Of whom is she the image?' And the reply will be: '*Demonii*—of the devil.' Then He will say: 'Let her who has followed the devil's fashions be handed over to him; and to God, those who have imitated the modesty of Jesus and Mary.' "[11]

Padre Claret was merely stating that it is we who daily crucify Our Lord not only by our more flagrant sins, but by our avid, or even careless, pursuit of the occasion of the sin of pride. But knowing so well that the plain statement would never galvanize the attention or capture the facile imaginations of the emotional Latins as would his arresting illustrations, he adopted the practice of drawing unforgettable word-pictures to emphasize his points. How well he understood his people is proved by the fact that the 144 works he wrote would, in less than a century, become *11 million* volumes totaling *500 million* pages! [12] Doubtless he took comfort in the realization that these were words which must long survive his hard-driven life; effect the "lasting good" he longed to achieve for God and his fellowmen. Certainly there is a note of obvious satisfaction in his affirmation: "All these books have been written, not for self-interest, but for God's greater glory and the good of souls. I have never made a penny of profit from them." (He spent $300,000 during his lifetime purchasing Catholic books for free distribution to the public.) "On the contrary, I have given away thousands of copies. . . . And with God's help, I shall distribute books until I die, for I consider this one of the *greatest* of all alms."

VIII

THE CELEBRITY

WRITING NECESSARILY REMAINED a side issue for a missionary in such demand. In September Padre Anthony embarked on another tour which, by April, would carry him across Solsona, Gerona and Tarragona. En route to the capital of the first diocese, which had been clamoring for his labors for two years, he covered five smaller towns. From San Lorenzo he was accompanied into Solsona by a group of followers. Eduardo Llohis, a student, described the general consternation when, an hour before his arrival, Padre Claret unexpectedly called a halt, saying that he needed a rest. Protests that this, for him, unprecedented notion was unjustified and uselessly prolonged the journey availed nothing. The apostle had divined that the *Solsenses* had prepared an elaborate reception for their long-awaited visitor. By delaying his appearance until the people, persuaded he could not now be expected until the next day, had retired, he avoided the well-meant but unwelcome festivities!

The civil war had reduced Solsona's population by four-fifths. An apostle of peace was therefore received with open arms and heard with eager ears. His fortnight there included a daily schedule of fifteen "painful" hours in the confessional. Unfailingly, he made his appearance at the church before daybreak to hear the long lines of penitents who had been waiting for him all night. (The more affluent occasionally paid "stand-ins" to hold their places.) Until noon, he withdrew from the confessional only for the time required to celebrate his Mass, make his thanksgiving, hold an hour's Exercises for the nuns, and preach another hour to the clergy. In the afternoon, following another sermon for the latter, he resumed the confessions until time to hold the regular evening mission. Thereafter, he was again at the penitents' disposal. Their queues extended to, and through, the Cathedral's wide-flung portals into the surrounding streets. To assure this blessing of unburdening their souls to "a saint," many of these patient folk had come in to Solsona from as far as ten hours' distance.

The doors were closed to the general populace only during the Exercises for the clergy which, though proper, served to alarm an overmeticulous military governor and his aide, an officious noncommissioned officer. In due course the "diligence" of this pair was reflected in an official inquiry directed to the *alcalde* by their superior.

Supreme Government of Lérida Province.
I have received notice that a *sacerdote* named Marín has recently arrived in your city and convoked all the ecclesiastics of the same and its vicinity in the Cathedral Church where he preached a sermon behind closed doors on the morning of the seventeenth of the present month. This act, of itself serious in the country's present circumstances, gives place for sinister interpretations. For this reason, I ask that, after making a thorough investigation in concert with the military governor, you inform me fully upon this matter. Please ascertain whether the above-named *sacerdote* mixed political ideas into the said sermon . . . as well as whatever can be learned of his political antecedents,

conduct, etc. I also wish to be told whether, from the expressions or political attitudes of the ecclesiastics, you judge that the preaching may have had any disguised object behind the inculcation of ideas for the better discharge of their duties.

God guard you many years.

Lérida, October 21, 1845—José Matías Belmar.

To the *Sr. Alcade Constitucional de Solsona.*[1]

This communication elicited a no less stern reply.

Office of the Constitutional Mayor of Solsona.

The *sacerdote* preaching in this city is the Reverend Anthony Claret who, authorized by the vicar general of the diocese of Vich to which he pertains, has been touring the province for some time, preaching wherever he is called, including the city of Barcelona. No claim has ever been made that he has either digressed in the slightest degree from the Gospel, nor touched upon any political issue whatsoever.

Each evening he speaks to extraordinary concourses of people in the Cathedral Church, and so pure and holy is his teaching that, were his hearers to comply with it, this would be the very best security against revolutions and disturbances.

The life of this ecclesiastic is exemplary. He does not associate with or talk to anyone, nor admit visitors. All day long he occupies himself in hearing confessions and preaching. And wherever he has preached all praise him to the stars.

He seeks only the good of souls; and to this end, is indefatigable. Long before daybreak he is in the confessional where he remains until ten o'clock—when he goes to speak to the MM. Sisters; and at eleven, to the clergy. In the afternoon he preaches again to these, after which he returns to the confessional until his evening sermon to the town.

True, his sermons for the ecclesiastics (attended not only by the priests of this city, but also by those from surrounding towns in compliance, as I understand, with the order of the provisor and vicar general) are delivered behind closed doors. But this is not because they touch upon politics. His exhortations are confined to attacking the vices and defects afflicting some of them; and to inculcating Gospel morals. Through them and edifying example he points out the road to salvation.

Actually, sermons have always been delivered to the clergy behind closed doors in this city, doubtless that the reproaches directed against failures and weaknesses in some cases may not scandalize the people. Nevertheless, it would be simple enough for anyone desirous of hearing them to conceal himself in the church; and furthermore, their content could be verified merely by listening at the window of the Episcopal Palace which opens into the temple.

It was an indiscreet zeal that sent you this complaint; for, in advance of taking such a step, your informant should have verified what was being preached to the clergy, either by entering the church prior to the closing of the doors, or by making inquiries of the attending priests. Then, had the facts borne out what has been unjustifiedly suspected, the proper procedure would have been to notify, not your excellency, but the authorities of this city, in the certainty that they would invoke the indicated measures.

The sermons preached here have been directed to nothing but the inculcation in all of their duty to comply with their obligations and, I repeat, *were* everyone to observe this missionary's teachings, there would be no more revolutions.

God guard you many years.

Solsona, October 23, 1845.

To the *M.I.S. Jefe Político de la Provincia de Lérida.*[2]

By the time this correspondence had passed between the civil and military authorities, the Solsona mission had come to a triumphant close and Padre Claret was on the road again. Within a few weeks he had labored across the province of Barcelona into Gerona. The populations of many smaller communities converged upon his missions at Bañolas and Figueres that they, too, might hear the "wonder-worker." In so titling him, the people had by no means been excessively optimistic, for there would indeed be miracles to see at these stations! The beneficiary of one was a small boy who, for seven years, had suffered excruciating pain from an affliction which caused his entire body to ooze pus. The medical attention he had received had aggravated it. The numerous novenas offered by his distressed family had been unavailing. His brother is our witness to the result of their parents' determination to present the suffering child for "treatment" by Padre Claret:

"The servant of God was hearing confessions when my father arrived at the church with my brother. They sent him a message that a sick person wished to see him. The sacristan returned with word that penitents came ahead of the bodily ill; but that they should wait. When Padre Claret emerged from the confessional he found my father holding my brother on the presbytery stairs. He observed the sick child briefly and then, after inquiring of my father what remedies had been prescribed by the *médicos*, advised that these be continued, and meanwhile, he said he would recommend the case to God. I cannot say if it was a matter of hours, but, within two or three days at the most, my father was astounded to see my brother completely healed. When he called out to my mother that the *chico* was well, she wouldn't believe it until she saw his body perfectly clean. They attributed the cure wholly to the intercession of the servant of God, because, in the interim, they hadn't even applied the medicine. . . ." [3]

The pastor of Figueres, Padre Comas, had, unfortunately, died before the taking of the testimony relating to the prodigy which favored him. However, one of the four witnesses who affirmed it was Carmen Ventós y Casamor, his close relative. She testified: "During Sr. Claret's Figueres mission, he one day had occasion to visit Gerona, a distance of some six or seven hours by foot, his customary means of travel. He asked the pastor, whose health was delicate, to accompany him a little way along the road. They set out, conversing as they walked, until suddenly Padre Comas was both amazed and distressed to find that somehow they had reached Coll d' Orriols, three hours beyond Figueres. 'Oh come on along with me,' urged the servant of God. So they continued on until, just before reaching Gerona, the pastor discovered a large tear in his mantle. Well known in the town, he was ashamed to make an appearance with his apparel in such a state. But, taking the mantle in his hands, Sr. Claret assured him: 'Don't worry—this isn't anything.' And to the pastor's astonishment, he saw that the rent had disappeared." [4]

I I

By the middle of January the missionary was deep in the heart of Tarragona, a province which would take most of his time during 1846 and most of 1847. In town after town he labored to achieve what were affirmed the greatest results he had yet obtained. The miracles were piling up and, although too numerous for recording here, we shall mention one incident which had the merit of humor. During one of the sermons at Valls three youths seated just below the pulpit began to be restless, to whisper, then, to complain audibly of the length of the preaching. Finally, the most audacious of the trio deliberately tossed an orange at the pulpit! Padre Claret ignored this disrespectful gesture and continued calmly on to the conclusion of his message. Later, as he prepared to close the church for the night, the sacristan saw someone tarrying in the building, sitting below the pulpit. The sacristan's request that he go on home and permit the locking of the church brought the reply, "I can't." This odd behavior was reported to the pastor who, in his turn, advised Padre Claret, now at his prayers in his quarters.

"Well, just tell the young man he may go now and to see me in the confessional at nine in the morning," he said.

After this message was delivered to him, the orange-tosser found himself able to rise and make his departure! [5]

The outstanding event of the Tarragona mission was the missionary-author's meeting with Canon José Caixal y Estrada,[6] the brilliant and erudite churchman in whom he believed he had found the ideal associate for his long-contemplated publishing project! In spite of the fact that the careers of these two had followed widely divergent paths, they held an identical estimate of the value of Catholic books in winning and developing informed Christians. And as their friendship unfolded through conferences on this mutual interest, it was soon obvious to both that they might expect to become complementary collaborators in such an endeavor. With enthusiasm they began to lay their plans for a work destined to be an outstanding achievement of their lives, and one that, incidentally, was to survive to our own day. This was the Religious Library. Padre Anthony could continue his tour in the confidence that the canon would leave no stone unturned in his search for ways and means to establish their press.

From Tarragona the apostle proceeded to carry the missions through the whole of Catalonia. His efforts were blessed by his notable success in bringing many youths into religion. Years later a canon of the Vich Cathedral would write: "When I was very young, I made a two-hour trip with some other lads, all more pious than myself, to Selva to hear him preach. Arriving at 3 A.M., we found a vast crowd passing the night in the open air before the church. In this way all sought to assure themselves places inside the following day in order to hear him and have the happiness of confessing to him. I recall very clearly the forcible call to an ecclesiastical career that I felt during his sermon on the Magdalen. I lived in Reus at the time and for me the multitude which had gathered at Selva to hear this missionary was most impressive." [7]

A highlight of the Selva labor was the affecting—and lasting

—reconciliation of the populace which Claret had found divided in bitter enmity over a purely local issue. Without going outside the church edifice he dissolved this long-standing contention merely through his powerful exhortations upon the command: "Love thy enemies."

Each community he touched would long cherish the blessings it knew through him. A generation later the senior priest of Falset reported to his archbishop: "Antonio Forcadell y Vadiella, forty-one years of age, a sandal maker by trade, married, and a native of this *villa*, has related an incident of his childhood, during the holy mission of the Reverend Padre Claret. One evening the missionary and some other priests chanced to pass the Forcadell doorway. Although, owing to an eye affliction, the Forcadell boy was unable to see even light, upon hearing a mention of the venerable missionary's name, he suddenly ran into the street, calling: 'Padre Claret, you must cure my eyes.'

" 'My son,' was the reply, 'I'm not a doctor.'

" 'That doesn't matter. You can cure me if you wish.'

"And thereupon, with the utmost kindness and sweetness, the apostle put his fingers on the sightless eyes, saying: 'Now just wash them well every day with clear, clean water.' The lad was cured instantly, and never again noticed the least thing wrong with his vision. . . ." [8]

Before the close of April Padre Claret had: preached and cured a paralytic seven-year-old girl at Porrera; gone on to benefit Prades and Montblanch (where in twelve days he delivered eighteen sermons to the people, nine to the clergy, three to the nuns, and one to the prisoners); held a week's mission at Espluga de Francolí, others at Palma de Ebro and Bobera.

In the midst of a sermon to an immense, soundlessly attentive concourse in Bobera's plaza, all were shocked to hear the rude shout of a mule train driver who had just entered one of the bordering streets. "How about a little water for the preacher, who must be good and dry!"

Unperturbed by this mockery, Padre Anthony digressed from his theme only long enough to quiet his hearers' indignation and prevent any retaliation. "Let it go, my brothers," he counseled. "All too soon this poor man and his animals are going to see entirely too much water." Following this enigmatic comment he switched back to his subject; while the unchallenged muleteer continued on his way. But within a few days Bobera learned that the man and his beasts had all been drowned in the Serós River!

After a rousing six-weeks' revival at Lérida, Padre Anthony started working his way back to Vich and what, in his parlance, at least, meant "rest"—another summer of writing. If he heard the reverent, oft-repeated word, "saint," on the lips of those for whom he was constantly securing favors and miracles that passed natural understanding, he gave no sign. He was just a little country missioner on his way home to his desk, where new books, revisions of earlier efforts for forthcoming editions, and necessary letters to printers and publishers awaited his attention. There would be two long months to devote to these things—and *in daylight!* Once again, therefore, he would be able to claim his two or three hours of nightly sleep!

However, he soon learned that Vich expected more of him than a literary summer! His name had become ever more renowned as the books rolled off the presses of several cities. The capital of the diocese in which he had been educated considered him her own son, as indeed, by adoption, he was. All Vich was clamoring to hear him; and, under this urging, the vicar general was already organizing the elaborate *fiesta* for which an outstanding attraction would be Padre Claret's dramatic sermons in honor of the Queen of Heaven. These and all his activities would be given full coverage by the newspapers which, hailing him as "another Vicente Ferrer," credited him with the "social regeneration of Catalonia." [9] Long before he had ventured outside his native countryside Anthony Claret had become a symbol of holiness throughout much wider Spain.

IX

THE VICTIM

SOON IT WAS SEPTEMBER and Tarragona was again calling him. He took the road once more, stopping briefly in Barcelona for consultations with his printers. At Tarragona he resumed the talks with Monsignor Caixal on the projected publishing venture. They outlined the indispensable propaganda campaign; agreed upon the figures whose cooperation might best forward their aims. Claret would labor unremittingly to turn out new books, and be on the lookout for additional material to publish. But as so much of his time was otherwise occupied, Padre Caixal must supervise the press work and the distribution details. Even now the new mission, the occasion of Padre Anthony's presence in Tarragona, was under way. When it was over his schedule would carry him on from station to station across the length and breadth of the diocese. However, he departed greatly cheered by the assurance that the Religious Library would soon be a fact!

He had tried to believe, with Balmes, that the recent comparative calm in Spain's political affairs meant a continuing peace. It did seem that the proposed marriage of the young

Queen Isabel to the Carlist pretender might settle the dynastic quarrel which, since their student days, had kept the nation either at war or on edge in anticipation of new outbreaks of violence. Such a union would appease the *Carlistas* and make it possible for the crown to dispense with the support of the radical element. Once free of the troublemakers, the way would be cleared for the restoration of Spain's traditional political liberties; the long years of religious persecution should be over!

But this solution was not to materialize. Europe was still resentful of the country which had, for more than three centuries, controlled a vast empire and the American gold so greatly coveted by her neighbors. The empire, to be sure, had dissolved and Spain was no longer rich—to everyone's intense gratification—but, in spite of the efforts of an astute and ruthless contingent of unbelievers, she was still unquestionably one of the strongest bastions of the Roman Catholic Church, now so implacably hated by the many Europeans who had defected from the Church. Therefore, anything serving to unify and strengthen the Spanish nation must be prevented at all cost! (This attitude, unfortunately, has continued unabated to our own day.) Other even more specific interests were at stake. Napoleon was no more, but France still carried the germs of his will to power; and she still had the influence to wreck the plan to merge Spain's contending houses. Pressure was applied to force Isabel into a marriage with her cousin Francisco, the candidate of Louis Philippe. On the supposition that Francisco was incapable of giving her an heir, the ruler of the French entertained hope that the Spanish throne would eventually fall to his own son, the husband of Isabel's younger sister.

The logical result of this interference was a new Carlist revolt! Catalonia was overrun by an insurgent band known as *Los Madrugadores* (Men of the Dawn), owing to its policy of attacking just before daybreak. This military activity was, in itself, a most annoying impediment to Padre Claret's work. What followed was worse. The plotting of the anti-clericals who had so long feared his prestige now utilized the Catalonian press to link his name with the new disorders. It was falsely alleged that the *Madrugadores* had admitted moving at the command of the peace-preaching Padre Claret! "The only reason they said such a thing was to jeopardize my reputation and give themselves a pretext for arresting me to prevent my preaching the Word of God."

Nothing of this sort ever alarmed Anthony Claret, but Casadevall, now bishop of Vich, deemed it prudent to interrupt the great mission saga. Reluctantly the prelate ordered Padre Claret to Manresa, where he would be less exposed to violence than on the road or at more remote points. He returned at once, and commenced a retreat for the St. Vincent de Paul Sisters of Charity at the Manresa City Hospital. There, ". . . the sister superior told me that their former director Padre Codina had just been appointed bishop of the Canaries. Then she asked me: 'Would you like to go and preach in those islands?' I replied that I didn't follow my own will, but 'liked' to go wherever I was sent by the bishop of Vich . . . under his order I would go there as willingly as anywhere else. . . . Thereupon the good sister personally wrote to Bishop Codina about my dispositions. . . . Bishop Codina immediately wrote to my bishop at Vich who, in turn, wrote me commanding me to place myself at the disposal of the bishop of the Canaries."

This unexpected development was doubtless welcomed by Casadevall as something more than opportune. That Anthony Claret had remained totally detached from politics throughout his ministry was obviously not going to prove sufficient protection from the impassioned elements now determined to hound so influential a figure from the pulpits of a newly agitated Catalonia. His very life might well be in danger. Thus any assignment that would temporarily remove him from so ominous a scene could be interpreted as providential provision for the preservation of his future labors. Today's loss to Vich diocese should be tomorrow's gain for Spain and, perhaps, the entire Christian world.

Deus providebit (handwritten margin note)

Padre Claret received his summons to join Bishop Codina in Madrid, where he arrived in time to attend the latter's consecration; and where, while their voyage was being arranged, he busied himself preaching and hearing confessions of the sick poor at the general hospital. On February 23, 1848, they left the capital—this new prelate and the calm-eyed, holy apostle who would be of tremendous aid in establishing Codina's spiritual rule over his distant diocese. They were accompanied by an ex-cloistered Carthusian, by the bishop's Capuchin brother Padre Salvador and four Sisters of Charity who, at the last moment, had been permitted to offer themselves for service in the islands. Via Seville and Jeréz, they proceeded to Cádiz (where the name of the "miracle-working apostle of Catalonia" was as well known as in Madrid). And here, too, he preached to large congregations. His hearers in both cities expressed amazement at the simplicity and humility of one who had attained country-wide fame by labors pursued only in the provinces.

They sailed on March 6 in the three-masted schooner *El Corso* and, from a quaint description by one of the accompanying sisters, it would seem to have been an agreeable voyage. A few days after their arrival at the Grand Canary, she wrote home:

> Very appreciable parents and brothers: I assume you have received my letters from Sevilla and have also heard from Sor Dolores. In Madrid I had no time to write, for we offered ourselves on the 22 and left the 23.

We had a happy voyage. It seems the Good Father always looks after the welfare of His daughters. We left Cádiz on the sixteenth and all of us were a little seasick, but only for the first day, after which we passed the remainder of the time very pleasantly, especially Sor Magdalena Febre and Sor Felipa Salarich [the writer], since we spoke Catalán the whole way. The *Sr. Obispo* was happy to see us all so content; and his brother, whom Sor Dolores already knew, is so humorous he almost made us die laughing with his *catalanadas* [regional jokes of Catalonia].

Our shipmates were both so prudent and entertaining that we couldn't have hoped for anything better. It was four days from Cádiz to Santa Cruz and all that time we heard not a single bad word either from the sailors or the passengers. . . .

Ay! beloved parents and all the family: you mustn't have the least worry for me, because we lack nothing; and while I am faithful to my Spouse nothing will ever be lacking either for the soul or the body. During the journey we didn't neglect our prayers, silence, confessions or Communion, and we were always watched over by the padres who are five in number— the bishop, his Capuchin brother, Padre Antonio Claret, a Carthusian, and another collected at Santa Cruz. If I tried to tell you about the trip in detail I would never finish. So I give only a few highlights. Everywhere we were greatly honored. . . . Thousands met us at Santa Cruz. All stared at us and exclaimed: "*Ay!* how young they are! Why, they're just girls!" Others said: "They're Dominicans." For our part we could scarcely contain our mirth at the women's strange costumes. They seemed made up for a masquerade. They wore white flannel mantillas such as Aunt Toña uses when it rains. And above the mantillas, black hats. . . . Eventually we re-embarked for the Grand Canary where, to reach the shore, we had to transfer to a launch and then, as it couldn't approach land either, be carried by the boatmen. Everyone was watching and I covered my face to hide my laughter. The man told me, "Don't laugh, we all have to do the same." Then we had to ride burros masculine-style on some rough pack saddles. The island sisters, who were there with all their girls, surrounded my burro and—I fell down in the middle of the road! After that I walked a little way, and when I finally mounted, did so in reverse!

Please give my best to all who ask for me and in particular to my beloved mother, sisters-in-law and brothers. This must serve for all . . . *a Dios, a Dios.*

Sor Felipa Salarich.[1]

At Tenerife the Sunday before their Tuesday sailing for the Grand Canary, Padre Claret had preached his first sermon to the islanders. Immediately upon reaching Las Palmas, the see city, he opened Spiritual Exercises for the clergy.

Lent had opened before their arrival, but, between March 20 and April 15, both the prelate and Padre Claret preached strong missions. Each delivered a series of twenty-seven sermons. All the meetings were thronged. Nevertheless, it was troubling to see that the capital's upper classes were poorly represented. It did not take the newcomers long to discover the reason. An Anglo-American enterprise had chosen precisely this holy season to organize and present a program of lucrative spectacles, gymnastics and equitation, for the attraction of the more affluent islanders. Understandably repelled by this badly timed diversion, Bishop Codina appealed to Las Palmas' *alcalde* to close the shows—an action within that official's legal powers. However, the *alcalde* decided that he could do nothing about the matter, and the performances continued up to Holy Week, when the foreigners, profits in pocket, set sail from the Grand Canary. A few days later the public was deeply impressed by the news that disaster had overtaken the Americans. Their ship was attacked on the high seas by pirates who, after robbing them of their gains, murdered everyone aboard except two young boys!

In other ways the situation in Las Palmas left much to be desired. The prelate's party was horrified to learn that Jansenism had made definite inroads within the seminary. By exaggerating the dispositions required for the reception of the Sacraments, some of the clergy had managed to confuse and discourage the people. The profoundly orthodox parishioners, who understood nothing of these aberrations, were supporting the unhappy effects of doctrines which left them abandoned and heart-sick in their accumulating guilt for sins unconfessed and unabsolved! In many instances, even the priests were neglecting their obligation to receive the Sacraments regularly. This remissness had inevitably brought about the most unfavorable spiritual and moral results. A notion which had commenced as an excess of zeal, seemingly, had ended in "suicidal indifference." So, while the bishop went to work to straighten out the seminary, Padre Claret exhorted the people to forget all about the delusions thrust upon them by their erring priests. As always all their dependence must be upon the goodness of God, Who had given His children but one sure and easily available route to His forgiveness and grace—in confession and Communion.

The Canarians immediately responded by descending on his confessional in droves. They were so anxious to be heard at once that considerable disorder and competition ensued. Marshaling the assistance of all the confessors, the apostle from Spain suggested a procedure he had quickly devised to speed this vital ministry for which such unmanageably large crowds were insistently clamoring.

"With the intention of eliminating the penitents' contention for first places, I made them form groups of eight persons each, four men and four women, whom I instructed to keep advancing toward the confessional while repeating the *Confiteor* and blessing themselves with the Sign of the Cross. The usefulness of this method was that it made it unnecessary for the individual penitent to keep me waiting until he had blessed himself and said the required preconfession prayers. With these said in common, the penitent had only to start confessing as soon as he entered the confessional."

At the end of April Padre Claret left Las Palmas to open his mission tour in the important town of Telde. The triumph he achieved there with a notably disordered population was hailed by Telde's *padre cura* in a letter to Bishop Codina: "This town has never seen anything like it! The bitterest enemies have been reconciled; both public and private scandals have been cut off and expiated; broken marriages have been re-established; restitutions have been made. And why? Because *no one* is capable of holding out against the fire of his discourses, the kindliness and animation of his manners, his energetic reprehensions, his dialectics, and the impact of his reasoning. The unction of his words breaks the hearts of his listeners, and all, even the most disdainful natures, fall at his feet weeping." [2]

He had found Telde in the midst of a disastrous drought and the rustics distracted with worry for their crops. One day he assured them casually, "I can promise you, my brothers, that before the close of these Exercises a copious rain will restore life to your plants, tranquillity to your homes, and happiness in your hearts." And so it did. [3] This is the type of prophecy difficult to identify as a prodigy inasmuch as it might easily be a coincidence, but there were others that could not be explained away. One of these involved an impious young man whom it pleased to mock the mission, which his sister was faithfully attending with the intention of securing the re-establishment of their mother's broken health. The skeptical fellow not only burlesqued the apostle's Catalán accent, but disrespectfully parodied his sermons. Finally, during what was indubitably the last of these "take-offs," the irreverent clown was in the act of waggling his index finger in a caricature of Padre Claret driving home a portentous warning when a sudden gust of wind slammed the door by which he stood with such violence that, his finger being caught between door and jamb, it was severed from his hand and fell to the floor! Simultaneously Padre Claret—in the pulpit and speaking of the Divine Judgments—announced to his listeners that a youth of their town had just been castigated for his mockery of religion—by the loss of a finger.[4]

In Telde, too, he cured an epileptic and a paralytic. As a result of such works, each evening found the church overflowing with penitents awaiting the dawn arrival of the famed confessor; and on the mission's final day, 2,500 received Communion. When he went on to Agüimes, the missionary was accompanied by thousands for some eight miles until he was met by an equally large welcoming committee.

As Agüimes' church could not begin to accommodate the mission's following, he was forced to preach in the public plaza. "Never has this place seen so vast a concourse. Almost all of Telde, the whole town of Ingenio, most of the populations of the districts of Cursival, Temisas, Sardina, Verga, and even those of Maspaloma and Arguiniguín converged upon Agüimes, bringing their food with them. And here they remained for the mission's duration, gladly supporting all manner of discomfort." [5]

His instantaneous, unprecedented success throughout the Grand Canary parishes became a legend. From Agüimes forward churches never were large enough to hold his enormous followings, while the gesture of his first island devotees in accompanying him along the road from one place to another became established custom. His long foot journeys here would never grant him the solitude for which he must occasionally have yearned! En route to any destination the crowd following him would be joined by those who had tramped long distances to hail his arrival, meetings invariably marked by emotional scenes. One contingent wept because this was *adiós* to a beloved padre; the other, with joy at his presence among them. The holy magic he had always held for his own Catalonia was proving no less effective in this isolated, sea-locked domain!

He who came to bring them the eternal truths of Christianity gratefully acknowledged that this flock also taught him some important lessons. One he would never forget materialized after the conclusion of the Grand Canary tour, on Lanzarote. This island's scarcity of priests had caused the bishop to order his brother to accompany Padre Claret there to assist with confessions. The Capuchin was an exceedingly corpulent man who, when they landed and learned that their destination lay five miles inland, inquired hesitantly: "How shall we manage it? Do you mean to walk or ride horseback?"

"You know I always walk," replied Padre Claret.

"Well, if you won't ride, then neither shall I!" declared Padre Salvador.

Padre Anthony paused to consider. Unquestionably this unaccustomed exertion under a blazing sun would be real hardship for his heavy companion. "No," he said finally, "that I cannot permit. If you insist upon walking because I do, we shall both ride."

As it turned out, their little trip was somewhat spectacular. For, in place of the anticipated horses, the natives produced a single large and ungainly camel for their transport! Perched one behind the other on this creature's less than commodious back, the priests were soon fully occupied by their efforts to adjust themselves to its strange, swaying gait. Perhaps they shared a certain embarrassment over the incongruous picture they presented, because, while still some way outside the capital, they dismounted and walked on into town.

Not until the close of the Lanzarote mission did anyone mention the means of their arrival. Then, however, Padre

Claret was approached by a gentleman who asked: "Is it true that you are the same missionary who lately preached all through the Grand Canary?"

"Yes, I am."

"Then I think you should know that hereabouts people believe otherwise. They had been assured that *he* always traveled afoot. Since you arrived on a camel, some have declared they wouldn't attend the mission because you aren't the Grand Canary preacher, after all."

So his consideration for the comfort of one man had lost at least several men the mission benefits! Even a seeming indulgence in behalf of his own convenience could turn people away from an apostle. He must make sure to avoid a recurrence of any such misfortune!

II

During more than a year spent in preaching missions in the Canaries he continued the night writing—of new books; of the imperative letters to Canon Caixal. Their Religious Library, under the protection of Our Lady of Montserrat and St. Michael, was now in operation and had issued its first offering, Claret's fame-destined *The Catechism Explained.* Both the Catalán and Spanish editions (4,000 and 5,000 copies, respectively) had been sold out within ninety days, and now reprintings were in process. It was an encouraging beginning, but in this early stage of its development there were many problems upon which Caixal and a third associate, Padre Palau,[6] needed to confer with Padre Claret. Would not the library's prime instigator be returning to Spain soon?

He sensed that Monsignor Caixal was growing somewhat disheartened over his confrere's protracted absence. Other considerations were also calling him home. He was convinced that the dearth of missioners was everywhere obstructing the spiritual good of mankind. If his fame for unremitting labor, poverty, the joyful acceptance of hardship had moved such multitudes in this strange land (in spite of the camel episode!), what might not be attained by ten, twenty, a hundred apostles whose hearts, like his, flamed with love of God and their brothers in Him? Was not his growing preoccupation with this thought of recruiting and training a company of such men as missionaries to the whole world an indication from Above that such a project might now succeed? As he finished the fifteen months of his ministry to the Canarians, he was giving this dream the study that would transform it into the most glorious of all his works. He knew that the realization of the missionary order he envisioned must be effected in his homeland—which was also, unfortunately, that of his bitterest enemies. In spite of their inevitable opposition, would God clear the way for him to transmute this exile they had forced on him into so great a victory, following his reappearance in his persecution-riddled country?

"I left those islands at the opening of May 1849. As a parting gift, his excellency wished to present me with a new hat and coat, but I didn't want them. So the only present I took away with me consisted of five rips in my old hat, made by the crowds which nearly crushed me [each time] I left one town to go to another. All the time I was in the islands I had worked every day, aided always by God's grace. Trials were not lacking, but these I suffered joyfully, knowing that crosses are the Will of Our Blessed Lord and His holy Mother. And so I offered them up for the conversion and salvation of souls.

"O my God, how good Thou art! What unexpected means Thou dost use for the conversion of sinners. Worldly men had planned to entangle me in everyone's disfavor, but

Thou didst free me from [the threat of] prisons by calling me to feed and instruct the sheep of Thy Heavenly Father for whom, O Lord, that they might live the life of grace, Thou didst give Thy very Own. . . ."

X

THE FOUNDER

Aᴺᵀʜᴏɴʏ Cʟᴀʀᴇᴛ's mid-May homecoming was saddened by the news of the death of his brilliant friend, Jaime Balmes, with whom he had been conducting a fruitful correspondence on the aims of the library project. But there was joy in being able to verify the reports he had received while abroad that, once again, the persecution had waned; that for the moment, at least, Spain's clergy and religious could labor unimpeded by official obstruction. Surely, he reasoned, this was a time to be improved, by himself specifically, through the foundation of his missionary congregation. So, after a consultation with his printers in Barcelona, he hurried on to Vich to lay his idea before his superiors.

He found that the enthusiasm of Canon Soler, rector of the seminary, and Canon Passarell matched his own. Both also approved his selection of a title for the congregation: *Missionary Sons of the Immaculate Heart of Mary*.[1] Emboldened by this encouragement, the newly returned apostle next submitted his plan to Bishop Casadevall who, recognizing its timeliness, added his full support. With his prelate's blessing Claret was free to accept Padre Soler's offer of space in the seminary during the organizational period, which would coincide with the approaching vacations. And if all went well, in the autumn he could move to <u>Merced</u>, a monastery the government had placed at the bishop's disposal. (Although the new regime had abandoned the drastic antireligious attitude of its predecessors, it appears to have largely neglected to restore the previously confiscated Church properties and was probably relying upon the relief and gratitude of a clergy now liberated from active molestation to prevent complaints on this score.) [2]

Now, while Casadevall undertook to secure the necessary civil licenses, Padre Anthony set about a study of the characters and dispositions of several young candidates. In the end he was satisfied to begin with five followers, confident that the outstanding gifts possessed by his selections would compensate for their limited number.

In his forty-second year, Claret was qualified by age, prestige and experience for the direction of the group, though he always insisted that his merits were *inferior* to the others'. "I was the last and least of all for, truly, they were much more talented and virtuous than I, and I held it a happy and esteemed privilege to be considered the servant of all." And, making due allowance for his characteristic modesty, he certainly *had* gathered together a company so <u>felicitously</u> <u>diversified and gifted</u> that it could hardly have been improved. Esteban Sala was a distinguished scholar; Domingo Fábregas, a brilliant preacher; a superlatively winning personality and exceptional holiness characterized Jaime Clotet; [3] José Xifré was clearly a man born to command and organize; while Manuel Vilaró, Claret's ardent admirer, had fully absorbed the founder's individual spirit during their association in the labors of the pre-Canary missions. One of the group's greatest advantages was its youth. Next eldest after Padre

Claret was Xifré, thirty-seven years old. The youngest was the twenty-seven-year-old Clotet.

The first assembly of this promising band was held in a simple seminary cell beneath an image of the Mother of Divine Love on July 16, 1849. It was a day triply precious to Spaniards for, besides being the feasts of Our Lady of Carmel and the Holy Cross, it was the anniversary of their ancestors' decisive victory over the Moors at Las Navas.

"Today," Anthony Claret exulted, "marks the beginning of a great work!"

"How can we be sure when we are so young and so few?" asked Padre Vilaró anxiously.

"You don't believe it now, but you shall see," [4] responded the founder from his prophetic insight.

And indeed their glorious future was clearly forecast by his moving definition of a Son of the Immaculate Heart of Mary: ". . . one on fire with love of God, who spreads this fire wherever he goes, and who ardently desires and proceeds by all possible means to inflame the whole world with the Divine Love. Nothing daunts him; he takes pleasure in privations, embraces all sacrifices, cheerfully welcomes all calumnies, rejoices in every torment. All his thoughts are concentrated on discovering how he can follow and imitate Jesus Christ in all his labors and sufferings, and how he can best procure the greater glory of God and the salvation of souls."

After approving the name favored by their founder, these original sons of Mary's Immaculate Heart made the Spiritual Exercises with intense fervor. Anthony Claret delivered a sermon from the appropriate text: *"Thy rod and Thy staff, they have comforted me."* And then, inspired by the retreat, they turned their attention to drafting the constitution. For the present they would not take the vows which would establish a formal order (and conceivably run them into difficulties with this or a succeeding government), but simply proceed to fulfill the spirit and labors of an order as a congregation. The community life of monastic poverty would be as strictly observed as though it had been vowed. Meditation must be the keynote of their striving for spiritual perfection. Hourly they would review the oversights of the preceding sixty minutes, say a *Hail Mary* and make a spiritual Communion. One another's suggestions for their individual improvement would be welcomed gratefully. Honors would be avoided; calumnies and injustices willingly accepted. They must love their enemies, respect the civil authorities, practice angelic chastity, eat little. Illness, however, must be promptly acknowledged to facilitate proper treatment. Their lives would be dedicated to preaching and catechizing. The reading of newspapers was prohibited.

Until colleges could be set up for the training of the congregation's priests, it would accept ordained applicants who, once admitted, might not be dismissed for unfitness before the end of a full year's probation, unless for the commission of a serious moral offense. These men, however, would be free to withdraw at any time.

Anthony Claret was unanimously chosen superior of the group which now remained at the seminary and commenced its labors. The summer heat was at its peak. To Caixal the busy founder wrote: "I greatly wish to see you to discuss matters relating to the Religious Library, but M. Esteban Sala insists I shouldn't absent myself a single day or take my attention from the state in which we find ourselves. . . . We are applying all our energies to learning and virtue. The devil has beset us with some terrible attacks, permitted by Our Divine Master for our testing. One *compañero* [Padre Fábregas] is ill and we must nurse him day and night. My knee is troubling me and has to be treated. . . . I am giving the Exercises to twenty-some young priests; M. Esteban is holding them for the Hospital Sisters, and between the two of us we must do the same for the Teresas, Carmelitas, Claras, Beatos de Santo Domingo and also those of the Escorial. . . . So far we have been living at this *Colegio*, but the seminarians will soon be returning, when we shall have to vacate the rooms without yet knowing where we are to go, inasmuch as the place we had planned to occupy is not yet ready for us. . . ." [5]

The two Barcelona priests and one layman charged with the library's management during his absence had done very well. Sales of the works issued had covered the cost of operation. Since it was quite as great a feat then as it is today for a new publishing venture to "break even" from the outset, he had reason to be most grateful. Even this much success proved that the faithful were hungry for books that would aid them to become finer Christians; and furthermore, as he had foreseen, the press's offerings were bringing about many conversions.

The next step, therefore, must be expansion—on the largest possible scale. As this would incur responsibilities too heavy to be borne by priests, he had already determined that the mechanical labor must be turned over to a commercial house. In seeking to utilize the greater resources and efficiency of businessmen, he realized, but did not recoil before, the fact that such interests would not be satisfied by the mere recoupment of their investment. But though profit would inevitably be an objective, he argued that the books would still be making more Catholics, or better Catholics, than money; while, though without a cent of his own, he would somehow manage to raise the funds to supply them to the poor. The whole point was to insure that, by one means or another, this inspirational literature received the widest possible circulation.

His heart was filled with gratitude before the goodness of God! How wondrously he had been blessed in the realization of his two dearest projects which, it seems certain, he well knew were to endure far into the future. Millions of instructive and soul-stirring volumes and thousands of diligent missionaries were sure to spring from the library and the congregation! It had been given him to fashion these important establishments for the rescue of God's children from that fearsome specter of eternal doom which, since his infancy, had challenged all of Anthony Claret's compassion and zeal! And to developing and perfecting these works he fully expected to devote the remainder of his life.

But insofar as he anticipated giving this double labor his undivided and on-the-ground attention, he was mistaken! For the pattern of sudden reversal which had periodically operated to change the direction of his life and work—usually at the very moment when he was savoring the sweet assurance of success—was now repeated. The lad who was "going to be a priest" had seen himself transformed into a factory hand; the young industrialist and master of textile design into a Carthusian aspirant. Later, by means too subtle for analysis, the seminarian whose monastic dream had been permitted full scope to develop unopposed was abruptly thwarted and redirected to the secular priesthood. And then, though his missionary inspiration was to achieve magnificent fulfillment, he had most unexpectedly been led to, and still more unaccountably, away from, the Society of Jesus.

Amazingly successful in all his undertakings, he had never been—and never was to be—allowed to linger over a *de facto* accomplishment! Now, less than a month after the inauguration of the congregation and immersed as he was in plans for it and the library, Anthony Claret was stunned and at least momentarily confused when he received the news. He had been appointed archbishop of a foreign see lying halfway around the world—Santiago de Cuba! His first reaction was, however, occasioned by a consideration quite outside his disappointment in an assignment that would throw a vast ocean and the demanding duties of a prelate between him and his cherished foundations.

It ". . . frightened me so much that I didn't want to accept. I deemed myself unworthy of so exalted a dignity and incapable of its discharge, owing to my lack of learning and the virtue necessary for an office of such importance. And afterward, when I had reflected more at length on the matter, I decided that . . . I ought not to abandon the Religious Library and the congregation which had just come into existence."

The circumstances that had culminated in Claret's selection to rule a distant and difficult New World jurisdiction were really complicated. Both the Church and state had long been deeply concerned by the moral corruption and social dissolution seen to be rapidly engulfing the "Pearl of the Antilles," which was now also manifesting an alarming political unrest. The see of Santiago de Cuba (vacated by the promotion of Archbishop Cirilio Alameda y Bres to Burgos) certainly stood in need of a spiritual director who was an expert in reform.

The privilege of nominating the Spanish prelates, subject, of course, to papal approval, still attached to the crown. But in this instance the queen's choice, Bishop Costa y Borrás of Lérida,[6] had declined to accept the post. His excellency did, however, make a suggestion which indirectly called the attention of the minister of grace and justice, Lorenzo Arrazola, to Anthony Claret. In a letter recommending Bishop Codina for Cuba, Costa y Borrás mentioned that the prelate's first assistant in the Canaries, Padre Claret, would be an ideal man to fill the former's present see. Coincidentally, the papal nuncio, Brunelli, casting about for a likely candidate for Cuba, took counsel with a holy and widely venerated priest, José Ramírez y Cotes.

"Padre José, whom do *you* think I should appoint successor to the see of Santiago de Cuba?"

Without hesitation Padre Ramírez said, "Your excellency, Cuba stands in need of missionaries, of a missionary bishop. You will find him in Catalonia. He is Padre Claret, the man you sent to the Canary Islands. None other is so well suited to carry this responsibility." [7]

In early August, during the congregation's first days, its founder had been nominated for this post. His spontaneous reaction to the news of this dismaying complication, as reflected in his reply to the nuncio, reveals the extent of his misgivings:

Most Excellent and Most Reverend *Sr. Nuncio Apostólico,* worthy of all my veneration and appreciation: Upon descending from the pulpit yesterday at the termination of the Spiritual Exercises I gave to 200 priests at the Vich Diocesan Seminary church, my most worthy Prelate Don Luciano Casadevall called me aside and informed me of my nomination by Your Excellency and the *Sr. Ministro* to the Archbishopric of Cuba. Your Excellency can have no idea of the grief such a nomination occasions in my heart: for two reasons. The first is that I have no liking for honors, nor am I adequate for them. The second is that this ruins all my apostolic plans—which I shall describe to Your Excellency in a few words. Seeing the scarcity of evangelists and apostles in our Spanish territory, the great desire of the people to hear the Divine Word, and the many solicitations I receive to go preach the Gospel in cities and towns in all parts of Spain, I determined to gather and train a number of zealous companions, and thus, be enabled to accomplish through others that which it is impossible to do alone. And thanks to God, my idea has enjoyed so fine a start that I already have fifty-nine ecclesiastical disciples—some of whom are sure to become excellent preachers. However, since all these men are very young, this realization [depends upon] my carrying them, so to say, on my shoulders. And if, owing to this nomination, I retire, all may fall.

Moreover, in accepting, I bind and limit myself to a single archdiocese when my desire is to serve the whole world. Even in that small section of the globe I would not be able to preach as much as I wish, for I have seen with my own eyes the many negotiations which demand the attention of an archbishop. It seems to me that it would be much better for another to be elected and then, if desired, I could go [to Cuba] and even take some of my companions along, to give missions.

Your Excellency can meditate upon this [suggestion] and if, after that and further observation, it is revealed that God's Will is for me to accept the prelacy, it shall be served only by commanding me who, in imitation of my Divine Master, will obey to the death, the death of the Cross with its most holy grace.

God guard Your Excellency many years, and [it is for you] to command your devoted and attentive servant,

Antonio Claret, Pbro.

Vich, August 12, 1849.[8]

These objections did not convince the nuncio or the minister that the see of Santiago de Cuba should be entrusted to other than Anthony Claret. And, after a rather involved correspondence between themselves, the apostle and Bishop Casadevall, the latter resolved the matter by writing his predilect missionary subject:

Manresa, October 1, 1849.

My friend and *Dueño:* Upon my arrival in this city I received various letters, among them one from the Minister of Grace and Justice, together with another from the *Sr. Nuncio Apostólico* enclosing a copy of the one he remitted to you. I believe that neither [of these figures] wishes to invoke the word: "command," but if you weigh with the requisite maturity the reasons they set forth, they equivalate a formal precept. Both charge me with insistence to obtain your acceptance of the archbishopric of Cuba; and, having consulted the Most Holy Virgin of Montserrat [about this] I can say sincerely that you will be resisting the Will of God by rejecting [this assignment]. Therefore inasmuch as, from delicacy, these gentlemen wish to abstain from directing a mandate to you, I am taking the lead to order *in quantum possum* that you accept the said archbishopric because God so disposes—for the good of those unhappy souls [which comprise it] who, engulfed by the clouds and shadows of death, stand in dire need of a zealous missionary who, in his episcopal character, will revive their almost extinguished faith, and put them on the road to salvation.

[margin handwritten note: In as much as you are able]

If then, in view of my words, based on what these *señores* have written, you decide to accept—as I hope you will—you may write your acceptance directly to the Most Excellent Minister of Grace and Justice and to the *Sr. Nuncio*, as soon as possible; and if you wish to know in what terms, you may contact the Sr. Bishop-elect of Teruel, who will preserve a copy of your reply. Also I hope you will communicate your decision to me, sending the letter in the care of my nephew, M. Javier, who will forward it to me at the first opportunity.

May your well-being be conserved. Order what you will from your affectionate friend and servant,

Luciano, Bishop of Vich (Rubrics)

P.S. When you write me, please return the Minister's letter remitted herewith.[9]

"This command filled me with dismay since, on the one hand, I did not see how I could possibly accept; and on the other, I wished to be obedient. I asked for, and was granted, several days in which to consider before giving my final answer."

Before making a retreat to ask Divine guidance, Padre Claret called together his old friends and advisers, Padres Soler, Passarell and Bach, as well as young Padre Sala, to beg their recommendation of his problem to God, so that they might tell him what he should do. Perhaps the counsel he eventually received was considerably influenced by the bishop's letter. But however it was, "those good Padres, after conferring amongst themselves on the last day of the retreat, agreed that God willed my acceptance of the appointment. So, October 4, two months after my election, I did accept the office."

II

While he waited for the arrival of the confirming bulls, Padre Claret settled down to accomplish everything possible toward the firm establishment of his foundation. His young followers were appalled at the prospect of losing their leader and their inspiration. Still lacking the most minimum material resources, with no house of their own (they were now at Merced), there were even difficulties with certain of the new men. So it seemed likely, indeed, that all might "fall" once the founder had placed an ocean between himself and his fledging missionaries! Nonetheless, it became known that he had been favored by a number of revelations relating to their future. He foretold at this time that, although another revolution [10] would scatter the company, it would, following its baptism by the blood of one of its sons, eventually flourish to write a magnificent chapter into the missionary annals of the Church.

Revolution of 1868

"Meanwhile I also busied myself with the customary ministries: retreats for the clergy, for the seminarians, the nuns and the laity. I remember giving one of these from a balcony to an immense throng which stood out in the open square, under the Cathedral arches, in the surrounding streets, on other balconies, looking out of windows and listening from the rooftops of adjacent houses."

And he continued his efforts for the Religious Library, which now had its own well-equipped plant.

In the midst of all this he suffered an aggravation of his old leg infirmity which had been troubling him intermittently for the past two years. A tumor had developed during 1847, and now the pain, originally localized in the leg, had spread throughout his body. In December, while in Barcelona to inspect a new printing press which had just arrived from Paris, his condition became so alarming that he listened to the advice of his friend Dr. José Bofill and submitted to surgery. Complete bed rest and a special diet were prescribed by the surgeon who, to insure the meticulous observance of his orders, left his patient in the care of Señora Bofill. When that good lady ascended to the padre's bedroom with a cup of broth, almost immediately after the doctor's departure, she was startled to find both bed and room deserted! Nor was the missionary anywhere in the house! No sooner had he found himself alone than he had risen, dressed and *walked* to the church where he undertook a long session of confessions. Hours later he reappeared at the residence of the worried Bofills, giving every evidence of well-being and, though on foot, wasn't even limping! He refused further treatment by the doctor—who later testified that such a routine was "very little natural or common." [11]

Finally, a year and two days after his reluctant acceptance, Anthony Claret was consecrated archbishop of Santiago de Cuba by Bishop Casadevall in the Vich Cathedral. Bishops Costa y Borrás and Fulgentius Lorente of Gerona were the witnesses. The ceremony took place on October 6, 1850, the feast of St. Bruno. It was also the first Sunday of October, the feast of the Most Holy Rosary.

As always with Antonio Claret obedience had won. It was a painful sacrifice that the first son of Mary's Immaculate

Heart must satisfy his own by counseling, praying for and watching her new congregation's glorious march into the future from afar. But he would use the merit of this pain for the benefit of his unknown Cuban subjects!

1854 Donoso Cortes prediction
that July 19, 1936
begin of civil war
between 2nd Republic
and Carlists

King Alfonso XII fled in 1931
leaving the country in hands
of Second Republic infested
with Communist revolutionaries.

Caudilo - dictator

XI

THE ARCHBISHOP 1850 - 57

absentia '57-60

Two DAYS after his consecration Anthony Claret left for Madrid where he received the pallium and was presented to the queen and her ministers by the nuncio.

Scheduled to sail from Barcelona at the end of December, he would have nearly sixty days for a swing through some well-loved towns. He must go to Sallent to take leave of his family. Would this, perhaps, be his last visit to them and to the scenes of his childhood?

When he left Sallent he set out by way of the Shrine of Our Lady of Fusimañya. As a small boy, hand in hand with his eldest sister Rosa (who "was the one who loved me most"), he had many times taken this road to visit the Blessed Mother in this little sanctuary. Now, in the same childlike simplicity, he asked her to make him a good bishop. He celebrated Mass before her image; preached a sermon on devotion to her. Then he journeyed on through Calders, Moya, Collesuspina and Vich to Barcelona, where he filled out the remaining time preaching in her churches and convents.

At eight-thirty on the morning of December 28, attended by a numerous party, he visited the Blessed Sacrament in the

122

Cathedral, looked once more at the chapels of Santa Eulalia, El Niño Inocente, El Cristo de la Agonía, San Olegario and La Concepción. From the cathedral they passed to the episcopal palace where Dr. Costa y Borrás gave the parting embrace to the missionary he had indirectly helped elevate to the hierarchy. And then, escorted by a constantly increasing company, he went on to the docks. *El Diario de Barcelona* [1] reported the impressive scene:

"When, following his custom, his excellency arrived at the wharf on foot to board *La Nueva Teresa*, he was cheered with enthusiastic affection from all sides. . . .

"The good prelate first blessed the crowd and later, giving rein to the impulses of his heart, he repeatedly extended his arms toward the surrounding concourse, almost as though he were offering these people his life's last *adiós*. The decks of the adjacent ships and an encircling swarm of smaller craft were jammed with the throng which had come to bid him farewell and pay a final loving tribute to one who, while remaining a model of simplicity, had ascended from a humble class to one of the highest offices of the Church.

"Aboard the steamer *Remolcador*, which towed *La Neuva Teresa* out of the harbor, were various ecclesiastics, gentlemen and ladies. By noon the schooner bearing the pious party had become but a dot against the horizon."

Those sailing with the new archbishop were: his vicar general, Juan Lobo; the congregation's Manuel Vilaró, acting as secretary, and Padres Barjáu, Sanmartí, Subirana, Coca, Rovira, Currius, Pladabella; the attendants: Betríu, Vila and Bonet. "There were also on board eighteen Sisters of Charity en route to Havana in the care of the Congregation of St. Vincent de Paul's Padre Pedro Planas . . . and some others. Hale and hearty, we all set out from Barcelona," wrote Archbishop Claret years later in the work he regarded as a task and a trial.

Young Padre Currius left us a more detailed, animated and, in certain passages, poetic description of those first hours on the deck that, for several weeks, was to bound the little world of some sixty-eight passengers and crew. All may have embarked "hale and hearty," but: "A few moments after the steamer left us, the seasickness began. It attacked Vilaró first . . . and the Sr. Provisor was so affected he couldn't eat a mouthful. But the victims endured with calm and gaiety, laughing together over this more or less anticipated affliction.

"The ship advanced before a moderate wind. We saw a school of dolphins. In the afternoon some of us, including a very seasick Lobo and certain of the sisters, prayed with the archbishop. I had held out very well, but what with the fumes of paint and pitch, plus the motion of the boat, I too began to notice some effects. . . . As the wind weakened, we were stuck for the night before the Garraf Mountains without even having passed Sitjes.

"At nightfall Vilaró and I bid farewell to our native land. [Then] praying the most holy Rosary with all the others . . . we made our voices resound upon the Mediterranean, whose waves were ensilvered by magnificent moon rays and the glittering stars that seemed to be rejoicing in our advance upon the other hemisphere. We sang the *Santo Dios*, which was to be our nightly practice. The sailors' devotion and respect were admirable, and proved to me that these men who live continuously upon water adore and serve God with more feeling than do many city dwellers who command abundant spiritual advantages. . . .

"Now, on the evening of the twenty-ninth, my friend, this is the setting in which we find ourselves: the heavens aglint with their lights, the sea in repose, the ship becalmed— inasmuch as Our Lord has paralyzed His elements (perhaps the better to hear the petitions of our devout ship's company). A complete little floating community, priests mingle with laymen, guileless virgins with sinners, the cultivated city gentlemen with rude seamen, as all pray together in the same words, the same modulations which make us, at this moment, equal in the eyes of God. With no covering but the heavens' immensity, no floor but the seas' immensity, we call on the Great God. . . . Surely in all the world there is no more suitable nor magnificent temple from which to render adoration to His Immensity!" [2]

They were not long becalmed. At Gibraltar they ran into a tempest. ". . . we had to await a change in the weather before attempting to pass the strait. The storm caused the captain to order us into Málaga harbor—where we were delayed three days. I occupied this time profitably," noted Anthony Claret, "preaching in the cathedral, the seminary, and the convent of that port."

The weather calmed, they continued to the Canaries in the expectation of a stopover at Las Palmas, where news of their favorite apostle's impending arrival brought a welcoming crowd to the shore. But again the waves began to toss ominously—and Captain Bolívar canceled the landing. Regretfully, they sailed on past the equally disappointed islanders. Lined up along the beach, they watched the vessel carrying their venerated friend toward a much more distant, larger and richer island.

"The deck was divided into two sections: the space between mainmast and stern was allotted to me and my companions; that from mainmast to prow, to the sisters who were left strictly to themselves, separated from the rest by doors with drawn blinds. All on our side arose each morning at a fixed hour, washed, dressed and made a half-hour meditation in common. Then I celebrated Mass . . . attended by all the passengers, including the sisters who, to do so and receive

Holy Communion, opened the dividing doors. Everyone received Communion excepting the priest who had to say the second Mass, which we offered in thanksgiving for God's protection. . . . The priests said this Mass in turn. . . .

"Following Mass and Communion we all went up on deck for tea. . . . At eight o'clock we assembled in the general cabin to say the Minor Hours. Then, until ten when we breakfasted, we held a conference on moral theology. Rest and study continued from breakfast until three in the afternoon, when we recited Vespers, Compline, Matins and Lauds, followed by another conference. At five we took dinner. We assembled again at eight to say the Rosary and other devotions. After this came a conference on ascetics; and before retiring for the night, we had tea." Nothing is surer than that Anthony Claret directed a school in Christian apostleship wherever he found himself!

"This was the ordinary program, but on feast days the second Mass was said at a more convenient hour so that the ship's crew might attend; and an afternoon sermon was also delivered by the priests in turn.

"On our arrival at the Golfo de Damas, I commenced a mission. . . . All the voyagers and the crew, from the captain down to the last seaman, attended, went to confession and received Communion. Ever since we have been close friends, so that on each voyage the captain and those sailors made afterward, they always dropped in to visit us."

The crossing took six weeks, but at last they sighted Cuba's emerald peaks. Soon they were coasting under the lee of its southern shore; then into Santiago's mountain-locked harbor. Although Havana had long since passed the old capital in size and importance, it remained the episcopal seat. From Santiago Anthony Claret of Sallent and Vich would rule over more than half of the island's four hundred and fifty mile extent.

[handwritten left margin: Sallent y Vich]

[handwritten note: Gallego / Portuguese spelling of ST. James]

[handwritten note: San Diego is Castillian for ST. James]

II

As he disembarked before a multitude deliriously enthusiastic to be able to greet the first prelate it had seen in fourteen years, he saw that his responsibility would be even heavier than the geographical statistics suggested. His subjects, massed beneath the banners and floral festoonings they had raised for him, ranged from those typifying his own countrymen through every conceivable shade to African black, not to mention a representation of Chinese coolies! Anthony Claret knew that Spain's just labor regulations for her colonies had been traditionally "overlooked" by interested Cuban officials; that during the epoch which had seen the loss of her other New World possessions and her further debilitation through her civil conflicts, she had been impotent to enforce her prohibition of slavery. Several countries, notably England and France, had taken advantage of her weakness to engage in a strong slave trade with Cuba, so that now the latter's 1,400,000 inhabitants included 600,000 Negroes, the majority bondsmen. The 60,000 Asiatics who had also been imported to augment the labor supply were living in almost comparable distress.[3]

By this time, too, there was an enormous intermixture of *pardos*, or mulattoes, largely the result of the illicit relations of Europeans and Negresses. Such circumstances had contributed heavily to the demoralization and worldliness which he had been warned were rampant. Nevertheless, the sincere enthusiasm with which he was met and accompanied to the cathedral was heartening. No missionary, least of all Anthony Claret, could condone the attitude of his predecessor— who had found what he called the well-nigh hopeless spiritual state of the Cubans so discouraging that he had refrained from visiting his see for more than a dozen years! And furthermore, here was indubitable evidence of his subjects' affectionate disposition toward the Faith. He was not a naïve optimist and therefore did not doubt that only too soon he would uncover the evil for which Cuba was famed, but he felt sure that wise guidance and strong discipline, elements he was prepared and determined to supply, were the prime needs of this long-neglected people.

His first concern was to acquaint himself with his native clergy. He immediately opened Spiritual Exercises for Santiago's priests. Then, before the Lenten mission to the public, scheduled to commence on Ash Wednesday, he improved a free day to make a thanksgiving pilgrimage with his missionary companions to the Sanctuary of Our Lady of Charity of Cobre, an image as enormously venerated by the Cubans then as it is today. Padre Vilaró described this interesting excursion, which introduced the Spaniards to an unfamiliar means of transport:

"At five o'clock in the morning the seminarians, all the *compañeros*, Canon Usera, and his excellency boarded a steamboat operated by the railway. It carried us a league's distance to a point where the trains unload [Cobre's] copper ore, where we transferred to a special train running to the foot of the mountain upon whose crest the sanctuary is situated. (This hill rises about 300 English feet above the level of the sea.) And do you know *how* we made the ascent? Without horses, without steam, but by means of an arrangement whereby our train was pulled to the top, balanced by another loaded with copper which was making the descent. They are controlled by a cable connecting with a pulley-block at the summit. . . . As one train descends through the force of gravity its weight lifts the other. If this means of locomotion surprised us, so did the strange trees we saw along the way. The landscape was very green. The sun was exceedingly hot, but we were refreshed by a soft breeze, the vista of the palm-covered plains of Coco and Níspero, and by the woodland scents. *Village*

"Upon our arrival at the *pueblo*, festive with flags which rippled from windows and doors of all the houses and above the church towers, the procession was organized for the ascent of another little knoll, the site of the rich and most beautiful shrine. There the Office of the Virgin was sung and all the priests celebrated Mass. In the afternoon we returned to Santiago well prepared for the mission," [4] which opened sensationally two days later. The populace of Santiago mobbed their five-naved cathedral to hear the sermons for which their new prelate was famed, as also the Church of San Francisco where Padre Vilaró was conducting supplementary services. Every available local priest and thirty seminarians meanwhile devoted themselves to catechizing the children in preparation for First Communion. The forty confessors, including the Spanish missionaries, were still too few to serve all the eager penitents (many of whom had not confessed in years!) who desired to be heard. Of a single day's Communions, Archbishop Claret reported in a letter to Caixal:

"It is believed that 2,000 received the Sacrament in the cathedral, and as many more in the other churches—those who were unwilling or unable to delay their breakfasts until eleven o'clock (a very heavy trial for our *delicate* Americans). But the cathedral was so crowded there wasn't room for a mustard seed. The Body of Our Lord was received in total composure by the noble *caballero* and the poor and *gentlemen* humble Negro slave at his elbow, by an aristocratic white native lady, next to a Negress born in Guinea. For [in church] there is no distinction whatever between classes or colors. God's grace can achieve anything." [5] Santiago had never experienced such a spiritual upheaval! Moreover, in many cases, its effects were to be lasting. The missionary prelate's introductory triumph was broadcast in numerous press dispatches, letters, even in the verses of Cuban poets that were duly reprinted by Spanish periodicals.

When the mission was terminated, he prepared to make the pastoral visit he must repeat at regular intervals in accordance with the Council of Trent decree. He convoked his missionaries for a division of the labors. Padre Lobo would, of course, function as ecclesiastical general during the archbishop's absence. Padre Currius and the Capuchin Padre Adoaín would proceed to Caney to open a mission; Padres Sanmartí and Barjáu, to Puerto Príncipe to teach catechism, while informing themselves fully upon the special problems of that distant and reputedly badly demoralized city. Subirana and Coca would commence with a mission at Cobre. Rovira and Pladabella were assigned to the seminary as professors of Latin and moral theology, respectively. Cuba's scarcity of priests was its greatest handicap, and there was obviously something amiss at the seminary which, though enjoying a large attendance, seemed not to be managing to ordain priests! The new instructors must locate the trouble for immediate correction.

"I myself remained in Santiago to open the visitation at the cathedral from whence I continued on to the parishes, administering Confirmation daily. Now, as such crowds waited to be confirmed, I . . . had papers printed and distributed, upon which all those to be confirmed were told to write their names together with their parents' and sponsors'. These were then handed in. This avoided confusion in the records and eliminated disorderly crowding at Confirmation ceremonies. I was to make this my procedure everywhere I went and it greatly facilitated the confirmation of 300,000 persons during [the ensuing] six years and two months." In June he visited Caney—and then Cobre.

Here he was met by disturbing news. In this town of pilgrimage where the island's most famous shrine was located, his missionaries had found hardly a dozen legitimately married couples! He praised their diligence in having substantially raised this figure prior to his arrival but—even so! This shocking situation required a strong hand—the hand of a patient but uncompromising prelate. The unhappy fact was that the Spanish-descended Cubans rarely condescended to marry their Negro and mulatto concubines, even when their half-caste progeny might number as many as nine or ten. Rightly suspecting that this intolerable state of affairs might prove typical, he attacked the problem vigorously. A committee was appointed to study each case individually. On its recommendations, he let it be known, all such unions must be regularized or, where impediments existed, dissolved!

It was a most trying undertaking, fraught with complications both tragic and absurd. Persons who expressed willingness, even eagerness, to legalize their unions were frequently not free to receive the Sacrament of marriage. Others, without the excuse of impediments under Church law were sometimes overcome with indignation to hear they were expected to make wives of their colored concubines. There were emphatic affirmations that Spain prohibited mixed marriages, a fallacy the archbishop had no need to consider. In all her colonial history Spain had never forced any such regulation. However, for any who persisted in this persuasion in spite of Padre Claret's assurances, his command was clear. They must immediately terminate their illicit unions. It would be a painful problem—the provision for their innocent children—but it would have to be faced. Although he praised God that many of these easy-going folk accepted their prelate's reprimands contritely and docilely obeyed his injunctions to amend their lives, Cobre had certainly given him a first-hand acquaintance with the repugnant moral deterioration that had engulfed a traditionally Christian nation.

III

His first word of the Puerto Príncipe revolt came from General Gemery who wrote to urge that he proceed to that place with all possible speed. The *comandante* believed that nothing could prove as effective in quelling the disturbance as the archbishop's presence. The captain general, José de la Concha, however, opposed the idea on the grounds that the clemency natural to a churchman might cause him to seek lenience for the rebel leaders of whom the government was determined to make an example. But an exchange of correspondence between the civil and ecclesiastical authorities caused De la Concha to reverse himself; and at the end of July Anthony Claret set out on the first of many long and arduous journeys across his diocese.

Although Puerto Príncipe, Cuba's third city, was no more than 180 miles northwest of Santiago as the crow flies, the trip proved twice that distance. The prelate's party proceeded by boat to Manzanillo, around Cuba's southernmost peninsula, and then, after a visit for the celebration of a *Te Deum* and his sermon on devotion to the Blessed Virgin, they re-embarked for Santa Cruz. This was the poor little port from which they must complete their journey by an overland march. (It was Padre Vilaró's impression that they were the first habited priests the *Santacruzanos* had ever seen.) [6] From here on their advance was along jungle trails that zigzagged through fifty miles of steaming wilderness. They were wholly dependent upon the settlements they happened upon for food and refreshment. Pushing along briskly at the head of his weary aides, Claret was considering more important reasons for this effort than a revolution. He knew that his subjects in isolated Puerto Príncipe [7] had never in their lives seen a bishop; that its clergy had been functioning for many years without supervision, and that scarcely any of the priests had

themselves been confirmed! These were circumstances to fill
any prelate's heart with trepidation; and this one was not
only a realist but a man endowed by God with the gift of
prophecy! He entertained no illusions that he might find
Puerto Príncipe in any state approaching satisfactory order.
Moreover, if, as he understood to be the case, its citizenry
were strong partisans of the insurgent leader Narciso López,
he must expect to be met with suspicion and ill-will.

This anticipation was entirely justified. After all, murmured
these long-abandoned people, of what moment was it to them
now, the sudden descent upon their little city of a Spanish
prelate? Would he have come at all except in an effort to
fortify the rule they were already seeking to throw off?
What would their chief inciters and supporters, the North
Americans (professional agitators for the United States' annexation of Cuba who had converged upon Puerto Príncipe),
think of them were they to succumb to the "wiles" of a foreign churchman? Of course they would attend his mission—
if merely to gather evidence that it *was* politically inspired,
but they were in no mood to be cajoled by pious admonitions
—or even the attractions of pomp and ceremony. Paradoxi-
cally, the conservatives, too, regarded his arrival with suspicion, for they were persuaded that one reputed to be "a
man of the people" would be inclined to protect, if not
openly favor, the rebels.

He studiously ignored both factions and quietly rented a
house in which to hold the Spiritual Exercises he would first
give his Puerto Príncipe clergy. Of his thirty-nine priests in
this area, he would commence with twenty; repeat the full
program for the remaining nineteen. In this way the parishes
need not be neglected during the Exercises.

"We all lived together in that house with a timetable set
for spiritual reading, meditation, recital of the Divine Office,
and for the conferences, all of which I conducted. Everyone

made a general confession, drew up resolutions and plans for future conduct. . . ." Discipline had come to Puerto Príncipe! Fittingly, it was first applied to the clergy. Only after the priests had been duly impressed and strengthened for the battle ahead did he turn his attention to the laity, whose emotions had meanwhile had time to cool. Then—"I saw to it that missions were preached simultaneously in three churches, in order to accommodate the crowds drawn from a city of more than three miles' extension. I ordered Padres Sanmartí and Barjáu to hold the one in Our Lady of Charity Church at one end of the city, sent Padre Vilaró to do the same at St. Anne's, at the opposite end, while my own was in the middle, that is, at Our Lady of Mercy, the city's largest parish."

As is still the case in Latin America, inducing attendance was no problem. The sentiments of these lands, like all their traditions, are centered in the Church. Her ceremonies are inevitably the most attractive of all public events. The situation in Puerto Príncipe, however, was charged with political passion. Claret knew he would be contending with a spirit of popular defiance which, though not directed against the faith, might readily challenge *his* motives. Actually, while dedicated to the cause of peace, he was as indifferent as ever to political issues. How could he best prove this fact to Puerto Príncipe? There was not time, nor the means, to convince the people individually or in intimate groups that he would have made this visit just as surely had there been no uprising; that his sole concern was for the good of their *souls*. Indeed, any protestation might only increase suspicion. Therefore, he must rely wholly upon the content of his sermons to clarify his position. In them he would ignore the local fuss and politics on any level, concentrate on the Gospel truths while, he hoped, giving these folk their first picture of an authentic bishop.

"In this state of affairs, I opened the mission. Crowds of

skeptical Cubans came to see if I spoke of the political upheavals which were tossing the land; but, observing repeatedly that not a word on politics escaped my lips either in the pulpit, the confessional or in public or private utterances, they were so greatly impressed that they began to trust me."

Thus, by merely adhering to a course he had always pursued as an itinerant preacher in nervous Catalonia, he soon won the confidence and affection of this people too, and so completely that four captured revolutionary chiefs under sentence of death ended by requesting to confess to "their prelate." He hastened to the prison to serve and console them. His compassion for the unhappy men indirectly justified General Gemery's belief that his presence would pacify Puerto Príncipe, because the rebels now entrusted him with the negotiation of an amnesty! If he would intervene on their behalf, they would lay down their arms and return quietly to their homes. He agreed to become the intermediary—thereby also proving Governor de la Concha's premise that "a churchman would end by soliciting lenience for the offenders." And although he failed to obtain a commutation of the condemned leaders' sentence to exile or imprisonment (for which he argued with energy and a wealth of Christian logic), he did succeed in securing pardon for all the other insurgents.

"After obtaining the general's promise that the conditions [of the amnesty] would be fulfilled, the armed bands broke up, ammunition stores were destroyed and the money gathered for the furthering of the revolt was turned to more profitable ends. Everyone was well satisfied and at peace."

With God's help, His bishop had secured the pacification of Cuba's largest diocese by remaining outside the conflict in which it was embroiled until the element which had thought him an enemy agent had turned to him and entrusted the conditions of its surrender to him.

XII

THE PROPHET

FROM THE TEMPORARY HEADQUARTERS he established at Puerto Príncipe Archbishop Claret pressed ahead with the visitation. He demonstrated an identical zeal in preaching to and confirming a half dozen farm children collected before a miserable wilderness hut, or to hundreds of city folk assembled in a prosperous parish church.

On strenuous trips to the north coast or into the vast wastes running westward to the limits of his jurisdiction he was content with whatever he might encounter. In priestless hamlets where there was an affluent resident to offer the episcopal party the hospitality of an ordered home, he accepted the courtesy with gratitude. But where normal accommodations did not exist, or where a would-be host was discovered to be living in concubinage, he accepted whatever shelter he could find. Sometimes in the more primitive villages he and his missionaries lodged and ate their improvised meals in crowded, earthen-floored shacks, unscreened against the clouds of fever-bearing mosquitoes. Nothing mattered except his assurance that, upon taking leave of any station, no reachable backwoodsman, woman or child had been left uninstructed, unconfessed or unconfirmed.

He opened the grinding program that would drive him until Easter, on November 15, at Nuevitas on the north coast, from whence, in looping back to Puerto Príncipe, he covered San Miguel and Baga. He went out again to Ermita Vieja, Banao and return before pushing west to San Jerónimo. This was the parish which, 75 x 150 miles in extent, had but one priest who was, moreover, ill, aged and blind! None of the people he confirmed by the thousands in these sections had ever entertained the slightest hope of receiving this Sacrament! For the instruction of the most ignorant Christians he had ever encountered he left missionaries behind him wherever practicable.

On his third return to Puerto Príncipe he found Padre Barjáu deathly ill with the black vomit, the horror which had already killed Padre Pladabella in Santiago! So now the prelate who had won his earliest fame as a healer abandoned all else to nurse his stricken priest. For a week he scarcely left the sick room. He even said Mass there. His rare ten-minute naps saw his head drooping upon the same pillow which supported that of his infected companion. As the dread plague ran its frightful course it would seem that even Anthony Claret nearly lost hope, because he wrote Lobo that Barjáu's burial might well take place before this letter reached Santiago. However, a postscript affirmed confidence that the Virgin would still bless his efforts to cure the dying man "with homeopathic remedies"! When, then, Padre Barjáu made a sensational recovery, both he and the provisor attributed it solely to the archbishop's prayer (though, as Fernández drily observes, the doctors might prefer to credit "the prodigies of homeopathy").

After celebrating the day of the Holy Kings,[1] the Puerto Príncipe headquarters were broken up and the party set out for Sibanico. As they moved out of the areas served by railway, horses were utilized for transportation; and since the prelate meant to complete the visit through this huge sector before presiding over the Holy Week functions in Santiago, the travel was literally achieved at a gallop! At Sibanico, where he gave a full mission, confirmed 700, and married fifty-eight couples, he was presented with a buggy. Escorted by fifty horsemen, he departed January 21 for Cascorro. There he also preached to a multitude, confirmed 300 and, leaving Padre Sanmartí to hold a mission, hastened along to Guaimaro, now attended by seventy *caballeros.*

The journey's rapid tempo was matched by an acceleration in the results of the labors, although it was certainly no help that, except in the most important towns, high-caliber priests were almost nonexistent. Guaimaro's was "very old, in his dotage and, far from aiding our work, merely impeded it. But this misfortune was compensated for by the docility of the people who, electrified by the person of Padre Claret, responded enthusiastically to the invitations to grace." [2] Five hundred Confirmations rewarded this visit. They moved on into prouder areas. At Las Tunas, its vicar and lieutenant governor came out to meet their prelate with a cavalry troop and orchestra, conducted him into town *bajo palio* in a solemn procession which included all the civil and military officials. There were 200 Confirmations.

In doubling back to the north coast port of Gibara, they covered Holguín, whose citizens expressed their jubilance by staging a balloon ascension. The mission opened on Ash Wednesday. It attracted an enormous following for which a prodigious labor claimed three weeks of the precious time remaining. But though on a tight schedule, they made Gibara and its adjacent *pueblos.* Claret even found an hour in which to preach a farewell sermon when they again passed through Holguín on the return journey. At daybreak, March 29, accompanied by ninety horsemen for many leagues, he continued south to be welcomed enthusiastically at Santiago on the thirty-first. Half of his initial tour was now behind him.

II

In spite of the unimaginable decadence of the territory through which he had been laboring among a people already infected by revolutionary ideas, social as well as political, he had, thus far, met no positive opposition. However, he did not deceive himself that all was likely to continue calmly. He foresaw the defiance he must surely encounter in a society addicted to self-indulgence and shot through with corruption. It was simply appalling that concubinage and divorce [3] were casually practiced by a large part of a public traditionally Catholic and certainly sentimentally attached to the Faith! True, he had already been able, with God's help, to regularize the lives of thousands of rustics and provincials, the simple folk who had flocked to see, hear and marvel over a real archbishop! But the situations he would inevitably confront in the more sophisticated localities were bound to demand more drastic measures than admonishment, loving kindness and holy example! How would he manage to convince the more affluent Cubans that their undeniable affection for the Faith must be earned by the sacrifice of their no less characteristic sensuality?

It was for an immense project of reform that he now armed himself and his missionaries during the Exercises he conducted for them immediately following Easter. He praised God for the excellence of the men who had accompanied him from Europe; for the zealous Capuchin Esteban Adoaín, a recent addition to the group. But death had already claimed Pladabella; and now the one who had been his most valuable aide was also alarmingly ill. For months his secretary, Vilaró, had been neglecting a persistent cold while attending to all the program detail. Following a long trip in a violent downpour, the cold had settled in his lungs. It became tuberculosis. Had Claret read God's sure will in this disaster? It would seem so because when treatment by Dr. Siga, a Chinese physician, failed to alleviate the malady, the prelate booked Padre Vilaró's passage back to Spain "that he might pass from this life amongst his dear ones." [4] There was to be no miracle for his beloved assistant. The archbishop took such consolation as he might in the conversion of Dr. Siga, whom he soon baptized.

Rovira became his secretary, with Currius substituting for the former as major domo. The tour was resumed. At Manzanillo, Vicana, Santa Cruz, Yara and Barrancas Claret was honored by elaborate receptions evidencing his subjects' affectionate deference. In all these places notable spiritual results were attained. It was a different story at Bayamo, where the atmosphere was frankly hostile. The mission did not go well; and meanwhile things were still worse at El Zarzal for Padre Adoaín who was holding another preparatory to the visit. The air of both communities was rife with calumny and resistance. The cause was not hard to run down. An influential El Zarzal merchant with strong connections in Bayamo, Agustín Villarrodona, had incited those who, like himself, were living in concubinage or apart from their wives, in a hate campaign against "this meddling Spanish prelate" who, in the surrounding towns, had been directing his vehement sermons against these two evils. To prevent mission attendance and the El Zarzal visit, Villarrodona's supporters launched a bitter attack upon Padre Adoaín, described in his *Memorias:*

"No group has ever shown such animosity toward the mission. It declared that we had come only to collect gold and silver, that the Capuchin was a politician, and that what he heard in confession he published. Oh what it cost us to overcome these evil rumors!" [5] Before they were overcome, he was forced to carry a report of the disgraceful doings at El Zarzal to his prelate in Bayamo.

Simultaneously, his denunciations of the unchristian customs prevailing in this area had been receiving much the same reaction. "Offended" citizens ranted against the mission and did everything in their power to force him to close it. When the archbishop finally, under his right and duty, demanded a list of all the divorced and those living in concubinage, even the civil authorities undertook to trick him with an obviously inaccurate report. The warden of the prison insolently escorted three pregnant women into his presence to inquire cynically which he was obligated to marry! This was the last straw. Anthony Claret demanded and obtained the warden's arrest. The man was admonished to devote his term on the less familiar side of the bars to meditation upon his "novel problem of conscience." Doubtless he would thereafter be able to decide for himself which of these "disgraceful females" held the most valid claim upon him!

The time had come for the drastic action reluctantly foreseen by the archbishop! On the evening of the feast of St. Lawrence, he delivered a crashing fulmination of major excommunication against all who had opposed the Christian marriage of any persons presently living in concubinage! This paralyzing pronouncement, rendered in "the accents of a prophet," induced a veritable panic among the astonished miscreants. "The very columns of the temple trembled to hear the terrible anathema from the mouth of so holy a prelate as Claret," wrote Padre Adoaín, "and for my part, I confess that just the thunder of his voice caused my hair to stand on end. . . ." [6]

If today any such reaction of consternation and terror in a public capable of flagrantly transgressing the commandments of God, and obdurate before the warnings and edicts of its ecclesiastical authority, seems incomprehensible, this is because of our unfamiliarity with the nineteenth century Latin heart and psychology. For, in spite of their frequent manifestations of disobedience and stubborn willfulness, the Hispano-Americans were believers to whom existence bereft of the consolations and protection of their mother the Church was unthinkable.

In their desolation they turned on the evil genius of their rebellion, Villarrodona, whose specific excommunication had been read on three consecutive feast days in the Bayamo and El Zarzal churches. The man whose arrogance had risen from confidence in his influence with his neighbors saw their doors closed against him, his business ruined and his house abandoned by his terrified companion. Soon, as convinced as any that this disaster was God's judgment upon his misdeeds, he hastened to Bayamo to sue for pardon and his prelate's clemency. The latter, however, having conquered the revolt with one brilliant stroke which guaranteed the progress of the Bayamo mission to a triumphant conclusion, had departed in answer to an urgent call from Santiago. The wretched Villarrodona had to follow him to the see city. There, after humbly confessing his sins and publicly acknowledging his culpability, he was conceded forgiveness.

III

Tragedy had fallen on the people of Santiago which was the cause of the clamor for their prelate's return. For months he had been publicly prophesying God's castigation of Cuba in the form of earthquakes and pestilence. Even so, he had paid scant attention to the light rocking he felt in the Bayamo pulpit on August 20. But the seeming insignificance of the temblor was owing to the distance between this point and the epicenter—Santiago. There the earthquake's violence surpassed any in memory. The first jolt leveled innumerable edifices, choked the streets with rubble and the atmosphere with a thick pall of dust. It left scarcely a house intact. And then one shock after another added its quota to the original destruction!

El Orden (Friday, August 20) reported: "We are barely able to inscribe this brief but terrible account, inasmuch as our office, like all [Santiago de] Cuba's houses, is overwhelmed by consternation over the earthquake suffered here at 8:30 A.M., today. This induced the flight of our horrified staff and prevented the publication of our morning edition. From every side the pious cry: 'Mercy!' is heard, and everywhere the people are on their knees imploring Divine clemency. All across the city clouds of dust mark the collapse of buildings. The streets are filled with fainting women, children pouring from their schools in terror, parents running in all directions searching for their little ones. At the temples the Blessed Sacrament has been carried out to the doors for the consolation of the attribulated populace which, with eyes and hearts lifted to the Divine Majesty, beseech the protection nothing else can afford. . . ." [7]

And on August 22: "All the thoroughfares are littered with the debris of [fallen] walls, cornices, entire buildings. All, all have been damaged to a greater or lesser extent; many so badly as to be rendered uninhabitable.

"Fleeing ruined or threatened buildings, the public has taken refuge in the plazas, at the gateways, in the Alameda. . . . The least movement of the earth, the slightest sound, evokes fresh alarms. . . . Severe temblors have continued. The worst were registered at: 3:30, 5:20 and 9 o'clock the same day. Others came at: 1 A.M. the second day, the heaviest of all at 3:30, and that which, at 5, totally obscured the atmosphere, greatly enhancing the terror. The altogether sinister aspect of the cloudy, rainy weather worsened matters still more; drew new and more fervent vows from the people who, from the first shock, had been converging upon the churches. The recurrences, however, forced the temples' evacuation, after which the prayers were offered up in the plazas. . . .

"Pray God to have mercy on this city, to stay His angry arm, pardoning our sins and conceding the aid we implore through the powerful intercession of His Divine Son Our Lord Jesus Christ and His most holy Mother, the Virgin Mary!" [8]

The quakes continued on each succeeding day. There had, as yet, been only three deaths, but this was owing solely to the fact that the entire city was existing in the open beneath drenching deluges. And meanwhile the continually heaving earth, accompanied by the sound of crashing edifices, had persuaded everyone that Santiago was doomed to annihilation. In this extremity they recalled their prelate's dire prognostications—and suddenly saw him as their single hope. If they could convince him of their contrition, surely he would intercede with God for their deliverance! The frantic appeal for his return to them was dispatched to Bayamo.

He arrived in Santiago September 2 and immediately took charge of the city. His authoritative calm tranquilized his hysterical subjects and, though the ground went on rocking, hope was reborn. As he moved about purposefully, organizing their devotions, he made no effort to conceal his conviction that the disaster was proving the finest missionary God had yet granted Cuba. Here, he said, was one reformer whose eloquence was equal to routing the superficial distractions which could divert a light-minded people's attention from a consideration of the fate in store for sinners! And if it seemed an insupportable affliction, once its object was achieved it would pass. Not so the doom awaiting the unrepentant evil-

blessing in disguise

doer, the impious, or even the merely "careless" Christian! *That* endured *para siempre.* If, in bringing them back to God, this agony saved them from damnation, should they not regard it as the greatest of blessings?

He rejoiced in the multitude of conscience-stricken parents who, clad in religious habits or mourning black, were now rushing their children to the baptismal fonts; in the whole city's participation in the rogative processions which daily wound through Santiago's littered thoroughfares. "All the world"—including the civil and military authorities—attended the Novena he conducted to the Virgin of Cobre before an improvised altar in the Alameda. His sermon was heard with "indescribable fervor and compunction. . . . Here where rain is so dreaded, since it is, in truth, more pernicious than elsewhere . . . absolutely all remained immobile throughout the preaching, notwithstanding the deluge [falling upon them]." [9]

rogare—to ask

Of course there was no way of determining just how much of the *Santiagüeños'* heightened devotion was induced by true contrition, how much by blind fear. For this reason Anthony Claret did not spare them another terrible prophecy: "God must treat some of us as does the mother a lazy son. When shaking the bed does not cause him to arise, she proceeds to castigate him physically. Now God is shaking the bed—the city; and if, even so, you won't awake, the physical punishment will come. As He has given me to know, this will be—cholera." [10]

There were many critics who deplored what they termed this "recourse to oratory in such lugubrious circumstances to intimidate vacillating consciences." But, close to God as he always was, Claret's words, as well as their moments of delivery, were not of his selection. Nor was he restrained by the prudence imposed upon apostles whose labor is for the conversion of preponderantly pagan or heretical peoples. His sinning subjects were already Catholic and thus, if unrepent-

sorrowful

ant, most certainly condemned! In utilizing their fear in behalf of their reform he was only improving a situation that was "lugubrious" by Divine intention. Furthermore, he himself was chronically frightened—not of earthquakes and cholera, the crude symbols of ruin and death—but of the sin which, unextirpated, would cast these pitiable folk (his spiritual responsibility) into unending hell! And lastly, the incontrovertible justification for his appalling warning of the infinitely greater tragedy lying ahead was the fact of its almost immediate materialization! For the plague he prophesied in September (one never to have struck Santiago before) was to be officially acknowledged on October 9; would soon be raging across the city, decimating a population that had just survived six weeks of devastation with a mere trio of fatalities!

Before this, however, the earthquakes' lessening violence had encouraged the *Santiagüeños* to commence the reconstruction of the city, a work of hope which, ironically, brought the fresh disaster. For it was the labor crew, comprised of convicts, sent by Governor de la Concha from Havana to do the preliminary wrecking and clearing, which introduced the plague into Santiago.

Although Claret had himself ordered the rebuilding of his demolished residence, he had opposed urgings that he also start reconstructing the damaged cathedral, saying: "It would be foolish, since it would only be redestroyed. I am reconditioning the palace, not for my convenience, but to house the workers sent us by the captain general. In the long run this work, too, will have been useless. I shall notify the council when it is opportune to proceed with the cathedral." [11]

Of this prophecy (dated from Bayamo where, with the improvement of Santiago's morale and prior to the cholera outbreak, he had returned to bring the mission so inauspiciously opened to a sensationally successful close), we read:

"And so it came to pass. On November 26, Santiago was struck by another earthquake so terrible that a merlon situated on top of one of the cathedral towers was flung into and onto the first floor of the same tower, while the edifice's façade, which had stood until now, collapsed completely. The very next day the servant of God convoked the *Cabildo* to announce: 'Now we may safely rebuild the cathedral church.' And indeed, there were no further consequences from the few ensuing light shocks." [12] His prophetic utterances, then, were not always pessimistic. Again: "The last quake came Christmas evening when the *pueblo* was gathered with the servant of God in the church of Dolores. Everyone cried out in alarm, but he arose and addressed the assembly: 'Have no fear. There will be nothing more.' And there *was* nothing more." [13]

IV

The cholera outbreak interrupted the pastoral visit a second time at Bayamo. Once again the prelate had hastened back to succor his harassed see city. The scene it now presented was incomparably more agonized than before. He saw the street fires' doleful blazing in the night air—with which, it was believed, they were "burning up the disease." He saw the coffin-laden carts that, together with the mules that pulled them, could only be obtained for the transportation of the dead through outright purchase by the bereaved. He looked upon the terror-haunted faces of the poor convicts condemned to drive them; and, at the cemetery, the hastily contrived "boxes" piled high for lack of men to handle the sepultures. He gazed down streets which, depopulated in a couple of days, gaped emptily away toward equally abandoned fields. He learned that in only one day this most repugnant of plagues had claimed ninety-four lives; may well have understood that before the end of the year

[margin handwritten note:] battlement — one of a solid interval between embrasures of a battlement parapet

2,734 fatalities—ten percent of Santiago's population—would have been registered! It was a colossal task Heaven had cut out for him on this occasion—described with his characteristic brevity for Caixal: "Breaking off the visit, I hurried here to serve the pest-stricken. In but one street and one night, sixty have died, none without the Sacraments. But though we are continually among the infected, none of us has experienced the slightest symptom. Moreover, Our Lord has conceded the same grace to all the city's priests who, without exception, have conducted themselves with superlative heroism." [14]

He himself visited each of the seven or eight fantastically crowded hospitals twice daily. And although his primary concern was for his flock's spiritual salvation, he did not content himself with hearing confessions, administering the Sacraments and consoling the dying, but exhausted his purse with his charities. Every cent he commanded, some 2,000 *duros*, went to provide care for resourceless victims.

Great as was his distress in the knowledge that this was one physical horror which must run its course, he was consoled by the obvious good it was effecting. "Very many," he wrote, "who refrained from confessing during the mission, have done so as a result of the earthquakes and the pest. . . . I can do no less than bless Our Lord and return unceasing thanks that He sent the plague so opportunely, which I *know* to be clear evidence of His adorable mercy!"

Touching upon his preknowledge of these disasters: "About the middle of May God revealed to me the approach of three enormous misfortunes: the earthquakes; the plague; and [Spain's] loss of the island. The first two I published from the pulpit in various sermons; but the third I reserved, since it is a political matter and I never mention politics. The fulfillment of the first prediction commenced August 20. We are now suffering the second. In the city alone cholera is killing an average of seventy persons every day. As for the loss of the island, I do not believe this lies far in the future." [15] Thus casually could Anthony Claret allude to the supernatural revelations by which Our Lord had confirmed his title: "the nineteenth-century prophet."

XIII

THE REFORMER

ARCHBISHOP CLARET's most outstanding service to Cuba still lay ahead. This was the reform of its clergy, necessitating the complete reorganization of the seminary he had found in a state which, had it not been so demeaning to religion, would have seemed ridiculous! "So undone that it even lacked courses in ethics and theology," explained Padre Currius, "it had not ordained a seminarian in thirty years. Most of Santiago's sixty lawyers, as was the case in many other professions, had been educated at the seminary's expense only to declare, when the time came to commence the ecclesiastical studies, that they had no vocations." [1]

This cynical exploitation was extirpated by the only possible means: institution of a complete curriculum; strong discipline by which an improved and amplified faculty might bring order out of chaos; the elimination of unworthy students. The archbishop meanwhile ordered the needful improvements for the pitifully run-down plant.

All this, however, was the merest start. He must create a nucleus about which to build a serious student body. To this end he solicited Spain for advanced seminarians,[2] a call

answered by ten Geronese and four others from Barcelona
and Vich. The former, having already concluded their studies, received Holy Orders at once. Other fine peninsulars
would follow; and meanwhile the prelate ordered his missionaries and such worthy priests as the diocese afforded to
be on watch for Cuban youths giving promise of *true* vocations. But he warned that the qualifications of all aspirants
would be severely tested. He already had a plethora of men
on his hands whose flagrant failures to fulfill their high calling had substantially contributed to the shameful state of
moral disintegration in which he had found his diocese.
Never would he ordain young men whose disinterested love
of religion, moral integrity and intelligence were open to
question. "It was a guiding maxim with him that it was preferable to leave the parishes priestless than to send them unworthy pastors. For he had observed from experience that
there was a better compliance with the natural law, and—
once Christian marriage had regularized their illegitimate
unions during the missions—the people were more likely to
be preserved in grace in places with no priests whatsoever
than in towns directed by bad priests, where depraved customs invariably prevailed. 'If God doesn't send me true vocations,' he contended, 'He will protect the [neglected] souls
by means of His angels. It is He Who gives the call; and not
for me to introduce unworthy [pastors] into flocks they will
devour rather than feed.' " [3]

Although, until they might be eradicated, his unfailing
compassion inclined him to bear with the relatively unimportant defects stemming from the careless Cuban temperament
or deficient early training, he was uncompromising when it
came to any sign of intransigence in his seminarians. Rightly
anticipating that the rigid discipline he instituted at the seminary would be resented by many, he wrote its rector: "Be
so kind as to inform me which students have shown their

displeasure, so that their places may be given to others who will find matters to their liking, and know how to value the grace of admittance to the seminary . . ." [4] And he straightway sent a group of "good, diligent and appreciative" young aspirants from Puerto Príncipe to replace the malcontents. Seminarians evincing undesirable weaknesses or lacking in enthusiasm were speedily dismissed, as well as several who, while comporting themselves with decorum, nevertheless aroused the doubts of an archbishop whose judgment was sensitized by the gift of prophecy. The reformed St. Basil's not only became a realistic training center but "the wonder of Cuba, and a cause of admiration in Europe."

The abuse of the chaplaincies came next. Benefices established by pious Spaniards had frequently fallen to laymen quite unprepared to administer them properly; again, to ecclesiastics who had been ordained, or sought to be, from no other motive than that they might appropriate a chaplaincy's incomes. It was little to be wondered that incompetence and immorality were rife in the parishes of such men. Anthony Claret abruptly disposed of this disgraceful situation with the decree:

"Each and every individual beneficiary must manifest a true vocation, or, lacking it, renounce his chaplaincy, freeing it for bestowal upon another more worthy to pertain to the clergy. All aspirants [for such privileges] must observe the sacerdotal obligation of chastity; practice the virtues, frequent the Sacraments, and bear great love for the things of God Our Lord; be assiduous in the functions of the Church, devotees of most holy Mary, zealous for the salvation of souls. They must edify the faithful in word and example; be teachers of catechism. And, inasmuch as an ecclesiastic without learning is like a bell which doesn't ring, they must be diligent students. The younger will dedicate themselves to the rudimentary studies; the more advanced, to Latin grammar.

Every three months their instructors will report their progress and application to us or to our vicar in this city. All
found deficient in application must understand that we shall
declare the chaplaincies they presently hold vacant. Those
prepared in Latin will pass into our seminary college at
[Santiago de] Cuba to undertake courses in philosophy and
theology, as well as other subjects whose mastery should distinguish a priest. . . . And since, lamentably, there are some
who, after wasting their boyhood and youth in idleness, and
the emoluments of their chaplaincies in extravagance, now
ask ordination with the sole recommendation that they hold
substantial chaplaincies ([a fact which] constitutes no proof
of either virtue or knowledge, but merely throws suspicion
upon their vocations, suggesting a speculation in the sacerdotal ministry), such persons will be refused Holy Orders,
a grace we shall concede only to those whose vocations, virtue and learning are unquestionable." [5]

Profit from office

The problem presented by men already ordained whose
failures varied from incompetence to dissoluteness was still
more onerous. From the descriptions left by his scandalized
Spanish missionaries it is clear that many of the native priests
had fallen into almost unimaginable depravity. And while
the prelate commented less freely upon this painful material,
he did confide to Bishop Caixal something of his dismay before the first intimation of his clergy's invincible ignorance:
"I have now closed the Synod of Examination, but with the
distressing conviction that, save a very few, they don't understand Latin. *Never* have I witnessed such struggles, merely
to translate what is found in the Breviary and the third noc-
turn of the common prayer starting with the Gospel bit.
Now, if they don't know the Gospel, or how to translate it,
how are they going to understand the rest?" [6]

Three years later, when soliciting the cooperation of the
Marqués de la Pezuela, Cuba's captain general, in behalf of

his reforms, he still bore the shadow of this early shock in his heart. "I should open this relation with a statement upon the condition in which I found the clergy, but it is exceedingly dolorous and humiliating for me to have to speak of the clerical group to which I pertain; so I shall say only that in the entire diocese I found but 125 priests . . . and most of these so ignorant that they comprehended neither the material nor the forms of the Sacraments." [7]

There were occasions, however, when he was forced to be more specific, as when refuting the attacks launched against him by resentful clerics who had earned what they were pleased to call his "unjustified severity." A letter addressed to De la Pezuela's predecessor, Valentín Cañedo, on June 3, 1853, is self-explanatory: "By now you have doubtless received my last confidential communication, wherein I sketched this worrisome situation. Since then the disgusts have been augmented by certain insubordinate and disorderly priests. As recently it served you to forward me an exposition by Padre Antonio Díaz, pastor of Bayamo, this may not surprise you. Well, let me say that, until my arrival there, this sly fellow had been living in open concubinage! . . . During my visit to his church he had the audacity to bring me the holy water, as prescribed by the rubric, accompanied by one of his sons who carried the container. . . . I do not know what greater impudence and disrespect might have been offered me. . . . I ordered him to the seminary for instruction, and that he might be detached from his evil life. . . . At the conference where, in the presence of the other priests, I examined him on the Mass, all witnessed his ignorance (excused on the grounds of 'faulty memory') of even the prayers of the Ordinary. If he forgets the Mass prayers, what is he likely to remember? After a short time he fled from Puerto Príncipe without a passport and lodged a legal complaint against me which, however, was rejected by the *Audiencia.*

"You will recall that when you were in [Santiago de] Cuba I was occupied giving Exercises to the clergy. There is no doubt that some took advantage of this for self-improvement, but others did not. . . .

"It is impossible to describe the evil state in which I found Mayarí, or the discourtesy and irreverence accorded me throughout the visit by its pastor. Every morning I was forced to wait for protracted periods for him to send the church keys so I might enter and celebrate the Holy Sacrifice, and the worst was that many [of the faithful] witnessed the scandal. Nor did this man once come in person, as he was obligated to do. . . . The continuous complaints I have received of his gluttony, gambling, and his arrogant, quarrelsome character, as well as the disobedience and contempt he offered me, obligated me to proceed as follows: I called him to Santiago to attend the Spiritual Exercises and, these concluded, kept him here in seclusion while I checked some of the scandals he had given. . . . Many of the facts verified were certainly repugnant. . . ." [8]

Aware that the flagrant abuses he had personally witnessed were indications of widespread disorder, the prelate delegated trustworthy ecclesiastics, and solicited the civil authorities, to report any clerical defections from duty they might note anywhere in the diocese. Such charges proved, if his initial admonishments were unavailing, the offenders were withdrawn from their parishes for a term of instruction and exhortation. Often this was enough, but when, after confessing their faults and declaring their intentions to amend their lives, certain priests returned to their posts only to relapse into the old errors, they were deprived of a substantial portion of their incomes, or even separated from their ministries altogether.

Besides the annual Exercises, all were obliged to participate in regular tri-weekly study and discussion conferences held wherever even two could be brought together. Claret's preoccupation with raising the intellectual standards of his men caused him to impose another measure which, however, he proclaimed with considerate delicacy: "It has been called to our attention that, your territory being so large, the exercise of your pastorate rarely affords time for the opening of a book on moral theology. For the remedy of this lamentable situation, you will report to our Seminario de San Basilio in this city each year where for one month you will devote yourself to the study of liturgy and moral theology. During your absence from your parish, it will be served by a substitute." [9]

By eliminating the hopeless cases and by supernaturally aided, unremitting effort to enlighten and discipline the rest, he eventually managed to whip this unhappy assortment of "improvised clerics" into an acceptable corps of ecclesiastics. "The clergy of this country has been completely transformed," he wrote back to Spain as early as 1852.[10] "All now dress in clerical garb, since the fine for each infraction of this rule is ten *duros*. So far, only one has had to pay, which was for appearing on the street in a Prince Albert!" And although he was still to suffer much from the abuses of certain of the less susceptible, the firm hand and diligent tutelage Anthony Claret's authority supplied would, in the end, effect a realistically "complete transformation" of his Cuban clergy.

As multitudinous and difficult as they were, these problems were soluble because they fell within his exclusive jurisdiction. But there were other wrongs crying to heaven for reform which he had to combat under the handicap of only partial authority. When an unchristian institution or practice was linked with civil law, no episcopal edict could assure its reform. Nevertheless, he would never overlook an opportunity to oppose, with his prestige, the evil customs which had overwhelmed and finally driven his less-fortified predecessor from Cuba. Several of the most repugnant aspects of Cuban life stemmed, of course, from the epic injustice of Negro slavery.

That, flouting the law of Spain, slavers were still discharging their cargoes of blacks in the island ports to swell its already enormous second- and third-generation slave population was primarily chargeable to "the interested or cowardly tolerance" of certain government officials. But also, as the prelate had instantly recognized, the rapidly spreading spirit of rebellion against the mother country was contributing strongly to the climate of moral corruption that favored slavery. And the general lawlessness had naturally infected the slaves themselves. Robbery, frequently accompanied by violence, even murder, was the Negroes' common recourse for securing the wherewithal to purchase their freedom, while their unrestrained sensuality facilitated that of their masters to produce a deplorable social situation and an ever-increasing class of illegitimate, disordered progeny.

Spain had always required her American colonists to supply all the native serving classes with Christian instruction. But as the Cuban slaveholders were already lawbreakers, few now bothered to observe the old beneficent regulations. There were many who even *impeded* their Negroes' attendance at Mass or catechism classes. All this pyramiding of abuse intensified their prelate's sorrow and posed problems more difficult to handle than was his deficient clergy.

Many anecdotes illustrate his consistent condemnation of slavery and discrimination; his efforts in behalf of his Negro subjects' welfare. At a time when few upper-class islanders believed themselves able to dispense with bondsmen, no such indulgence was countenanced in any circle close to the archbishop. He had brusquely clarified his attitude on this wrong for a surprised townswoman soon after his arrival. Knowing his fame for almsgiving, she had applied to him, as casually as though her need were for food or medicine, for money with which "to buy a little slave."

"Señora," he replied severely, "know that I do not keep slaves, nor funds to be employed in any such acquisition."

On another occasion he dramatized his opinion of racial discrimination for the edification of a slaveholder. Taking two sheets of paper, one white, the other black, he applied them to a candle flame. When they had been reduced to ashes, he stirred these together and then demanded of the *caballero:* "And can you distinguish the ashes of the white paper from those of the black? Well, that is how God sees us all."

At his personal cost he published two pamphlets (*Proclamation of Good Government* and *Basic Laws of the Indies*) which, circulated throughout the land, did much to improve the living conditions of thousands of slaves. He was denounced in some quarters as "a meddling abolitionist," but this was an opprobrium of which he was proud.

From the beginning he had perfectly comprehended the connection between the abhorrent practice of concubinage and slavery. Spaniards who had come to the island with the intention of returning, sooner or later (in some cases to wives and families), had fallen into illicit relations with female slaves or their half-caste daughters, of whom—owing to poverty, ignorance, and less excusable causes—there were so many readily available in the Antilles. Then, whether or not they eventually did leave Cuba, the brazenly temporary nature of their alliances supplied no deterrent to abandonment of the women and the unfortunate offspring of their associations. In time, the fatherless, materially insecure children, having grown up largely uninstructed in religion, and in the

miserable customs which would today be termed predelin-
quency, came to form an exceedingly large segment of the
population. As haphazardly as the baptismal records had been
kept in some instances, they still proved to the archbishop
that at least two-thirds of his subjects were illegitimate! That
many were destined to crime was hardly surprising. And in
the background of this class there was certainly little to en-
gender respect for the Sacrament of marriage. Then too,
as it became ever more widely scattered throughout the island
and in isolated regions, baptismal certificates of some became
all but impossible to trace. Even those who might be inclined
or persuaded to legitimatize their own unions were frequently
impeded by inability to meet Church requirements for reception of the Sacrament. Sometimes poverty was the obstacle.
There was no money for the parish fees. Discouraged by such
complications, many of these in any case only semi-instructed
Christians simply skipped the 'formalities" and, setting up
their own illicit households, proceeded to live as they knew
their parents had lived.

Claret revised the requirements. He decreed that, in cases
where certificates were unobtainable, two affidavits might be
accepted in substitution; in those where poverty was reasonably cited as the cause of sin, the marriage fees be canceled.
These two measures could not be expected to extirpate Cuba's
besetting, perhaps predilect, evil, but they did rectify numerous cases. This much accomplished, he fortified himself for
the major battle.

II

An 1805 royal decree had ruled that all persons pertaining
to "families of the nobility and of pure race" might contract
marriages with mulattoes, Negroes, or other castes only upon
receipt of permission from their parents, through the author-   *civil*
ities. This was an understandable requirement. However, by

Claret's day, this law was being very differently interpreted. Now *all* so-called "whites" were forced to seek *official* consent for mixed marriages, and such solicitations were customarily denied—a manifestly unjust procedure in a land where white males greatly outnumbered women of their race. This "convenient" impediment had done more than any other to enmesh Cuba in the degradation of concubinage. While it existed no revisions of parish regulations, exhortations of missionaries, nor even the interdict, could restore the Christian home in Anthony Claret's diocese!

When this situation had first been called to his attention (in Cobre) he had commenced an intensive study of all Cuba's marriage legislation. Just as he thought, there was *no* basis in any of it for the prohibition of the average mixed marriage! For certainly, all these petty officials who staunchly defended the erroneous interpretation of the old decree could hardly claim noble ancestry! But they were the first to resort to concubinage on the grounds that the law made this a "necessity"! Their prelate was not one to be hoodwinked by any such hypocrisy. He had witnessed these same men's shameless evasion of Spain's antislavery legislation. Obedience was hardly a distinguishing virtue of the revolution-minded Cubans. In behalf of the salvation of his humbler subjects it was his duty to denounce this deliberate misrepresentation, as well as publicly to reprehend the sins held to be excused. He immediately ordered his clergy to witness mixed marriages (particularly those which regularized illicit unions of long standing), with or without official permission!

As might have been expected, this program was attacked bitterly. All the elements which loved their disorder had savagely denounced the Bayamo interdict. The *Audiencia* had been swamped with indignant protests of the archbishop's severity. Indeed, one of the judges of that body recorded his own *amazement* at the harshness with which the troublemaking Villarrodona had been dealt "in view of the insignificance of the man's offense." All the missionaries saw themselves made targets of the most malicious obstruction. During one of the prelate's periods in Bayamo, he learned that, on complaint of a petty official, the pastor of Cobre, Francisco Mirosa, had been arrested and carried off to Santiago. The archbishop immediately addressed an energetic protest to Santiago's governor, Field Marshal Joaquín Martínez de Medinilla:

By the last mail I received notice from my vicar general of the controversy which has arisen between you and himself in respect to the concubinage of D. Juan Simón, lieutenant of Cobre. From the enclosed communication I have also seen all that has been done against the ecclesiastical judge of that jurisdiction, the Reverend and most *virtuous* Padre Mirosa, whom I love as a predilect son *because of* his faithful dispatch of his sacred duties.

It is impossible to express my surprise and sorrow upon learning that your excellency has fined him and that, when ill and during a rainstorm (what inhumanity!) he was made to accompany a military escort as a prisoner [to Santiago] where he is presently detained. . . . And why? In favor of Lt. Simón, this functionary who, instead of offering a good example as required by the royal dispositions, has a number of children by a concubine, and is a relapsed sinner. For, if his representation that he has separated himself from the house is true, he certainly has not severed the relationship but, to the scandalization of the neighborhood, continues to scorn the ecclesiastical authority and the laws of the kingdom, a fact I have communicated to his excellency Captain General Cañedo. Upon my arrival in Santiago I shall be pleased to show you his reply wherein you will see what he tells me of this employee and certain others I have encountered in my diocese during the mission and pastoral visit; and that your procedure in this case has been the antithesis of what the said captain general promised it would be.

Before leaving [Santiago] at the beginning of June, I passed his word on to the ecclesiastical judge of Cobre. . . . But because he did not wish to betray a confidence, and for other reasons he did not consider it prudent or just to reveal, the invariably meticulous vicar merely requested time to consult his superior. This was denied and he was promptly fined the sum, no less, of fifty pesos, whereafter he was arrested and taken to Santiago without the least consideration for the sacerdotal dignity, the authority of an ecclesiastical judge, his illness, or the inclement weather that prevailed—a thing unheard of in this island, a thing entirely new. . . .

This most disagreeable occurrence obliges me to suspend the pastoral visit and, nothwithstanding the heavy rains and the intransitable state of the highways, proceed to the city to settle this affair, secure a refund of the fine, and the liberation of the reverend judge of Cobre! I shall abstain from complaining to the higher authorities until I have spoken with you, because I should deeply regret having to demonstrate the inflexibility and character of a Spanish Catholic prelate (who would gladly lose his life before receding one inch from anything he deems a duty of conscience) in a conflict with a friend like yourself, whom I have loved and consistently defended to critics of your method of governing. Doubtless such a spectacle would delight your enemies, reason enough for us to reach an accord and deprive them of this satisfaction.

Attentively—Antonio María, archbishop.

P.S. I expect to arrive in Cobre Thursday night and shall anticipate your kindness in restoring Reverend Mirosa's liberty, that he may receive me in his parish and jurisdiction; but if, for any reason, you are hesitant to extend me this favor, know that I will take full responsibility, offering myself as bond.[11]

These lines, proof that Anthony Claret could be quite as formidable in defense of his clergy as in its correction, needless to say, attained his desired ends. But opposition to the moral regeneration he was determined to effect in Cuba continued. There were even two attempts to poison him, both frustrated, Fernández assures us, "miraculously." Nothing prevailed to daunt him, of course, and he seems always to have been able to count upon the support of the Captains General Cañedo and De la Pezuela. The exposition of the whole marriage code he finally wrote incorporated a sharp, practical analysis of the relationship between the abuse of the law and Cuba's current ills. It was set down for the elucidation of the *Audiencia Pretorial de Habana*, which conceded that justice, logic and legality were all on his side; and forthwith proclaimed that, excepting in cases involving minors and the nobility, Spain had certainly never decreed any impediments to mixed marriage. Anyone after that opposing such marriages would be the lawbreaker, and punished accordingly. Claret's singlehanded reform of this abuse worked marvels in the suppression of Cuba's greatest, and allied, evils: concubinage, bastardy, and racial discrimination.

This victory was all to the glory of God, and he rejoiced in it. But there was no joy in the knowledge that it had spread his personal fame throughout Europe. "Spain's wonder-working prelate in America" was still the simple Catalonian missionary who had recoiled before the very thought of episcopal distinction. He had experienced small satisfaction in his prelacy and, as early as the end of the first pastoral tour, had petitioned Minister Arrazola's efforts toward his release from the archepiscopal office. "I beg you to support as strongly as you can my renunciation of this cross, because I have now done all I am capable of to institute here a general reform of customs; nothing more is possible." [12]

Knowing that His Holiness Pius IX would be duly informed of his desire, he refrained from repeating his plea in the report on the labors, achievements, pains, and frustrations of the visitation he remitted to the Pontiff. This noted the efforts described above and, additionally, that, in the two years he had spent in America, he had: attained the rectification of 9,000 notorious cases of concubinage through marriage; the legitimization and religious instruction of 40,000 children; the restoration of 200 broken marriages; the free distribution of 98,217 pious books, 89,000 holy cards, more than 20,669 rosaries and 9,831 medals. Countless heretical and immoral books had been collected and destroyed, all replaced by Christian works.

If he had hoped that this reassuring report and his application to Arrazola would obtain his freedom to return to the direction of his Missionary Sons of the Immaculate Heart of Mary, to the writing, the preaching to men of his own country, he was soon to learn better. Back came the instructions of the Vicar of God: "Our heart has been flooded with joy to read the testimonies and proofs of your great solicitude and vigilance, truly pastoral; and, lifting Our eyes to the Lord, We pay tribute to Him Who, in the extreme necessity in which the Church finds itself today, has so most clemently aided a pastor of His Own Heart. We congratulate you and Ourself, venerable brother, for the most zealous will with which you have complied with the duties of the episcopal charge. Continue with high spirit the work you have initiated for the growth of the number of ecclesiastics who, through adjusting their customs to the rule of the canonical discipline, healthy doctrine, and zeal for the salvation of souls, will be enabled to serve the Cuban faithful through example, while cultivating its piety and virtue. Continue, day by day, correcting and forming the faithful in the Christian life, now with the holy missions, now with all the other religious auxiliaries. . . ." [13]

He had by no means been granted the desired respite; but rather the highest possible stimulation for the continued pursuit of his prodigious labors in behalf of Cuba. Had he really believed he might return home thus soon? Probably not. He could hardly have forgotten his casually confident reply to the inquiry put by one of the missionaries during the crossing from Spain: "We shall spend six or seven years in America."

XIV

THE SOCIAL CONSTRUCTOR

Aㅜㅜ NTHONY CLARET fulfilled every labor of a prelate and an apostle before the end of 1855 in a schedule so strenuous as to challenge the imagination of any reporter. It is almost inexplicable that at the same time he was brilliantly carrying out spectacular reforms and resolving savage controversies.

To save precious time on the tours he did now make use of such sketchy stretches of railway as existed; but just as often he and his priests had to fight their way on foot to their destinations through jungle tangles and over miles of mountain wilderness. Usually they covered their grueling ten to twenty-league trips on spirited horses selected for their ability to "eat" such distances at a brisk canter. Catalonia's Padre Claret, who had rejected any means of transportation, was now an expert horseman. Whenever a steed proved too temperamental for handling by the man to whom it had been assigned, he would claim it for his own and instantly bring it under perfect control. As his party sped up the steep passes or plunged into the swift, unbridged rivers, he was always in the lead.

He unfailingly provided the impressive ceremonies, colorful pageantry and pomp so dear to the Latin heart and so attractive to the aborigine. But the processions, *Te Deums* and other solemnities concluded, he reverted to his most natural role: the humblest and hardest-working of padres. Occasionally, however, he administered a gentle reprimand to his more pretentious or careless clergy. One evening he went into a parish church and found the sacristan conducting the Rosary. Kneeling alongside this lowly functionary, the archbishop of Cuba, rosary in hand, took over the prayer. Arriving on the scene before its termination, the pastor was covered with confusion to see who was compensating for his neglect. Later, when they were alone, the prelate observed quietly: "For the duration of this mission, padre, whenever you find yourself too busy to conduct your Rosary, as I assume must have been the case today, just advise me in advance, and I shall be happy to substitute for you." [1]

His long labors in the confessional spread the fame of his clairvoyance throughout the island. Padre Barjáu wrote that, on countless occasions, his own "little Negro penitents" met his: "And what have been your sins?" with a naïve: "Why don't you just divine them like the *Padre Santo* does?" [2]

The most glorious event of these years was the immense jubilee in celebration of the definition of the Doctrine of the Immaculate Conception. For the Missionary Sons of the Immaculate Heart of Mary this was the height of joy; while to their founder it was the crowning of his lifelong devotion to the Mother of God, who had brought him all this way and blessed him in everything! Although the proclamation had been issued in December, 1854, the Council stipulated the following March 19, St. Joseph's Day, for the Santiago celebration. This date gave the archbishop time to wind up his current tour and return to his see city where he must, in any case, preside over the immediately following Holy Week functions. The magnificent jubilee honoring this historic triumph was attended with unprecedented enthusiasm by all the civil and military, as well as the ecclesiastical, dignitaries.

II

Anthony Claret's expenditures in behalf of the poor exceeded the cost of maintaining the palace, even though that was usually crowded by resourceless visiting priests and people engaged upon the reconstruction of the cathedral or other diocesan projects. "With Our Lord's help, I protected the needy," he noted in passing. "I always collected all the poor of whatever place I found myself and, as they were likely to be still more impoverished in soul than in body, each received his peseta *after* I had personally given them a lesson in Christian doctrine. Following the catechism, I also invariably exhorted them to receive the Holy Sacraments of Penitence and Communion. So many confessed to me because they well knew how greatly I loved them, and truly, Our Lord has given me an overwhelming love for His poor."

There was a regular distribution of alms each Saturday at his Santiago residence, which followed the same pattern: catechism instruction, a brief sermon, almsgiving. Sometimes Padre Major-domo Currús complained that the canny mendicants were making two appearances each Saturday; or that the religious books they were given with the alms, they sold. But the prelate's unvarying reply to these reports was: "It doesn't matter. If the poor folk come back for a second alms it's because one doesn't suffice for their needs. And if they sell the books, then the buyers will receive the benefit of them." The souls in his care were equally worthy of any effort for their welfare, spiritual and material. Repeatedly he warned his sometimes harassed administrator that *no* beggar was ever to be dismissed unaided. Obedience to this dictum and the free distribution of more than 200,000 books soon reduced the episcopal household to rather chronically straitened circumstances.

III

The archbishop drafted an ambitious welfare program. It contemplated the establishment of schools for both sexes, to be available to the poor without charge, to the young of the comfortably situated at a modest tuition. ". . . I built first a convent for the teaching sisters charged with educating the girls, at a cost of approximately $12,000." His list of projected works also included: orphanages, hospitals, homes for the aged, other shelters for the needy of any age group and an educational program for the convicts. This would go beyond religious and moral teaching to train the inmates in trades of their own selection, which would enable them, upon completing their sentences, to start life afresh in the most favorable circumstances they had ever enjoyed. (For lack of cooperation by the civil authorities this plan was not realized, but the prelate personally taught prison classes in morals and made these pupils, too, the beneficiaries of his charity. "As a result [of the peseta he gave each upon the conclusion of the lessons] they heard me with pleasure and attention.")

One of the major and most difficult achievements was the parish savings bank system he set up under the protection of "three individuals of proven probity and dependability" in each parish. Savings accounts might be opened with deposits of from two to two thousand "hard pesetas" at any time. Loans were also made available to worthy persons desiring to acquire small farms, stock, or independent businesses that might be expected to improve their economic situations. A negligible interest rate (3% per annum) defrayed "the absolutely indispensable costs of operation."

This innovation was motivated by his ceaseless concern for the welfare of the Christian families he had worked so hard to create from the shambles in which he had found Cuba's domestic life. Their children must be decently maintained, given the education that alone would preserve them in virtue and honorable independence. No economist and quite uninterested in the "science of finance," he knew he must, nevertheless, procure every possible aid for the material security of his families. And he believed that nothing would serve this end so well as individual ownership of "the little farms and businesses." It had been the huge Cuban estates' concentration upon sugar and coffee alone which had reduced the majority to hopeless dependence on its poorly paid labor for the few. Even this was only seasonal. Except for the short harvest and processing periods unemployment had always been widespread. Now the big planters were even uprooting the coffee groves (in view of dipping profits) to make more land for sugar. Things were bound to be still worse. The archbishop wanted to see his Cubans producing their own vegetables, dairy products and meat and—on their own lands. This was the idea behind the savings banks. Both plans were sound; both notably in advance of the times. That they found favor with the people is evidenced by the survival of the banks for many years after Claret's return to Europe.

Somehow he found the time for the study and writing of two books dealing with the latest agricultural methods, books in which he also stressed the attractions and benefits of the rural life. *Reflections on Agriculture* (1854) and *Rural Delights* were given a wide distribution both as books and by being reprinted in *El Diario Redactor*. The latter enjoyed exceptional success, was highly recommended by the authorities in this field, became a classic reference for even the most experienced landholders. There was a Puerto Rican edition and a gratifying demand for it in other lands. In its preface he explained his motives in undertaking labors that might seem unusual for a churchman: "Perhaps it may seem strange that I should speak of agriculture. It may well be asked: 'To what has a prelate come to occupy himself with such a subject when his proper fields are theology, canon law and Christian morals?' That these constitute my first obligation is unarguable, but I do not consider [the work here introduced] as unreasonable in my situation inasmuch as the propagation and perfection of agriculture can be made a powerful influence for the improvement of customs, which *is* my principal obligation. Good agriculture also obtains the abundance and felicity I am duty-bound to procure to the fullest possible extent for those who, as their prelate and spiritual father, I so greatly love. To love is to desire the well-being [of the beloved], which is why I must give [my people] this benefit and utility. It is this love and desire for their welfare which obliges me . . . to teach the best methods of planting, cultivating and grafting—to the end that, with the same labor and likely less, my subjects may harvest larger and better crops."[3]

His next great project merged this wish to improve life through improved agriculture and his concern for Cuba's countless orphans and abandoned children. The tragic fate of the little ones left to their own devices in the city streets and rural wastes of this island was one of his deepest sorrows. In all Cuba there was only one orphanage—and that in distant Havana! Moreover it could accommodate only an infinitesimal fraction (200) of the waifs produced by the colony's 1,400,000 population. General de la Concha admitted that this situation was appalling, but he also maintained the problem to be beyond solution by a captain general! There wasn't the personnel, nor the necessary money. "So," observes Fernández, "that which the governor, amply subsidized by the [Madrid] government and absolute master of all the dominion's resources, esteemed a chimerical aspiration, a humble prelate shouldered with decision, valiance and dispatch . . . in the face of his exceedingly limited incomes, lack of appreciable aid, and the combined opposition of the corrupt, the malcontents and the ambitious." [4]

What was it that Anthony Claret now attempted for a cause too costly to be tackled by the civil authorities? "The plan was to collect the poor lost boys and girls who lived in the streets by begging, and there to feed, clothe, and teach them religion, reading, writing, etc., and, afterward, an art or trade, whichever each preferred. . . ." "There" was a plantation strategically situated not far from Puerto Príncipe, which the archbishop had pieced together by adding to the original purchase of a farm, several adjoining *fincas*. The entire property he ordered enclosed by a wall. Its entrance was centered in the 8,400-foot frontage behind which, at a distance of 850 feet, he constructed an edifice so planned that its dimensions (225 x 280 ft.) might later be easily extended in both directions. He put Padre Curríus in charge of construction; the farm installations; the planting of banana stands, extensive citrus and other orchards; a botanical garden. Much of the holding was subdivided into squares which could be allocated to the children for their individual vegetable plots. "All the children will be required to work an hour daily, no more, in their gardens . . . and what they may gain from their crops beyond the provision of the table will be deposited in the savings account." These profits would be their contribution to the waifs who would succeed them when, armed with a basic education and their special arts or trades, the time came for each group to leave the home.

"The house was divided into two large sections, one each for the boys and for the girls, with the church in the center. . . . The house had two stories. The shops were on the first floor; the dormitories, etc., on the second. Across the front on the boys' side were the physics and chemistry laboratories, the agricultural apparatus and the library. This had an entrance for the general public which would be permitted to use it two hours each morning and again for the same period in the afternoon. All so desiring could attend the agriculture classes held three times weekly, but the other courses were to be exclusively for the resident children. . . . The trees in the botanical garden were numbered and, in a book under corresponding numbers, the names, descriptions, origin, utility, methods of propagation and improvement of each species could be read. To achieve [the orchards] I myself planted more than 400 orange trees which thrived admirably. A part of the farm was allotted to the animals, those native to the island and others we would import for the improvement of the strains."

With high hopes for its future he expended $25,000 on construction and organization, a sum eked out of his inadequate resources. He eagerly looked to the day that his orphans, after a healthy, well-ordered childhood, would go forth, prepared to make good lives for themselves and a better Cuba. His head was filled with plans for securing the government aid he would require to bring this work to its peak development; and, beyond that, for another forward-looking proposition. He would seek the subdivision of Cuba's idle lands for acquisition by small farmers on easy terms. But at this point he received disheartening news! A new political upheaval in Spain had brought to power the *Progresistas,* a [*Progressives* — handwritten] party whose platform demanded a new expropriation of all Church holdings! Useless now to expect aid from the crown [1856 — handwritten] for any of his welfare foundations in distant Cuba!

"Just see how things go in this world!" he wrote in bitter disappointment to Padre Curríus. "Here we are raising this establishment of beneficence while, according to the papers which came yesterday, in Spain they are selling up [the Church]. . . . It surely seems that the exterminating angel is free to do anything he likes in that unfortunate nation. . . ." [5]

Hope dies slowly and some remnants of his own must have inspired his exhibition of the farm orphanage to the governor general, who inspected the lands and edifice with lively interest. However, instead of the encouragement for which Anthony Claret certainly longed, he heard only the callous comment: "Magnificent, magnificent. This will make a magnificent barracks!" And soon after the rumor was circulated that the archbishop's grandiose enterprise was a trick after all! Did the poor Cubans really believe it was for them? Whenever had such extravagant charities been launched in their behalf? (When indeed!) They had been taken in. What Anthony Claret was actually erecting with such fervor and at such a cost was nothing less than—the Inquisition! And feeling began to run so high in some quarters that he wrote Curríus: "I believe that if tomorrow I were to leave the island, they would raze the building." [6]

1856

In order to understand how this absurd distortion of the motives of a prelate whom tens of thousands referred to only as "*el santo*" might have gained credence with even some of the people, we must remember that his triumphs in the cause of Cuba's moral regeneration had vastly annoyed certain factions composed of prominent figures. To those who resented having lost, through him, their so-called "legal justification" for concubinage, Anthony Claret seemed the personification of the bigot. He was equally detested by a few clerics whom, when he was convinced that they were hopeless cases, he had deprived of their functions and privileges. Such men tirelessly propagated the idea that he was a rude peasant lacking the erudition and class requisite to a prelate. In dismissing or disciplining them he had been demonstrating ignorant fanaticism, or simply giving vent to jealousy of his "betters." Last, never least, the revolutionary and Masonic interests consistently pushed their calumnious campaigns against "this overbearing foreign churchman" whom they accused of despising all Cubans. According to them, his "hatred and contempt" for "a race he considered mongrelized" was reason enough for his "odious railings against its time-honored customs and traditions!"

The significance of the irrational attacks by his several-sided opposition was not lost upon him. The very preposterousness of the arguments proved what they were: the machinations of the devil, thus, the persecution Our Lord had promised His disciples. Therefore, he must see it as a greater cause for gratitude than were his hardest-won battles for the reform of his diocese! Could one ask that the sign of God's favor be an easy thing?

That he went determinedly ahead with all his works, ignoring the attacks and obstructions, while the decent elements in the population rendered him ever-greater reverence, drove his enemies to desperation. Everything he stood for, his least achievement, they regarded, quite logically, as threats to their personal desires and group ambitions. And when the evil-hearted were forced to look upon the multitude of desertions from their own ranks through the conversions of those who could not resist the archbishop's persuasive powers and the impact of his holy example, it was determined that he must be eliminated—if necessary, by assassination!

IV

There had been threats against his life from the beginning. Now, as he prepared to open his fourth pastoral visit (1856), tour anonymous letters warned him not to preach or appear at Holguín. Padre Barjáu was one of several witnesses who testified later that he had examined these messages: "Ordinarily the servant of God didn't take the trouble to read them himself. His attitude on the subject was summed up: 'I fear nothing but God . . . and though I should see the blade descending upon me, I wouldn't be stopped from fulfilling my obligations to Him.' " [7]

He promptly set out for Holguín. En route he preached at Gibara where he was to pass the night. After the sermon the archbishop, his vicar, Antonio Lladó, who had come down from Holguín to meet him, and the chaplain-secretary Lausás were halfway across the plaza on the way to their lodgings when Lladó noticed that the bells were not ringing, as they should, to mark a prelate's exit from the church precincts. So, while the others continued on, the vicar turned back to call this oversight to the attention of the pastor.

At the first toll from the towers, a thin, stooped figure of most unprepossessing appearance emerged from the night before the portal of the parish church. When no one came out, he stepped into the doorway and peered into the empty building. His coarse exclamation of surprise, followed by savage muttering, was overheard by several bystanders who, in the light of later events, recalled this singular behavior and interpreted it as annoyance at having missed the prelate's departure.

Early the next morning (February 1), the archbishop's numerous party took the road for Holguín, to be met almost immediately by the Guardia Rural escort Governor Dolsa had dispatched ahead of his personal welcoming committee. The presence of the soldiers and then of the governor himself doubtless caused the second frustration of the furtive-eyed stranger who had been tagging along on the fringe of things all the way from Gibara! When this man arrived at the Holguín residence of Chaplain Castorense, he was so indiscreet as to quiz a servant about the prelate's program. Was this where his excellency expected to lodge? When he found

1856

this to be true, the pursuer loitered about until his intended victim emerged to commence a series of calls at the hospitals and cemetery. From this moment, as he dispensed blessings and consolation to those in danger of death, offered prayers for those already dead, Anthony Claret was never free of the shadow of murder!

One may wonder why these overt acts, or the very presence of a man so suspicious might have been ignored by persons well aware of the latest specific threats. After all, this was Holguín, the city their archbishop had been melodramatically warned not to approach. Moreover, given his gift of "second sight," how was it that he, himself, "missed" the proximity of malice? Perhaps by one of those coincidences so rare as to seem certainly destined, the whole circumstance actually passed unnoticed; that only later, after they had become the very symbols of infamy for the entire public, did anyone recall the revolting figure and depraved countenance so incongruously included in a company of distinguished clerics, civic authorities and prominent laymen. But as for the apparent failure of the apostle's intuition, who can say what might have been revealed to him; or from what motive he did, in any case, ignore the situation? As a matter of fact, during the course of his evening sermon honoring the Virgin, he did seem to hint of trouble anticipated. After relating the incident of his miraculous escape from the tidal wave at Barceloneta, he paused briefly and then exclaimed: "Who knows but that this very night the Most Holy Mother may not preserve me from another such danger?" [8]

He left the church flanked by Padres Lladó and Castorense, and preceded by a priest bearing a lantern. Once they turned into San Isidoro Street there would be no other illumination. The page Betríu followed some paces behind. As they took the middle of San Isidoro they were kept busy acknowledging respectful salutations of disembodied voices, the dispersing congregation. The shadows were much too thick for the identification of individual faces. When they had been following their little spot of light fifty yards or so along the street a thin, hunched figure detached itself from the gloom on their left. This was a man whose attitude and posture suggested a desire to kiss the episcopal ring, a conventional procedure that, given the numbers by which they were surrounded, caused Claret's companions, at least, no premonition.

The light of the lantern was far ahead. Did a faint flicker shine on the blade driven directly toward the throat of one who, in the execution of duty, knew no fear of daggers? If he saw nothing, how did he happen to incline his head, raise the hand that had been beneficently extended to an assassin to cover his mouth with his handkerchief, in the split second which sufficed for the fierce lunge of a weapon long prepared to deal instant death? The razor-thin steel which opened his arm to the bone and slashed on to part his face from chin to cheek-bone had missed its mark—the jugular vein—owing only to the victim's still faster reflexes!

It was all over before his companions had sensed the danger. So they were at a loss to account for his backward leap, while his terse command: "Rid me of these!" was even more mystifying. But as they swung about they saw his hand clutching his cheek; that his clothing was heavily splashed. Had acid been flung on their prelate? The color of the blood "gushing with equal force from the inside and outside of the face" was neutralized by the dark. But as soon as Padre Lladó had drawn close and thrown his arms around the obviously injured man, the nature of the drenching was clear. Anthony Claret was holding his severed cheek together. Consciousness and life itself might soon run out of him! His distraught priests' exclamations of alarm immediately attracted the crowd. In the ensuing confusion only the wounded man preserved serenity. "Let's get into this pharmacy where there will be remedies," was his quiet suggestion.

As he leaned on Lladó, and started toward the little corner drugstore, the assassin again lunged out of the night in a frenzied attempt to consummate his crime! Instantly he was fallen upon by a policeman and, in a matter of seconds, another had him securely shackled with a belt. Hearing the menace to the criminal in the yells now raised by the mob, Claret stopped outside the pharmacy door to forgive and protect: "He has my pardon. Leave him alone." This effort greatly accelerated the hemorrhage.

When the commotion had broken out in San Isidoro Street all Holguín's physicians, civilian and regimental, were homeward bound from the church. But they soon gathered at the pharmacy where they found the holy little figure seated on a stool holding his face together above a stream of blood. They quickly transferred him to a cot in an adjacent room where they administered the indispensable preliminary treatment: disinfection and stitching. During these painful procedures the single nerveless man of them was the patient whose eyes, as they moved from one to another of the worried faces bent above him, never lost their reassuring smile. His only apparent anxiety was aroused by the discovery that he had lost his ring. Indicating his bare finger, he gestured that Lladó must go look for it. The vicar obeyed at once—and was deeply affected to find it, entirely smashed, lying in the street alongside the blood-encrusted knife!

When the emergency measures were completed the patient asked if he might sit up. Was this risk permitted because none cared to oppose the wish of a prelate or, what is more likely, that of a saint? This effort, however, brought on his first sign of weakness. He fainted. But he regained consciousness almost immediately, whereupon Governor Dolsa assigned four soldiers to carry him on a stretcher to his quarters. At the chaplain's house, following a redressing of the wounds which continued to bleed copiously, the greatly concerned doctors held a consultation in the hall. They estimated that he had lost five pounds of blood! With the town's leading citizens and officials, they kept an all-night vigil.

The chaplain and page stayed in the sickroom. The protracted silence during which their eyes never left the wan visage on the pillow was broken by his excellency's question directed to the priest: "Didn't you see that pair of gigantic Negroes wrangling and exchanging blows as they approached us? It was when neither of you did anything about them that I pushed them off saying you must rid me of them."

"Your excellency's servant saw no Negroes," replied the perplexed chaplain, "only the man coming from the sidewalk on the left. He was stooping rather, seemed about to kiss the ring. Then I saw him fling an arm up toward your face."

"Enough," sighed the tired voice from the bed. "I just wanted to know whether you had seen them." In the stillness that again enveloped the chamber, the chaplain pondered this strange disclosure.

Padre Lladó took over the watch and, stationing himself at the head of the bed, commenced to pray silently. Suddenly he heard cool chiding: "Ah, you rascal! There you stand praying for my recovery while I lie here longing to die for *Jesucristo!*"[9]

Betríu recorded his impressions of this fearful evening in a letter to a Vich nun. "You can't imagine, Sister Rosa, my horror at seeing the prelate's cheek in two pieces, all bathed in blood. '*Ay, Dios mío!*' I thought, 'tonight you are to lose your prelate!' And when, over the spouting blood, *el Señor Arzobispo* said: 'Thanks be to God it didn't happen until after the Most Holy Virgin's sermon,' I was convinced she would take him up that very night . . . I was inconsolable. While I was holding his head during the operation, he asked in the calmest manner conceivable: 'What are you afraid of? This is nothing.' I asked who *wouldn't* be afraid? Then, hearing mention of the prisoner, he who hadn't uttered a complaint or a single 'ay!' declared: 'I've quite forgiven the poor fellow!' " [10]

At Holguín's jail "the poor fellow" had been identified as Antonio Abad Torres, a native of the Canary Islands whose black record included one murder indictment in Cuba. On that occasion when, for lack of evidence, the crime was not fully proved, Anthony Claret had been the influence to effect his release from prison! Although Abad now stubbornly resisted police efforts to elicit the motive for the dastardly assault upon his benefactor, later it was found that he had been hired to assassinate the archbishop by a combination of Masons and renegade priests. In spite of the failure of his attempt, he was forthwith condemned to death by garroting. That this sentence was eventually commuted to a penitentiary term was another favor he would owe the long-suffering prelate, who would even offer to defray the expense of the criminal's deportation to his own country.

Actually, Anthony Claret was deeply grateful for this sad experience. It was his opportunity to offer reparation for the sins of Cuba—of all the world. In his own words: "I cannot describe the pleasure, the enjoyment, the happiness my soul knew in the attainment of what I had so long desired: to shed my blood for love of Jesús and María; to seal the Gospel truths with the blood of my veins. Still greater was my content in the belief this might well be but a sample of what time would yet achieve: the shedding of it all, and the consummation of the sacrifice in death. . . . My joy persisted all the time I was in bed and was so great it also rejoiced all my visitors. . . ."

Longing for martyrdom, he rallied with amazing rapidity. Just a week after the attack Lladó was able to reassure Santiago (where the news of "the archbishop's death" had been so promptly and assiduously circulated as to appear suspicious): "Today his excellency may sit up in a chair. . . . His sweetness of disposition, religious unction and the cordiality he exhibits toward all have filled us with admiration." [11]

"Nevertheless," wrote Dr. Garófalo to Padre Lobo, "there is a circumstance which is giving us cause for concern. This is the likelihood that a salivary tumor will form in the section of the channel proceeding from the paratoid gland. Inasmuch as the cicatrization is well advanced, we hope to avoid this danger, and perhaps today will see it covered. I wish to say in closing that the prelate's life was saved by an inch, because, had the wound been that much lower, its profundity would have occasioned death in a very few minutes. Thus I can declare without fear of error that, in effect, this holy man has been born a second time." [12]

The physicians' concern was justified. The salivary glands had been severed and, as the cheek healed more rapidly on the inner side, the liquid was forced outward through the center of the exterior wound. Besides preventing a clean closure on that side, this procedure caused the patient incalculable annoyance from the constant drainage. His surgeons finally decided they must submit him to a painful and complicated operation whereby, with a gold needle, they would attempt to open an artificial passage to lead the saliva back into the mouth.

It is possible that modern medicine would not describe this project "drastic," but we should not minimize its seriousness to Claret's nineteenth century doctors. This fact assuredly increased the magnitude of the prodigy that now lifted it out of their hands. The miracle was related with the brevity and candor characteristic of Anthony Claret. "The painful and doubtful operation being scheduled for the following day, I recommended myself to the Most Holy Virgin, offering up my resignation to God's Will—whereupon I was instantly cured, so that when the surgeons examined me the next morning, they were astounded." Then, "by a second prodigy, the scar on my right arm was granted the form of a half-length image of our Mother of Sorrows in two colors, purple and white. For two years it was perfectly recognizable . . . but later it began to fade slowly and now it is not readily distinguishable." [13]

By the close of the calendar's shortest month, he had made a complete recovery from his dangerous injuries and, on March first, was ready to resume the pastoral visit!

XV

THE QUEEN'S CONFESSOR

So, for the fourth time, the shaken but rejoicing populace of Holguín gained the benefits of their archbishop's visit. This was brought to a resounding conclusion on March 11; and, amidst an elaborate demonstration, the episcopal party took its departure from the city. If Anthony Claret suspected that his ingenious enemies were unlikely to accept their hireling's fiasco as a final defeat of their determination to secure his liquidation, he gave no sign. No effort had been made to conceal his itinerary, and the whole town knew he was to pass the first night of the journey at *Hacienda Altagracia*.

By nightfall, however, the travelers were still far short of the proposed stop. They therefore accepted the hospitality of *Naranjo*. It was this change of plan that once more preserved the prelate's life. Padre Lausás described the circumstances: "After a tranquil night and an early start the following morning, they comprehended what had been prepared for them when they reached *Altagracia* to discover it reduced to ashes!" [1] At midnight a terrific blaze had broken out in the great house where, it was supposed, his excellency was sleeping! That no lives were lost was doubtless because, save for an old grandmother and the caretaker who had managed to carry her to safety, everyone was away attending the harvest at another holding. But nothing else on the place escaped the conflagration. *Altagracia's* buildings, furnishings and animals were all destroyed.

Clearly Anthony Claret was a marked man and could never be confident of leaving Cuba alive. Since he coveted martyrdom, he did not share his companions' consternation. But it was also true that for other reasons he deeply desired release from the burden of his office. He was still convinced that God had destined him to be the plainest and humblest of missionaries, which is why he had insisted upon living and maintaining his household in poverty. For unhappy Cuba he had done more than seemed humanly possible in the most perfect obedience to Our Lord's inspiration and the orders of His Church. But the fulfillment of the Cuban assignment had never afforded him the joy he had known as an equally diligent, equally overworked itinerant apostle to his beloved Catalonia.

His second report to the Holy Father (written just before leaving Holguín) was touching in its exposure of his longing to return to Europe and the ordinary missionary life. It described the enmity his best efforts had generated in America and continually increased until it had culminated in the Abad attack. He cited his reasons for the belief that his usefulness to this turbulent diocese was past. But even now he did not ask release from his discouraging charge, merely that Pius IX consider his situation and advise him whether it were not best for him to renounce the miter. This letter was dated February 23, 1856.

During the nine months that elapsed before the receipt of His Holiness' reply,[2] Claret discharged his accustomed duties to the fullest possible effect, while taking account of the need

for greater precaution than he had formerly observed. The
fire had persuaded him that his presence anywhere jeopardized lives and property, that he had no right to endanger the
generous landholders upon whose hospitality he had always
been able to depend during the visits. He therefore revised
his schedule for this one and returned to Santiago. For the
time being the visit would take the form of short journeys
out of that base.

"Know *Holguiñeros*," said *El Redactor* in a special dispatch [3] to the city of his suffering, "that upon the evening of
his arrival the population [of Santiago] assembled to receive
its prelate completely filled all the streets leading to the palace. To the accompaniment of jubilant cheers and ringing
bells, many [could be heard] rejoicing: 'Now he is with us
again! Now we have him here!' " The same periodical had
already reported the fervor of this welcome: [4] "Attended by
the Cathedral Council, the clergy, many prominent persons
and an immense crowd, his excellency proceeded to the seminary chapel from whence, after prayers and the bestowal of
his blessing upon the concourse, he repaired to the palace by
way of the cloisters. In the parlor we saw the mingling of
magistrates and lowly Negroes, all vying for places close to
the revered pastor; and he, with his unfailing kindness, winning courtesy, and genial happiness, satisfied them by speaking with them all."

The next day was Dolores Friday, the Cubans' predilect
fiesta. At six o'clock the prelate was at the Church of Dolores. If the 150-mile trip he had undertaken so soon after his
injury had fatigued him, he did not show it. He celebrated
Mass and personally distributed Holy Communion to the
vast assembly which approached the rail in huge, consecutive
waves; thereafter he conducted other devotions, including a
Te Deum for his recovery. It was noon before he retired to
the palace in the midst of a surging multitude "whose excited

manifestations of joy in his presence, and of indignation at the sight of his frightful scars, could not be restrained." [5]

The love and reverence he inspired in the hearts of good men were as vividly expressed as was the hatred that fired his many enemies. No one, it seemed, could regard Anthony Claret dispassionately. To the pious, the oppressed and the just, he was the living symbol of righteousness and hope; to the licentious, the devious and the selfish, an implacably hated nemesis. Though he saw his persecution by avowed foes as a surer sign of God's favor than was the approval and esteem ever accorded him by the majority of his subjects, it was, nevertheless, a blessed relief that, within the palace his immediate "family" was imbued with a spirit of total affection, not only for him, but for one another. The harmony that reigned in his household, and its cheerful acceptance of poverty, had created a little island of virtue and peace where its members were fortified for all their labors. Even this haven of love was not, however, immune to the invasion of trials and anxieties. In June he opened the Exercises with the prophetic words: "Owing to the possibility of our dispersion during the coming year, this may well be the last time we shall see ourselves gathered for the Exercises. Let us therefore improve it by transforming coldness and tepidity into the fire of fervor. . . ." And when, five days later, he was suddenly stricken with yellow fever, perhaps his assembled clergy may have wondered if this were not the beginning of the "dispersion" to which he had alluded. Once again, through the prayers with which the diocese stormed Heaven and the heroic efforts of his physicians, he made a sensational recovery. On July 1: "He is already well and today took dinner with us at the table, thanks be to God!" [6]

Although he had yet to hear from His Holiness, he seemed confident that he would receive permission to renounce the miter. His friends were urging, in behalf of his health, a vacation in Spain. It was a tempting proposal, if only because, by carrying him closer to Rome, this might facilitate a clarification of his future. But regretfully he concluded he might not properly abandon Cuba, even temporarily, until his Pontiff had spoken. He pressed ahead with the tour.

It was, then, with mingled feelings of deep gratitude and sharp disappointment that he read, in November, the message Pius IX had signed some six months prior to its delivery. For, while the document was an affecting eulogy of his works for Cuba, his virtues, character, gifts, and defense of the faith, and moreover, was phrased in so intimate a style as to prove the Pontiff's special affection for this splendid son, it certainly did not constitute a release from the archepiscopal burden! Rather, the Holy Father delicately affirmed that such was his confidence in Our Lord's nearness to Anthony Claret that he could not bring himself to make an order in this matter. However: "In view of your virtues and the great good that with the Divine aid your zeal has achieved for this diocese—and must continue to achieve—We should certainly wish, venerable brother, that you might continue ruling it if, in your prudence, you believe you can do so without endangering your life. Do not cease, venerable brother, to offer the Father of Mercy your assiduous and most fervent prayers that He may aid, strengthen, and confirm with His Omnipotence, Our human frailty during these days when the pastoral solicitude for all the Churches is so especially heavily-laden. Nor shall We fail, humbly and perseveringly, to beg the same Most Clement Lord to guard, defend, and, with His Divine Hand, pour out upon you all the most abundant gifts of His bounty, which will descend upon the lambs confided to your paternal protection. And, as a presage of all this and a testimony of Our most ardent love for you, We give most affectionately, O venerable brother, from the intimacy of Our heart, Our apostolic blessing—to you and all the faithful, clergy and laymen, of this your Church.

"Given at Rome in St. Peter's, May 8, 1856, the tenth year of Our Pontificate. Pius IX, Pope." [7]

This was a masterpiece of holy psychology delicately applied, in the light of which the subject could but abandon all thought of separating himself from his episcopal responsibility. Moreover, though he had already spent years in prayer over this problem, the conflict between his personal persuasion that he had been born for the simple missionary life and the vowed obedience which had made him a prelate—there had, thus far, been no clear inspiration. Did he sometimes wonder how he might have erred in one of those moments when "the Spirit of Our Lord was upon" him, in recalling the confidence in which he had said: "We shall be here six or seven years"—in 1851? Already it was 1857 and now he had no assurance whatever that he would ever leave Cuba alive, though, of course, by the portal of death, he might well go on any day! At any rate, as he reshouldered his burden, he found it had noticeably lightened. The testimony of his Pontiff's love and trust which he carried with him on the visit to Baracoa had renewed the heart and had revivified the spirit of Anthony Claret!

On the eighteenth of March he was back in Santiago and, while delivering a sermon at San Francisco, was handed an envelope marked "Urgent." However, having neglected to carry his glasses, he did not open it until after his return to the palace.

"Please read me this message which I was handed in the pulpit," he said to one of his canons when he went in the door.

Santiago's Comandante Vargas had forwarded an official communication from Havana, signed by De la Concha, which, surprisingly laconic, set forth news equally surprising. "It is the queen's pleasure that you leave immediately for Madrid. I believe you are to be made archbishop of Toledo. Tomorrow I shall forward the formal order and place a ship at your disposal." [8]

So here it was again—the recurring pattern of reversal upon which he had been forced to erect his entire career! Having just sacrificed the desired renunciation in deference to his Holiness' intimations, he was now commanded to return to Spain. What had prompted this recall by the queen? The governor general's surmise could be discounted as mere speculation, suggested, doubtless, by the recent demise of Bonel y Orbe, cardinal archbishop of Toledo. But if this was Isabel's reason for issuing the order it would have so cited. The crown's nominations for prelacies had to be submitted to Rome and in the procedure became known. Likelier— and rather disconcerting—explanations occurred to Anthony Claret. Some of his Cuban enemies enjoyed considerable influence. Might they not have found a means to pursue their animosity toward him right up to the throne? In the circumstance of the recently revived Spanish religious conflict had he been made a pawn in the desperate game the adversaries of the Church were playing for that coveted prize—complete political control of the peninsula?

"What shall I reply to her majesty?" he asked his counselors.

"That you will go to Madrid," they concurred. "The requirements of rulers amount to precepts. Disobedience to, or neglect of, them could prejudice the Church." _endanger_

"Enough," he answered—and instantly commenced delegating authority for the period of his absence.

Only the unavoidable necessity to order a new soutane and mantle prevented him from departing the following day. However, as he could hardly present himself at court arrayed in the much-mended apparel which for years had been traversing Cuba's humid jungles, he was forced to concede his tailors four days in which to make him presentable.

These final hours in Santiago, in the ports touched by the boat which bore him to Havana (March 22-28), and the busy fortnight's stopover there witnessed his incessant ministrations to huge gatherings of his greatly affected subjects. Dozens of dramatic incidents and moving moments impressed the public with the magnitude of its approaching loss. There was at least one prodigious cure; and the occasion upon which, while speaking to the convicts of Havana Penitentiary, he stood face-to-face with, but apparently unnoticing, his would-be assassin Abad. Everyone now recalled that Anthony Claret was the only prelate in Cuba's history to have visited *all* of his diocese (and on four occasions); his long list of great works for her; the countless sacrifices and trials he had offered in her behalf. Thus, something very like consternation had swept the island before his Easter Sunday embarkation on the *Pizarro* which was to carry him back to the Old World. What if this really were a final *adiós* to their protector, their stalwart bastion against eternal condemnation?

"Today we are counting those during which he whose impending departure has evoked so many tears will be absent from our midst," wrote a celebrated journalist. "Today's loss is immense, irreplaceable; one of those blows that destiny deals nations, perhaps that they may be brought to an appreciation of the good they have possessed without recognizing it. If the Cuban public must acknowledge the inclusion of some who have failed to cherish this treasure of the virtues . . . if this [loss] had to be, we cannot disaffirm the castigation, nor the Hand that metes it out. If his excellency has been abused by the ingratitude of some of us . . . if he is too holy to have been loved by the evil, at least the sincere tears of the majority upon receiving, for a last time, the benediction of so worthy a prelate, such an exemplary *sacerdote*, a father so solicitous and loving, today offers proof of its love and profound veneration." [9]

II

Such was the tenor of Cuban sentiment when, accompanied only by Padre Rovira and Betríu, he headed out to sea, April 12, 1857, terminating the labors which had claimed six years and two months of his life.

The voyage would not be concluded without mishaps. The *Pizarro* was forced to put in at Cayo Sal until the source of a mysterious leak was located [10] and the damage repaired. And hardly was she again underway when it was discovered that most of her fuel had been saturated. This occasioned another delay in Bermuda to take on a fresh load. Were these annoyances, which might easily have resulted in disaster, accidents—or evidence of foul play? Whatever they were, Anthony Claret refrained from conjecturing upon the causes of "the many dangers we encountered on the trip home to Spain," or mentioning his fellow passengers' conviction that their lives had been preserved miraculously. His conjecturing during this protracted voyage was concerned with the reasons for the queen's summons. Save for De la Concha's gratuitous speculation, which he had discredited from the first, he had been given no hint of what might lie in store for him once the *Pizarro* had negotiated this vast waste of water and berthed at Cádiz.

This she finally achieved, docking on May 18. After brief stops in the port, Seville and Córdoba, he arrived at Madrid on the twenty-sixth. He went directly to the quarters he had requested of Padre Fermín de la Cruz, pastor of the Church of the Italians, where he had been installed less than two hours when the carriage of her majesty's major-domo appeared at the door. He had come to escort the archbishop of Cuba to the palace. The queen wished to see him at once. So, for better or worse, he was now to learn the reason for his presence in Spain!

And it was certainly *worse* than anything his imagination had conjured up during the long weeks of suspense! He who had desired to renounce the miter and come home to his missionary sons was "left petrified" by the information that he had been called to listen to Isabel's importuning that he become her confessor! [11] To him nothing could have been more appalling than the prospect of the slightest participation in the superficial life of the court. He had always considered worldliness an insult to God and abhorred politics. How could he assent to any such assignment? On the other hand, in view of the argument advanced by the queen, how was he to refuse?

With disarming frankness she had unburdened her heart to him, exposing its "disgusts" and uncertainties in the midst of the latest political controversy through which the Church stood to lose so much ground in their country. The constant jockeying between the demands of the powerful influences scheming against the Faith and the dictates of her conscience had left her exhausted and confused. Surrounded by fawning courtiers and flattering ladies, bullied by a bevy of treacherous or interested ministers, she was totally alone, and close to heartbreak. Her ten-year marriage to her cousin Francisco had been unrewarding; now the king had withdrawn from the palace to live with his particular coterie at El Pardo. He was a sufficiently good-hearted man, but they had been unequal to making a success of the union which, at the age of sixteen, Isabel had been badgered into accepting against her inclination. She had now taken a resolution that, at any cost to the dynasty, her soul and that of the five-year-old Infanta Isabel must be saved. She was convinced that none of Spain's prelates or religious could so well further this end as he whom *even Cuba* had been impotent to defeat. Hadn't she repeatedly heard it declared that Anthony Claret was a saint? Surely only a saint could guide her through the perplexities and frustrations by which she was beset! Almost childlike she had seemed, solemnly promising always to tell him the exact truth! Dare he rebuff the humble appeal of this deeply troubled woman whose youth and patently sketchy preparation were so clearly unequal to her inherited responsibilities?

It was a terrific problem—reflected in his letter to Lobo, written while he struggled for light by which to make his decision. "What shall I do, *amigo* Juan? . . . I, *I*—confessor to the queen! . . . In the entire episcopate there is no one less suited to this office, none with less affinity to the palace. . . . Let me carry on missions and confess monsters and wild men; there are others to confess queens." [12]

And what about Cuba? It was a charge upon his conscience. Had not His Holiness indicated that its welfare lay in Anthony Claret's hands? Thus had he been answered when seeking encouragement to renounce the miter in favor of the missions, a field, perhaps the *only* field, his gifts and inclination might serve as God would be served! But to abandon his diocese, all his works for a neglected nation, merely to hear the confessions of Isabel and teach the little princess her catechism . . . ?

Already he was receiving an avalanche of correspondence and editorial opinion lamenting the retrogression being noted everywhere in Cuba as the result of his absence. He knew that Padres Dionisio González and Curríus, left behind as governor of the jurisdiction and assistant, were making a valiant fight to hold it together and develop the projects he had instituted. But the former's poor health was being aggravated by the Cuban climate and, altogether, as Curríus wrote to Rovira: "Things go along, but not with the former certainty, because there is but *one* Claret." [13]

Just as no one before him had been able to handle the complications confronting the Cuban Church, it was apparent that neither González nor any succeeding provisor was going to prove competent to fill the vacancy he had left. This he recognized in all modesty, for he well knew how especially Heaven had aided him "in favor of that unfortunate island." Currius had also reported that local ecclesiastics of doubtful merit were ambitiously eying the episcopal authority. Could the queen's spiritual needs outweigh any such threat to a million of her subjects?

The confusion in Cuba had been anticipated by the Jesuit Juan Puigdollers prior to Claret's sailing in a letter to Vich: "The archbishop's departure, if satisfactory from the standpoint that it may well spare him the martyrdom which, at all hours, threatens him here, is exceedingly sad for this island because in losing a great prelate it loses a saint who may well be the only arm strong enough to detain the just ire of God before so many varieties of evil. It is to be feared that, in his leaving, lies one of the great scourges this holy man prophesied God is going to visit [upon Cuba] for its lack of appreciation of His abundant blessings. We pray Him, Our Lord, that He will deign to grant this unfortunate Church a worthy successor to Sr. Claret, that the works instituted by this extraordinarily virtuous prelate shall not perish before realizing their fruit." [14]

Anthony Claret found he could not make his decision unaided. He told the queen he would abide by the counsel of the papal nuncio and other advisers. Then, as all consulted vigorously urged his acceptance, stressing the benefits his direction of Isabel must work for religion, he resigned himself to undertaking a post that, more than any other, was personally repellent. There would be conditions, however. The queen must agree he need not reside at the palace, or present himself there save to hear her confessions and instruct the infanta. He simply would not countenance having to attend court functions; and he demanded full liberty to preach, visit the hospitals, welfare houses, et cetera.

Rejoiced by her victory, Isabel made these concessions; proved her gratitude not only by seeking the Sacraments frequently but by attending the princess' classes in religion.

But there was no trace of delight for the prelate in this abrupt latest switch in his career. At first he even entertained strong doubts of its justification. The news from Cuba continued to be lugubrious. He suffered sharply in the knowledge that now he had little means of helping, except by prayer and good counsel, the country whose archbishop he still was. Was there not much irony in this, the narrowest restriction he had yet supported, when it had been greater liberty in which to pursue the good of souls for which he had consistently longed? Should he not regard it as God's reproval of his unworthy dissatisfactions, his chafing under the duties he had called so "limiting" while he had at least been moving rapidly from place to place administering the *certain* good of Confirmation to 300,000 of his island subjects?

Perhaps his pain was somewhat assuaged by his provisor's gallant assurances that in this new sacrifice, ". . . you are more greatly benefiting the Church than you might by governing many dioceses, or by devoting your whole life to missionizing. After all, despite fewer molestations and the lesser noise attending his labors, the architect must precede the stonehewer; and it is more important to form maestros than to instruct children." [15] Even so, Claret was not to be reconciled to his "architect's destiny" until the Vicar of Christ had approved it:

". . . We know, venerable brother, how you were called by Our most beloved daughter in Christ María Isabel, Catholic queen of Spain, elected by her to be director of her conscience. It is a fact that We very much regret seeing the Metropolitan Church of Cuba orphaned by the absence of one whose most excellent religion and zeal invigorated him to fulfill all the obligations of a good pastor. Nevertheless, We rejoice that in this new charge confided in you, your piety is offered a wider scope for the defense of the most holy Faith in Spain. . . . Thus, by virtue of these letters and Our Apostolic Authority, We hereby absolve you of the tie which unites you to the archbishopric of Santiago de Cuba. However, fearing that the same Church, deprived of its archbishop, may be exposed to grave dangers, it is Our will that you continue to administer the diocese under each and every one of the faculties you presently hold and in which We confirm you by Our Supreme Authority, until such time as the new archbishop whom We shall name shall, with the ritual, canonical formalities, take possession of the archbishopric. . . ." [16]

This disposed of his conscientious doubts, if not his natural aversion to the new post. In His Holiness' letter he read God's will in his acceptance for, among other ends, his own discipline (or purgatory?). He had only to make sure that, through this onerous assignment, he would obtain an increase in meekness. The lack of this virtue, he was convinced, was his very *worst* sin!

He also inferred that his only recourse was to renounce the archbishopric forthwith, clearing the way for his successor's appointment. But in their habitual jealousy of the crown's prerogatives of patronage (which precluded papal intervention, direct or indirect, in colonial Church affairs), this was gruffly opposed at first, and later postponed for their own reasons, by the government ministers. The resignation was not submitted until June, 1858, after which two more 1860 years were to pass before he received Rome's acceptance of the renunciation and verification of his election to the titular archbishopric of Trajanópolis, *in partibus infidelium.*[17] At the same time he was requested to suggest the man to succeed him in Cuba. His first choice was his own confessor Esteben Sala, the brilliant and holy son of the Immaculate Heart of Mary who, during the founder's long absence in America, had become "the very soul of the congregation." Sala's gifts and virtues had gained him wide fame throughout Catalonia; and Anthony Claret deemed him the finest possible choice for a post whose difficulties might defeat a lesser character. But Padre Sala tenaciously maintained that he was unworthy to accept so distinguished and responsible a post. When urged to reconsider, he declared: "As men will not, I pray God will hear [my objections]." This enigmatic expression was clarified for all when, following "a few days of fervent prayer [over this matter], Our Lord called [Padre Sala] to Himself." [18]

After this greatly lamented death, Claret successively proposed two other worthy candidates, and when these also declined, a fourth, Manuel María Neguerela, *catedrático* of the Valladolid Cathedral, who was finally elected. But until this was settled, he continued to direct his provisor in the administration of the Cuban Church, a fact which irritated his old enemies. This totally disinterested prelate who, in behalf of Cuba's poor had impoverished himself and exposed his aides to every inconvenience, who had never possessed more than one soutane at a time, was accused of *causing* the delay in his substitution because of material considerations! He did not wish to relinquish the diocesan incomes it was declared and repeated in whatever newspaper columns were available to the malice of his detractors! The fact that he was meeting all the archdiocesan expense, as well as carrying a second household in Madrid, while much of the time these same incomes were months in arrears, or only remitted in part, was assiduously ignored by his opponents. But Anthony

Claret offered no rebuttal. Persecution had long since become a very old story; and anyway, he was entirely too busy to bother with it.

His zeal for reform had, of course, already been turned upon the palace. And there, besides the anticipated problems, he encountered a most embarrassing one he had not expected. Apparently Isabel II, in her first recital of the anxieties oppressing her well-intentioned spirit, had avoided mentioning one infelicitous detail. For it seems to have been some weeks before her new confessor learned of a scandal which the court gossips had based on the queen's indiscreet friendship for a certain young engineer attached to the entourage. The general belief that this man was the "favorite" had given rise to considerable agitation, not only among the ministers, but in ecclesiastical circles. In the unfortunate circumstance of the existing estrangement of the rulers, the situation was regarded as a threat to the queen's good name, and, perhaps, to the dynasty. There had been demands for the engineer's banishment to which Isabel had, thus far, turned a deaf ear.

Whatever may have been the archbishop's estimate of the facts or potentials, he took drastic steps to clear up this matter. He added his insistence that the young man must go, and told the queen that she must either return to her husband, or lose her confessor! And while her highness was cogitating this ultimatum, he did withdraw from his office. This course obtained the desired result. Isabel found that her hope in Anthony Claret's counsels was too great to risk their loss. She acceded to his conditions and, furthermore, made a point of showing him, in many other ways, a convincing improvement in her customs and piety. Most gratifying of all, she persisted diligently in these.

"Every day she reads the lives of the saints, says the rosary, hears Mass, makes a visit to the Blessed Virgin; and she receives the Sacraments with fervor and devotion. . . . She never tires of good works, is most charitable, giving generously and with all the good will in the world. There is no sorrow or affliction her compassionate heart does not induce her to aid," he wrote. "The one thing she has had to fight to master is her reluctance to clash with the customs of high society, but, little by little, she is prudently correcting these idiosyncrasies which, after all, are slight faults.

"Up to the time of my appointment as her confessor, she attended the theater every evening. . . . Today she seldom goes and when she does it is only out of ceremony and courtesy. By her command, only plays conforming to good morals may be presented. . . . Formerly, too, balls and banquets were held frequently at the palace. Now they are few and, according to what the participants tell me, good order is invariably maintained. I myself never attend such gatherings; rather, try to convince others to remain away. But, in any case, these events are held more for political reasons than as pastimes. From this point of view, they may be tolerated, and perhaps are even necessary for the ironing out of political questions.

"My greatest endeavor is to convince the court ladies to wear more decent clothing, to cover themselves better for flocking all over the palace on reception days. . . . They protest . . . that it has always been customary to use apparel such as theirs for court levees everywhere in the world, etc. Though the queen is always the most decently dressed of any at the royal functions, I am still not content. I complain; I manifest my sorrow and disgust, giving this as one reason for my wish to leave. . . ."

As a matter of fact, many writers of the period noticed the definite change toward conservatism that appeared in Isabel's dress following Claret's arrival in Madrid, a fact that may be verified by a comparison of her portraits from the earlier and later years. All in all, he doubtless recognized

that he was accomplishing more than might have been anticipated, not only with her majesty, but with the court. He
had won the lifetime love of the infanta whom he was preparing for First Communion; the queen's ladies constantly
sought him out for confession; while the monarch, herself,
meticulously made the annual retreat. What more could he
ask? Temporal rulers are not frequently saints here on earth!
All these things did not, however, render his position agreeable to him.

"I simply have not the makings of a courtier or aristocrat,
and thus my life at the palace is a continual martyrdom. I
often tell myself that God sent me to this place for my
purgatory, that I may atone for the sins of my past life. . . .
Sometimes I try to analyze the situation by asking myself:
'Why do you so dislike the court? Everyone here respects
you; all the royal family appreciates and honors you; her
majesty shows you great deference. Why, then, are you so
ill at ease?' And I cannot answer. My only explanation of
this enigma is that the repugnance I feel is a special grace of
God—that I may not center my affection on the honors,
riches, and vanities of this world . . . and I thank Him for
this constant repugnance. . . . Woe to me if the court and
world _were_ delightful to me! This alone pleases me: knowing that I take pleasure in none of it."

But there was one concrete cause for his annoyance. He
was incessantly pursued by persons coveting the benefit of
his known influence with the queen. Such self-seekers understood, as did he, that Isabel would gladly grant him any
favor. She had told him as much. "But I have never made any
requests and have no intention of ever making any. What am
I saying? I have repeatedly asked her to permit my retirement from Madrid. And this, my single request, has never
been answered. . . ."

As might be expected, his undeviating rule to remain aloof

from all matters of politics and interest won him new enemies. The numbers who swamped his study with calls and an average of a hundred letters daily resented his refusal to serve as intermediary. Others, fearful that he might exercise his influence to the jeopardy of their current privileges, hated him for the power they knew he could wield, if he so desired. Such people eagerly grasped at the old calumnies and, by repeating them, kept them in circulation. But, ". . . in the midst of all this, I have suffered in silence, rejoicing that Our Lord has offered me a drop of the chalice of His Passion. Pardoning and expressing all the love of my heart for my calumniators, I commend them all to Him."

Perhaps it was natural that many refused to believe he was not a power in the selections of the bishops at least, since Isabel always solicited his counsel in this important question. "With regard to the provision of bishops, I shall try to outline the procedure. . . . From time to time, the minister of grace and justice asks the prelates whether they have any priests endowed with the requisites of a bishop. . . . When the reply is affirmative, it is accompanied by the names and ages of the likely candidates, the studies they have covered, their virtues, personalities, and other qualities. This information is filed and when a vacancy occurs the minister submits his list of suitable priests to her majesty. Hearkening to the voice of inspiration she seeks from God, she isolates three names from the number. Next, invoking God's help once more while seeking nothing but His glory and the good of the Church, she selects the best of the three. I can personally assure everyone that the priest who may manifest the desire to be made a bishop has done the one thing that will forever exclude him from that rank. . . .

"Would that every priest sought the last place among the clergy, as Our Lord taught! The best canonicate for the priest is to love God ardently and save souls, that he may gain a high place in Heaven. He will have more security and less to account for who has been a missionary than he who has been a canon. . . ."

If Anthony Claret did have a hand in the selection of the Spanish prelates, he had, in any case, never aspired to another life than that of a missionary.

XVI

escorial — mound of stones from mine

THE PROTECTOR
AND THE PROTECTED

Philip II

San Lorenzo del Escorial

1563-84

built in the plan of a gridiron to honor Saint Lawrence

THE UNIVERSALLY celebrated Escorial, Felipe II's magnificent legacy to Spain,[1] had not escaped the tragedy of her disastrous nineteenth century. Following the eviction and dissolution of its traditional protectors, the Fathers of St. Jerome (1837), the sale of a portion of the Escorial holdings and the addition to the royal patrimony of title to the edifices, these had suffered a scandalous neglect. So vehement had been the public's outcry against the depredations and threat to the classic structures and their treasures of jewels and books, that it had forced intermittent efforts of the crown to provide an adequate administration of the massive monument. None of these, however, had been efficacious in preserving it, and at the time of Claret's return to Spain, the famed "Eighth Wonder of the World" which, for three centuries, had been the nation's greatest pride, was standing in a semi-ruined state, the remnants of its furnishings and its priceless library decaying or rapidly being lost through other causes.

This unhappy situation had recently incited a renewed

204

clamor for the Escorial's return to the custody of the religious. The general opinion that this was imperative for its preservation was expressed by *El Diario Español*[2] in a June, 1857, editorial: "Certain periodicals of this capital have reported that her majesty the queen is conformable to the proposition that monks be re-established in the royal monastery of the Escorial. *Nothing could be more appropriate and beneficial for the conservation of this sumptuous monument than to return it to a community.* Actually, its present minimum staff contrasts most uncomplimentarily with the magnificence and gravity of the work of Felipe II. . . . Every Spaniard, regardless of his political persuasions, who loves our national glories, *is convinced that the Royal Monastery of San Lorenzo del Escorial is nothing and can never be anything without the monks.* Well good: let the monument today so poorly attended and *at a very great cost to the royal patrimony* be returned to the care of its traditional occupants so that it may endure forever to command the respect of the ages. . . . And, at the same time, let the religious there dedicate themselves to the instruction of youth by the establishment of a conciliary seminary in which young men may be formed and educated for the priesthood."

Since the ministers, while evincing no enthusiasm for this plan favored by both the queen and the king, did not openly oppose it, it was not surprising that while she was journeying to Asturias in the summer of 1858, Isabel suddenly announced to her confessor in the presence of the court: "The Escorial will be your charge."[3] Under this order Anthony Claret undertook its administration, conservation and restoration. On August 7, 1859, *La España* (San Ildefonso) reported: "Under the presidency of the virtuous Sr. Don Antonio Claret there has been established in the Royal Monastery of San Lorenzo del Escorial, a corporation of priests which will live there in community, consecrating itself to the celebration of the divine cult in the magnificence and religious spirit appropriate to these immense vaultings, and dedicated to imparting primary and secondary education which will serve to prepare [its students] for all the professions.

"The royal patrimony has assigned to these ecclesiastics the incomes formerly enjoyed by the suppressed Jeronymites for the support of themselves, the cult, the school, and to defray the costs of the edifices' conservation and reparation.

"According to reliable sources, their majesties, who appointed Sr. Claret to study and determine upon the best solution of the [Escorial] problem, so long their constant concern, more than a year ago . . . are very pleased with the most worthy prelate's recommendations."

Because of the demands of his office as court confessor, Anthony Claret could not join the company which now moved into the Escorial, but his was the guiding hand in everything there. He closely supervised the organization of the secondary school, soon inaugurated; and by January 1861, had obtained Her Majesty's decree for the re-establishment of the seminary originally installed by Felipe II during the sixteenth century. So greatly did it prosper that, by 1865, it reported the matriculation of 152 paying boarders, seventy-four free students and seventy-eight holders of scholarships, who were taking fully accredited courses in: philosophy, theology, canon law, Hebrew, Arabic, Greek, advanced Latin, English, French, Italian and music—both vocal and instrumental.

Bishop Francisco Aguilar, Claret's great admirer and contemporary, listed his achievements at the Escorial as follows: maintenance and repair of the monastery and its dependencies; maintenance of the community of from sixteen to twenty priests who revived in the Basílica "a majestic cult, complying with edifying exactitude and solemnity to the pious duties with which they had been charged by their majesties"; restoration of the sacred ornaments and the replacement, through new purchases, of those lost during previous epochs; organization and maintenance of the secondary school, which he provided with fine laboratories and extensive museums; and of a choir supplied with professors in singing, music [theory], and one for its exclusive service, in Latin; formation of a new library consisting of some 4,000 volumes covering all branches of learning carefully selected from the most recent offerings of Spanish, French, Italian, German, and English publishers.[4]

The queen's confessor must have shared her gratification that he was able to work so much positive good at no greater cost to the crown than that formerly allocated merely to maintain, very poorly, this priceless monument.

His provisor for Cuba, Dionisio González, and Padre Barjáu, whose life he had saved in Puerto Príncipe, were back in Spain. The former, he now made supervisor of the Escorial improvements; the latter, rector of the seminary. They and the entire community could affirm that the protector never benefited by one *centavo* of the Escorial fund. He would not even accept such insignificant compliments as fruit or cheese from its farms. "Not a pear!" he would protest to any argument on this point. "Why? I need nothing." Once when the vice president dispatched a few pounds of chocolate to his Madrid residence, it was returned forthwith, accompanied by a notation that the archbishop couldn't consent to receive anything for which he had not paid from his own pocket. And still he was persistently accused by his busy critics of enriching himself from the Escorial budget!

Concurrently, also as official protector, he had been working marvels of betterment for another venerable institution—the Hospital of Our Lady of Montserrat.[5] After renovating the building and reorganizing the staff to insure the finest obtainable care of the patients (who, numbering precisely *two* on the day he accepted this assignment, thereafter rapidly mounted to eighty), he cleaned, redecorated, and strengthened the devotions in the hospital church. The better to attend the spiritual needs of his sick poor, he took up his residence at Montserrat. Just as no project for the good of men exceeded his capacity, no occupation nor concern was too small to command the meticulous attention and deep-running compassion of this amazing man. While ordering new linens, the replenishment of the pharmacy, and hiring personnel, Anthony Claret could always manage to "make time" to hear his lowly, devoted patients' confessions and administer the Sacraments. And meanwhile, besides administrating two complicated institutions, he was carrying a daily schedule so heavy that, alone, it might well appall the most industrious priest.

"I . . . arise at three. . . . After reciting the Divine Office, Matins and Lauds, I read the Holy Scriptures, prepare myself for Holy Mass. Following its celebration, I spend some time in thanksgiving. This over, I hear confessions until eleven o'clock, when my appointments commence. From eleven to twelve I am overrun by persons chock-full of petitions that I help them secure, by hook or by crook, better jobs or greater influence with the higher authorities which, of course, I cannot grant. From twelve to twelve-fifteen, I make a special examination of conscience. At twelve-fifteen we have dinner, after which I recite Vespers and Compline. In the afternoon and evening I visit the hospitals, prisons and similar establishments, preach to nuns and religious, study, and write books and pamphlets.

"These are the ordinary daily occupations, in addition to which, I give, extraordinarily, retreats to the clergy, to the Society of St. Vincent de Paul, preach missions to the laity, etc. But all this doesn't satisfy my longing for more work. . . . I am almost envious of those fortunate missionaries who are able to preach the Gospel from one city to the next. I do have the consolation, however, that, when the king and queen are in residence in their country home, I am afforded time for preaching to the people in the mornings before their majesties leave the house. And later I go preaching to the nuns, priests, seminarians, Catholic societies, etc., since, save for the hours I must give the royal family, my time is my own.

"Since my arrival in Madrid, I have been constantly occupied writing and printing books and leaflets which I personally distribute in the confessional, the institutions I visit, and in the streets and schools I pass along my way.

"O, my God, would that I might prevent all from offending Thee! Rather, would I could make Thee known, loved and served by all Thy creatures! This is the sole object of my desire, for all things else are unworthy of my attention." That this was, indeed, his sole desire is the only adequate explanation of the brilliant achievements in organization and administration, of the indubitable ascendancy over the court in moral and spiritual matters attained by one born into, and reared by, a simple provincial family of meager resources.

II

Reunion with his congregation had been his dream when he embarked for Spain. He knew that the little community laboring under Padre Sala at Merced in fondly remembered Vich was still struggling for existence; that though he had, from America, kept it supplied with sound advice and the assurance of his incessant prayer for its welfare and utility to God, the Sons of the Immaculate Heart of Mary needed his presence for the realization of the expansion that, overdue, had as yet been denied them. It had been sad that the demands of his immediate appointment to court had frustrated his plan to hurry straight to Vich. Nevertheless, the very fact of the proximity of its father and founder, and the certainty that he would visit Merced at the first opportunity, served to electrify the group of but ten men remaining to the congregation following the necessary elimination of several who had proved unsuited to its rule and specific aims. The tiny community finally had, and literally, "a friend at court." The previous lack of any such support (as well as of money and, perhaps, of initiative on the part of the saintly Padre Sala) had barred its logical increase, so greatly needed by Spain at this time of trial for religion. Now, through an exchange of correspondence between Claret and Padre Sala's successor, Padre Xifré, much was accomplished. The constitutions were amended and submitted to Rome for papal approval. Means of strengthening the membership through judicious selection were discussed.

But it was 1859 before the queen's confessor secured her permission to make the eagerly anticipated visit to Vich that enabled him to preside over the congregation's first general chapter meeting. Now at last, solid bases were set for the important expansion. With funds largely supplied by Anthony Claret's influence or from his private means, houses were soon established in various sections of Spain; and the congregation possessed its blueprint for its valiant march into the future!

Their founder knew his missionaries to be his finest aides and, among men, his principal blessings. But even more numerous were his supernatural consolations. Before leaving Cuba while thanking the Blessed Virgin (on July 12, 1855) for her help in the writing of a pastoral letter on the Immaculate Conception, he had suddenly heard distinctly the words that seemed to issue from her image: *"You have written well."* Can we doubt his affirmation that the knowledge that

Our Lady had actually spoken her approval of his effort inspired him with an ardent desire for perfection?

"While meditating upon Our Lord's Sacred Humanity, at five o'clock on the afternoon of January 15, 1857, I pled: 'What dost Thou will of me, O Lord?' And Jesus Himself replied: '*You must work a while yet, Anthony. Your hour has not yet come!*' " How could he fail to rejoice as he fulfilled this cherished command?

On various other occasions during that perplexing year which had brought him home to Spain, he had been blessed by direct messages—in *words*—from the Blessed Mother. In October: "*Now you know; be sorry for the sins of your past life, and watchful in the future. . . . Do you hear me, Anthony? Be watchful in the future. This is what I have to say to you.*" And later: "*You must be the Dominic of these times in propagating devotion to the Rosary.*" In December she gave him four counsels. He must pray more; continue writing; direct souls; be more tranquil in the post God had willed him to fill in Madrid.

"On Christmas Day God infused into me the love of persecution and calumnies. . . . I dreamed I was imprisoned for a crime of which I was innocent. . . . To one who would have defended me, as St. Peter wished to defend Our Savior, I said: 'Shall I not drink the chalice my Father has given me?'

"On January 6, 1859, Our Lord made known to me that I am like the earth . . . which is trampled upon, yet doesn't speak. I, too, must be trodden underfoot and say nothing. The earth suffers cultivation. I must suffer mortification. Finally, to produce anything, the earth needs water; I, for the performance of good works, divine grace."

How consoling it must have been to hear Jesus promise him divine love, while tenderly addressing him as: "*My little Anthony*"—on April 27, 1859! And how he strove, ever harder, to obey his Redeemer's injunction, given at 4:25 A.M. on September 4, of that same year: *"You have to teach your missionaries mortification, Anthony,"* to which, a few moments later, Our Lady added: *"Thus will you reap fruit in souls, Anthony"!*

And now, conditioned to receive supernatural messages in *precise words and audible tones* and, when they were precepts, to obey perfectly, he was ready for the most glorious promise and the most portentous revelation of all. "At 7:30 on the morning of September 23, Our Lord told me: *'You will fly across the earth . . . to preach of the immense chastisements soon to come to pass.'* And He gave me to understand those words of the Apocalypse: [6] *'And I beheld and heard the voice of one eagle flying through the midst of heaven, saying with a loud voice: Woe, woe, woe to the inhabitants of the earth; by reason of the rest of the voices of the three angels who are yet to sound the trumpet.'* This meant that the three great judgments of God which are going to fall upon the world are: 1) Protestantism and Communism; 2) the four archdemons who will, in a truly frightful manner, incite all to the love of pleasure, money, reason and independence of will; 3) the great wars with their horrible consequences."

Can we read this prophecy, set down for us a century ago, just when our world was entering upon the "golden age" of industry and commerce, of the scientific achievement that our grandfathers were assured was destined to create a life so good for all peoples that war would be banished forever, and doubt from whence it came? And do we dare to trace it from the Protestant Reformation to the curse of Communism; from the conquest of materialism to the deification of poor weak human reason and self-determination into "the great wars and their horrible consequences"! Upon the clean tablet of Anthony Claret's selfless spirit Our Lord engraved the warning His servant was to spell out for us: the incredible but inevitable graph of the "progress" of one century—*our* century!

A day later he was granted a second revelation. This too, from the Apocalypse: [7] "*And I saw another mighty angel come down from heaven, clothed with a cloud, and a rainbow was on his head, and his face was as the sun, and his feet as pillars of fire. And he had in his hand a little book open; and he set his right foot upon the sea, and his left foot upon the earth. And he cried with a loud voice as when a lion roareth. And when he cried, seven thunders uttered their voices.*" These thunders, Anthony Claret saw, were the Sons of the Immaculate Heart of Mary, "because like thunder they will shout and make their voices heard by their love and zeal," as indeed they have done from that day to our own. It was this righteous Claretian thunder which would gain 275 of them the victory of Heaven, martyrdom, before 1950; and it requires small imagination to note a relation between the outrageous slaughter of Claret's modern-day sons by the Spanish Reds during the most recent of that nation's *1936* civil wars and the fact, too little appreciated, that the single *Communism* European country ever to have fallen beneath the Russian heel thereafter granted the will and strength to drive the archenemy of Jesus Christ back across its borders, is Spain, homeland of Saint Anthony Claret and the Sons of the Immaculate Heart of Mary!

It was their founder who was marked for extinction on the feast of Santa Teresa, October 15, 1859! That morning a man entered the Church of San José with the full intention of murdering Anthony Claret. Moreover, he came with the certainty that he must take this prelate's life or lose his own! His secret society had given him forty days in which to "eliminate" its victim, and his time was running out. "If he failed, he would be killed, just as he had killed other defaulters in assassination." But once inside the church this man of violence experienced an unaccountable change of heart. Only Claret knew that it was St. Joseph who worked the miracle which brought the "poor fellow" weeping into the presence of his quarry to confess his motives and explain that now he, himself, would have to pay with his life. "He embraced me and set off to hide from the society, but not before revealing that regicide was a part of the plot. Isabel, too, had been signed for death! This warning, relayed by her confessor, invoked the protective measures which likely saved her life."

There would be several such incidents. Not long after this, a well-dressed man appeared at Montserrat requesting an interview with the protector. It was most urgent, he told the attendant. Informed that his excellency would doubtless see him at the close of the sermon he was delivering in the hospital church, the stranger observed blandly that, while waiting, he might as well go in and hear the preaching.

What he heard, at the instant he slipped into the temple, was: "If the enthusiasm with which I speak of the glories of my most holy Mother Mary surprises you, know it could hardly be less, inasmuch as all my life long she has been my Protectress, and even at this instant she is freeing me from a greater danger that threatens me." [8]

Can we imagine, then, that Anthony Claret was much amazed to see his guilty auditor very soon kneeling before him, extending the dagger, ugly evidence of his errand to Montserrat? The shock of the prelate's prophecy had gained the repentance of another who must now flee the secret society's wrath. Following the man's general confession, the archbishop assisted by Betríu supplied him with a disguise, a passport, money and recommendations to residents of the foreign country to which they sent him. When Claret was asked how he had come to speak the words which had converted one so far gone in crime, he replied: "As a matter of fact, I have no memory of *having* uttered them."

The secret societies' next attempt against his life was frustrated by his quiet injunction to a man who had borne into his confessional a heart laden with murder, rather than contrition: "If you wish to confess, please lay your weapon outside first." There was a clatter of steel on the tiles; a real confession; the absolution of an assassin by his intended victim!

On another occasion Claret unhesitatingly stepped into the dark city streets with a furtive-faced stranger who had brought a nocturnal summons to the bedside of a "dying" sinner. It was enough for him that anyone, known or unknown, held a claim on his ministry. He permitted the messenger to lead him across the sleeping city to a black alley where, before a squalid doorway, he heard that the dying man would be found in the room at the top of the staircase rising just inside. His guide would await him below.

The aging prelate felt his way up the unlighted steps, knocked on the barely discernible door. Receiving no reply, he turned the knob and entered. Not until he had struck a match did he discover the motionless figure bunched beneath the blankets on the bed. He crossed to it and still the form did not stir, not even at his touch. For, although yet warm, this was a dead body! Thoughtfully, Anthony Claret turned back the bedding, and may not have been surprised to see the pistol clutched in a hand that, now, would never fire it! He returned to the alley.

The astonishment of his escort when he was faced by the wrong man was immense. Whatever had prevailed upon his co-conspirator to permit the churchman's escape? And where was he who had bragged he would put an end to this detested preacher in that dingy slum bedroom?

"You should have called me sooner," the archbishop admonished gently. "Your friend was already dead."

"All hell has conspired against me," wrote the target of so many evil plots. He also knew that all Heaven was marshaled in his defense; and that the dagger or the pistol would never be equal to silencing the holy thunder Heaven would demand of him always. For had not Our Lord promised him (on August 26, 1861) the incomparable grace "of retaining the Sacramental Species" forever thereafter? Since then: "Day and night, I have the Most Holy Sacrament in my breast."

XVII

THE ZEALOT

H<small>E CHAFED</small> under the queen's insistence, sometimes tearful, upon holding him, if not literally at her side, always within range of her call. Nevertheless, these years of his "exile at court" could not have been more productive. Besides the exceptional works—the books, the vast Escorial and Montserrat projects, the consolidation of the congregation— his day-by-day ministries far exceeded any schedule that might reasonably be expected of the most diligent and unfettered missionary-prelate. Certainly they demanded more strength than nature apportions to any man.[1]

He was the most tremendous attraction in Madrid. His pulpit appearances invariably crowded the temples to the last foot of floor space, as the public competed for the privilege of standing for hours beneath his resonant voice. And truly, the dynamic words God put into the mouth of His servant exerted an unearthly pull. They were converting, or reconverting, literally uncountable numbers, including many highly placed and influential natives of Madrid. They were also winning from heresy or paganism large groups of the capital's North American and Arabian residents. But as

217

divergent in background, class and condition as were Anthony Claret's converts and reanimated Christians, they were one in declaring that, at their moments of self-surrender, each had known this amazing man to be speaking to him alone, from an intimate penetration of his individual state of soul! [2]

While "all the world" clamored for instruction and baptism by Madrid's most revered figure, several of its most distinguished archbishops and order prelates also chose him to be their spiritual director. His profound insight into the problems of monarch or prelate was matched by his understanding of the schoolboy who would attribute his religious vocation to his weekly day's-long journey to confess to his "Padre Antonio." Each human being was of equal consequence to the archbishop of Trajanópolis—which is to say, every soul was of the *utmost* consequence. He who had not a free moment, somehow made time enough for all.

This is how it went, from 1857 to 1865, while he also watched over the actions and secured the domestic harmony of the royal family. He rejoiced with the rulers in the birth of the heir, Alfonso; in the advents of the younger princesses. He gave all of them their earliest religious instruction; saw the Infanta Isabel grow into a lovely, intelligent girl devoted to the Faith and charitable works, docilely obedient to his counsels. In the salvation of thousands and his achievements for his nation and Church he recognized the Madrid assignment as God's will; that even stronger evidence of His approbation must be read in the continuing attacks of the die-hard revolutionary elements and the many more attempts upon his life than we have had the space to recount. Knowing unchallenged success in this world to be the very antithesis of the Promise, an absence of injustice and abuse would have rendered him uneasy over the state of his own soul.

He had, of course, been heartened to find Spain enjoying comparative, if not a fully confident, calm, under Prime

Minister O'Donnell's astutely formed coalition of the more
moderate *Progresistas* and the conservatives. But this situation underwent an abrupt change with the launching (in
1860) of Garibaldi's aggression against the Italian States.
Aware that this exploit was powerfully backed by Napoleon
III, England and International Masonry (all enchanted with
the heady prospect of seeing the Pope stripped of his temporal prerogatives), the Spanish radicals noisily espoused
the invasion—to the intense disgust of their Christian compatriots and the sorrow of Isabel II. A faithful daughter of
His Holiness, the queen deplored the wrong to him, and
furthermore, the deposed king of Naples was her kinsman.
All too soon came the news that Garibaldi had overrun the
peninsula, vanquished the princes, and annexing the papal
territories, had proclaimed the less-than-Italian Cisalpine Victor Emmanuel king of a consolidated Italy. The horrified
Catholic peoples of the world were forced to look on im-
potently while most of the European nations engaged in a
precipitate scramble to recognize this imposture and all its
implications. While Pius IX was decreeing the excommunication of everyone "guilty of participation in the rebellion,
invasion, usurpation and other aggressions against the Church
States," the Spanish Reds, however, were heatedly hailing
this victory of a professional soldier-of-fortune as a triumph
for their vaunted "new democracy."

The Spanish hierarchy, solidly backed by both the old
and the neo-Catholics, the Carlists, and all moderates, were
demanding that their own rulers stand firm on their initial
refusal to recognize Victor Emmanuel. (The queen and
O'Donnell had both avowed themselves invulnerable to any
pressure to swerve them from their opposition to the un-
seemly Italian developments.) But the impetus supplied by
the *fait accompli* and, it is likely, the machinations of Napoleon, effected the temporary overthrow of O'Donnell in

1863; whereupon, in order to return to power, he compromised his principles, committing himself to secure Isabel's approval of the upstart regime. And meanwhile, Francisco's 1864 visit to France was used by Empress Eugenie to maneuver the consort's defection from the cause of the Church. Thus, in rapid succession, was the distracted Isabel bereft of the support of her most trusted minister and her husband in her determination against recognition!

There could be no question of her duty, religious and familial, in this affair. But while the majority opinion of her subjects backed her natural inclination, O'Donnell was relentlessly pressing for the disloyal act, which he affirmed to be her single recourse against a revolution that would depose them both. And Francisco was urging it in defense of the dynasty, her clear obligation to their children! Her world was divided into two equally vociferous, bitterly opposed forces, with herself the lone target for the dire warnings of each. She could satisfy but one side and whichever it was to be would still leave her—this open-hearted queen who so coveted the love of all her people—hated by a powerful sector of her nation!

For his own, and good enough, reasons, Anthony Claret alone had refrained from publicizing his opinion on this painful matter. He had, however, made his position clear in many interviews with Isabel. "I had continuously exhorted her to avoid all responsibility for recognition. She promised me [Victor Emmanuel's government] could never win her approval, since to grant it would be to wrong the Holy Father and also the king of Naples, her close relative. Sometimes she declared she would relinquish the crown rather than to agree to such a thing; again, that she would give her life before her approval. As I came to understand that, in the end, she would receive the same treatment accorded the king of Naples, which I told her, I exhorted her to die indeed with her honor, rather than to stain it with so ugly a blemish. And besides . . . I went so far as to threaten, on two occasions, the thing that, in view of her attachment to me, she would most feel: should she recognize the kingdom of Italy, I would forthwith retire."

From this it is seen that while, at the time, he could not demean his royal daughter of the confessional by making public his counsels to her, he had certainly not merited the charges that he had kept "comfortably" aloof from an inconvenient participation in the energetic campaign being waged by the hierarchy against the recognition. He well appreciated that his failure to raise his voice in the pulpit or to publish his convictions in the press was attracting considerable comment. It wounded him to know himself an object of the censure of many Catholics for this reason, while it was downright repugnant to him to hear his silence hailed by the radicals' unprecedented plaudits. But, in the belief that his influence on Isabel might better serve the Pope than the deluge of excited protests that were showering upon the palace, he replied to neither faction. Even so, he could feel small confidence in the outcome of the argument because, although he knew the queen's conscience thoroughly, and that its dictates could not be altered, he also knew her weaknesses—upon which, for reasons of interest, O'Donnell and Francisco were determinedly working.

To Isabel's credit, she did withstand the pressure until she had written the Pope. The letter, which assured him of her undying allegiance, was also a plea for the Pontiff's concession that her advisers might be partially right in affirming that the principles involved were not as serious as she had believed; that, in sparing the Spanish faithful the rigors of revolution and, perhaps, the suppression of religion, her capitulation might realistically prove the lesser evil. But if she had been so naïve as to hope that Pius IX could be lured into condoning the sacrifice of right to expedience, she was soon disabused of this notion. His Holiness' reply, though couched in the most paternal and understanding terms, uncompromisingly condemned the course that the queen of Spain was now obviously debating with herself, and it only served to increase her agony of mind to the breaking point. Constantly besieged from both sides, she was also ill—four months pregnant—and, altogether, the whole thing suddenly became too much for her.

The day of shabby decision was either July 14 or 15, 1865. (Claret said "July 14, the day of St. Bonaventure"; Fernández gives it: July 15.) The ministers had assembled at La Granja where her majesty was in residence, and there O'Donnell subjected her to every conceivable argument in favor of recognition in a trying interview protracted from 9 to 11 P.M. "He assured her that the question of Rome's annexation by the king of Italy was not as grave as had been supposed . . . that it was not a question of approving the rights [involved], but merely the fact. . . . There were vital commercial reasons for the approbation and, besides this, she could not refuse to grant it since, if she did, the army would surely revolt. In this way, it can be said, the queen was deceived and threatened into it."

Expedience, as it so often does, had won the day against the better instincts and judgments of rulers and leaders. And, as would soon become evident, expedience wasn't even going to serve the ends for which it had been invoked! But quite apart from such general considerations, for Anthony Claret, who had sacrificed eight long years to the spiritual welfare of his queen: "This event was like a sentence of death. Presenting myself before her majesty, I asked her: 'Señora, what have you *done?*' She told me, and I replied: 'Well, they have deceived you.'

" 'What could I do?'

" 'Señora, a stone may easily be thrown into a well,' I answered her, 'but getting it out again is a more difficult problem. . . . Now I must go.'

" 'If you do, I shall die of sorrow,' she said. And I left her sobbing."

If Isabel's act in approving the wrong to His Holiness had put her into a fever, as she declared to her confessor, its verification brought upon him an intestinal ailment for which La Granja's water was considered fatal. He himself believed that to delay there even briefly would be his death. This was the explanation he now gave out for proceeding to Catalonia to take the cure. It was the truth but, as the queen rightly inferred, he would have gone in any case. Even she, however, did not know that his departure had been commanded. "While praying before the image of the Holy Christ of Pardon in the La Granja church at seven o'clock on the morning of July 17, 1865, Our Lord said to me: '*Anthony, retire.*' " [3]

Isabel's dismay at the prospect of being deprived of the benefits and consolation so long supplied her spirit by his ministrations brought her to the brink of desperation. On the twentieth she sent her humble appeal to Vich:

> Señor Claret, *Padre mío:*
> My object in writing these lines is to beg that, by the affection you bear us, you will come to Valladolid on the second of next month so as to accompany us from there to Zarazuz. You well comprehend what I shall be going through, and what will be said when it is seen that you are not with us. If, after Zarazuz, you still need more baths, you can leave for a few days, and return afterward. Do make this one more sacrifice for your spiritual daughter who owes you so much!
> If you will grant my request, I implore you to send me two lines, which will give me immense happiness.

Pray God and the Virgin to preserve us all in good health. The king is slightly ill, but you will pray it is nothing serious. We all have the greatest trust in your petitions, and hope for everything from them.

Your loving and respectful daughter, Isabel.

It seems sure that the realization that her confessor's absence would cause gossip and, perhaps, be regarded as his judgment upon her conduct in the matter of the recognition was but a secondary cause of the queen's distress. To her ministers, however, it was of primary importance. Already there had been rumors that his withdrawal from court would prove permanent. These they had countered by emphatic denials through the Madrid papers which assured her majesty's subjects that nothing but his indisposition had taken the archbishop of Trajanópolis to Catalonia. He would rejoin the court in a matter of days.

El Diario de Barcelona (July 21) commented: "If her majesty's confessor has not separated himself from this office, it is because, as the public believes, he stands firmly with the government on the Italian question. If so, nothing could be more logical than that he continue exercising his elevated and important responsibility. . . . But this will not overcome the disgust in which some of the exigent will view such an unexpected transformation." And, on the following day: "The bishops continue directing expositions and more expositions against the recognition of the kingdom of Italy, with only the cardinal archbishop of Toledo [at this time charged with the crown prince's education] and Padre Claret distinguishing themselves by their silence on this subject. How shall this [fact] be explained? However it may be, it certainly suggests that the archbishops of Toledo and Trajanópolis highly disapprove the attitude and conduct of [their confreres]; and they have, in any case, manifested to those soliciting their opinions upon the Italian question that it is merely a political issue having nothing to do with religion."

Here, at last, was the slander Anthony Claret could not let pass unchallenged. If his silence had exposed him to criticism, that was one thing, but it had been a total silence. To have words which might give scandal falsely attributed to him, was another. He therefore permitted *La Regeneración* (Madrid, July 26, 1865) to print his rebuttal:

"Sr. Claret is desolated to hear himself accused by the progovernment periodicals of *worldly prudence* and impious ideas.

"Sr. Claret says to all that he would tear out his tongue a thousand times before risking the wrath of Heaven by approving the currently projected [evils of] secular education, an unlicensed press, *or* the recognition of Italy without the previous consent of the Sovereign Pontiff.

"You may believe and declare that Sr. Claret trembles only to hear that he is supposed capable of temporizing with the enemies of the Holy See.

"Sr. Claret believes in hell and, for nothing or none, would he risk eternal damnation. He knows that he who is not with Peter is not with the Church, and that he who leaves the ark will perish in the time of flood.

"Sr. Claret approves all that the Pope approves, reprehends all that the Pope reprehends. Contradict those who would calumniate this venerable prelate in saying anything else!

"Sr. Claret has always lived apart from the ministers, neither seeing nor listening to them, never authorizing them to use his name in anything. . . . Certain reporters know that Sr. Claret has suffered to the extreme of heroism while letting the years pass without denying nor declaring apocryphal the infamous things attributed to him simply to dishonor him. However, know that everything has its end, and that the time is near when Sr. Claret's calumniators will be given the lie in a manner as terrible as it will be solemn."

Four days later *La Esperanza* (Madrid, July 30, 1865) carried his signed statement: "During my stay in Catalonia I have read press notices to the effect that the archbishop of Trajanópolis does not share the sentiments of the other Spanish prelates, has reprehended their representations relative to the recognition of the Italian kingdom. As such a deception could occasion my disestimation by my most beloved brothers the bishops, I wish to say that I feel as they feel and that, had I found myself in their places, I would have done what they did and have said what they have said.

"Antonio María Claret, archbishop of Trajanópolis."

This unqualified statement doubtless caught his maligners, accustomed to abuse him with impunity, off guard. In any case, it served to end the speculation of the faithful, the crowing of the opposition. All Spain knew that when Anthony Claret deigned to make a flat affirmation it was not open to question. If he had never before bothered to defend his motives in print, Our Lord knew them; the Holy Father knew them. His followers were well aware that his labors were all for God's glory and their good. The baiting of interested factions or the gossip of the ignorant and superficial had not been pleasant to absorb, but unless, as in this case, such things jeopardized the Faith by casting suspicion upon the integrity and obedience of Our Lord's minister, they had been endurable. His missionary's heart had not the will to combat the injustices directed exclusively against himself; nor had he ever commanded the time for it. But this latest injustice had reflected on religion. Also, for a while, at least, he might have considerably more time! For the presumably red-faced *Diario de Barcelona* rightly interpreted his intention in its prognostication (July 31): "The Reverend Padre Claret's manifestation of his adherence to the opinion of. his brother bishops on the Italian question, as quoted by last evening's *La Esperanza* and copied by all today's papers, has been received in political circles as a sure indication that the prelate will not be resuming his delicate functions [in behalf of] her majesty."

The churchmen were in complete accord in approving his statement and sympathizing with his withdrawal from court. They perceived that by this gesture he had "made his point" more dramatically for the people's edification than had all their fulminations. However, there was less unanimity on the question of his duty, or even right, to make his retirement permanent. True, his endeavor to hold Isabel firm against the recognition had failed, but, as no one could be expected to equal his influence with her, it was insisted that his retirement must inevitably weaken the queen's recent fine relations with the clergy and the faithful, Spain's only visible guarantee of religious stability. And had his advice in the matter of the elections of bishops not been invaluable? The papal nuncio was himself pressing for, though by no means commanding, his return to his post. For, while repeatedly soliciting his undertaking of most difficult and onerous charges, the Church had never asked Anthony Claret to do anything in violation of his conscience.

At Vich he was weighing these opinions, praying over them. He seems not to have been much affected by Isabel's emotional appeals, even less by O'Donnell's efforts to induce him to return to Madrid, but he was bound to give the nuncio's valid arguments serious consideration. For a month, in the grateful seclusion of his only real home, the cradle of his congregation and most important work, Merced, he sought to know the desire of his Lord, Who certainly had dictated his withdrawal!

With Padre Clotet (on August 14) he prayed for enlightenment before the Blessed Sacrament at Santo Domingo, his

favorite temple during the seminary years. As their visit
had not been anticipated by the sacristan neither dais nor
chair had been prepared, and the two old friends knelt side
by side on the pavement. Their devotions concluded, Claret
turned a glowing countenance upon his companion and announced: "My indecision has been dispelled. Jesus Christ,
from the Blessed Sacrament on the altar, has deigned to tell
me I must go to Rome." [4]

II

He marveled that he had not seen this as his one sure course!
The long journey in the midsummer heat would be dangerous for an invalid, but he would leave as soon as possible.
And though his convalescence delayed his departure until
October, from the moment that he had seen his problem resolved for him he was at ease. Meanwhile, just being able,
for a few weeks, to share the beloved community life with
his missionaries was reason enough for rejoicing. Needless to
say, the presence of their founder was a privilege which inspired all the brothers in their labors. There were long con-
versations during which they came to know his whole spirit.
Perhaps in some amazement, they heard his quiet prophecy
that, regardless of whether his visit to the Holy Father resulted in his return to court, the hour of Isabel's overthrow
was drawing near. The compromise that had jeopardized her
credit in heaven had not, as would soon be seen, served to
secure the dynasty. On other occasions the Missionary Sons
listened to his comments on the futility of the brilliant political and military career of Napoleon III, since he, too, was
moving inexorably toward a most humiliating fall! If his
fascinated auditors might have preferred a glimpse of their
founder's own future, now so shadowed by uncertainty, so
seemingly handicapped by illness and the old age they could
see settling upon his little figure like a gray mantle, none

had the courage to ask; and on this one subject he maintained silence.

Padre Xifré accompanied him to Rome, where they arrived November 5 and, the following day, were received by Pius IX. His Holiness' cordiality in greeting this faithful, long-embattled son was very affecting. Explaining that he had just received a letter from Isabel piteously pleading his influence for her confessor's return, the Pontiff asked Anthony Claret to fill in for him all the circumstances of this painful case and to bring the Spanish political picture up to date.

Apparently there were various meetings between the Vicar of Christ and his holiest of nineteenth century apostles, for the latter wrote Padre González on December first: "His Holiness has received me with the greatest demonstrations of love each time I have visited him. He spoke to me of the Escorial with intense interest." [5]

Every day he spent in Rome lifted his spirits to greater heights. He felt his heart composed and, rejoicing that he might now consign all responsibility to the one he was vowed to obey in simple love, he shed his problems and cares. He heard with perfect equanimity that the cardinals, under the Pope's minister of state, Jaime Antonelli, thought it best for him to return to Spain prepared to resume his office of confessor to the queen. However, he was not to proceed to Madrid until such time as she had acceded to certain contingent stipulations.

Carrying an exposition of these conditions, he embarked for Barcelona, November 27. The way ahead, at least to the next turning, was completely clear; his composure so firmly rooted that he only smiled at Xifré's lugubrious sallies anent this latest direction of events. (The superior had consistently opposed the return.)

Remaining in Catalonia until notified that Isabel had commanded the execution of all the Pope's dispositions, the prelate then departed for Madrid, arriving in time to witness the fulfillment of the principal condition. This was that the queen make a public, official declaration of her full adhesion to the Roman Pontiff and his imprescriptible rights—which the recognition of Italy might have seemed to place in doubt.

With the reconvening of the Cortes on December 27, Isabel's discourse was immediately read: "Diverse motives, founded upon the material interests and sentiments of the nation impulsed my recognition of the kingdom of Italy. But this recognition by no means indicated a cooling of my sentiments of profound respect and filial adhesion to the Father of all the faithful, nor the impairment of my firm intention to observe and protect all the rights pertaining to the Holy See." [6] After this reading, which they both heard, Isabel II received absolution from her confessor and returned to the Sacraments.

So Anthony Claret made the "one more sacrifice for the spiritual daughter who owed him so much." He made it compassionately and, of course, calmly. The time had passed for worrying about where it would all end. He knew well that his reappearance at court could only augment the fury of their foes, "the Protestants, the Communists and the materialists" of whom God had warned him, the Masons and all other revilers of the Faith in these quite frightful times. In fact, unless his wonderful respite had sharpened his sensitivity to the noises of combat, his return had already vastly aggravated the opposition. He knew he was inhaling the atmosphere of holocaust!

Let the poor, frustrated souls accuse him—as they relentlessly were—of having suborned the Vicar of Christ by a contribution running into the millions to effect the absolution of a silly female whose authority they would soon overthrow. Let them revile him for an "ignorant and bitter zealot"; demand ever more insultingly the explanation of his resumed ministry to "this excommunicated woman"! (There it was—the heart of the matter. That was precisely what they had intended her to remain: "an excommunicated woman"—no better than they! It had been hateful delight to see her bereft of hope and the spiritual resources which had fortified her through too many crises since, as a child of thirteen, she had ascended the throne of her fathers, presumedly to become no more than a pawn in their nefarious games.)

Anthony Claret, "that crude little weaver of Sallent who presumed to rule a nation of his betters through his preposterous hold upon their queen," was equal to the worst they could do. And if the royal family were hailing this reunion with nothing but joy, let them have the brief satisfaction of their innocence. His own must center in the possibility that his return might work the fortification of Isabel II for her spiritual survival of the next—and determining—crisis!

XVIII

THE EXILE

AFTER SO MANY miraculous escapes from blades, guns and bombs, Anthony Claret now had to face the most dastardly attack of them all—by those sworn to assassinate his reputation. The weapon they selected was ridicule. During the mid-1860's Madrid was flooded with slanderous doggerel purporting to unveil "the real character" of her majesty's confessor. According to the ear-catching jingles, he was a scheming cynic, bent upon using his important office for self-enrichment and to forward his political ambitions. It was "exposed" and then propagated into a legend that the queen was but the puppet of a pernicious cabal consisting of the archbishop of Trajanópolis, her friend, the saintly Sor Patrocinio (foundress of the Franciscan Conceptionists) and, as a sort of inconsequential adjunct, the consort! Ergo—the "progress" of la Patria was being blocked by the "reactionary objectives of a pair of power-mad papists"!

Everyone having the slightest contact with the court knew perfectly: that Claret was barely acquainted with Sor Patrocinio; had, during all his years in Madrid, spoken to her but twice, but briefly, and in public; that he had neither the time nor the inclination to cultivate close friendships outside the congregation; that he despised politics in any form. But these facts impressed the nineteenth century Spanish radicals precisely the way truth impresses today's "people's courts" in Moscow or Peiping, and for the same reason. They weren't remotely interested in the truth. Nor would Claret's accusers be content with their own fabrication until they had invoked obscenity to infer his "indecent relations" with both the queen and the nun!

The wicked verses were too well turned to have been produced by other than professional talent; too bitingly clever to be overlooked by the coarser elements of irony-loving Spain. On the tongues of the vulgar "wits," they speedily ran through Madrid's alleys and saloons, from where it was the usual brief circuit into the kitchens, my lady's boudoir, and finally, the halls of, occasionally, even respectable houses. The yellow press fell into line with malicious innuendo and caricatures. Many soon "had it from unimpeachable sources" that the real secret of Anthony Claret's popularity was the sensational content of his sermons. To think, exclaimed the prurient self-righteous, that, on the pretext of denouncing immorality, this man hailed a saint has all along been attracting his vast audiences by lurid expositions of abominable sins! It was even "discovered" that he had sung—from the pulpit, no less—an example of the salacious songs he pretended to condemn!

The momentum attained by this vicious campaign could have only one explanation. Madrid's welter of political factions, whose diverse ambitions had, so far, prevented their accord on anything but enmity toward the regime, realized that, to bring it down, they must first strike out its strongest moral support: the court confessor. And to achieve this they must: 1) embarrass him with the queen; 2) alienate his enormous following.

From slander and lascivious gossip, it was only a step to criminal libel. The opposition press came into the open to lend the powerful corroboration of print to the heretofore anonymous inventions. Then, having (they hoped) prepared a climate of serious mistrust, the Socialist and Communist newspapers proceeded to drop their bomb! If the hero-worshipers still needed to be convinced of the horrid nature of Anthony Claret's "great mission" to the nation, they headlined, let them examine the latest edition of his work, *La Llave de Oro* (The Golden Key), a shocking volume in text and lavishly illustrated with pornography! Needless to say, thousands rushed to act on this suggestion and were duly revolted to find the accusation apparently only too true!

The Madrid clergy was as thunderstruck by this attack upon his little book as was the author. For more than a decade they had been using *La Llave de Oro* most profitably in the work for which it had been composed, were familiar with its every page. They knew it as a fine exposition of simplified techniques for the religious instruction of beginners. To what, then, could these raucous editors possibly be alluding? It seemed that a spurious burlesque of *La Llave de Oro*, prominently featuring the authorship of Claret, had just been issued by one of *their own presses*. And so insane was the plotters' daring that they proceeded to the extreme of carrying their imposture before the ecclesiastical authorities with a demand for the castigation of a prelate "capable of such vileness"! This impertinence was, logically, their undoing, since a simple comparison of the two versions of the book readily exposed the crime, if not the criminals. "Nevertheless," writes Fernández, "the pernicious seed had been sown and it grew and propagated itself to give origin to a thousand insults and nauseating impudences against the calumniated archbishop." [1] Nor did his official exoneration prevail to discourage the foes whose villainy it unmasked from publishing another volume under one of his best-known titles; or a flood of spurious ironical subjects to which his name was also libelously appended which soon appeared under such titles as: *The Confessional, Salvation in the Hand,* and *Spiritual Alfalfa for Christ's Sheep.* So was his lifelong work of Christian publication mocked!

As climax, there now appeared two "biographies" of the archbishop of Trajanópolis, both fabricated from the rough cloth of calumny. These estimates of his life and work attributed to him all, and even more, nefarious motives and deeds than had the doggerel. The first, by a pair of professional slanderers named Funes and Lustonó, was run serially in *La Iberia.* The second, signed merely: "Señor O," was generally considered to be the work of either the disgruntled minister Olózaga, or his brother, both close associates of Clavo Asensio, *La Iberia's* editor.

It was only natural that the clergy and especially the congregation bitterly resented these outrages; it was supernatural that the victim did not. When urged, not unreasonably, to defend himself by refuting the villainous lies, he declined. To his intimates he maintained that, properly evaluated, persecution must be seen as "the corrector of the bishops," whose friends and subjects rarely offer them the needful reproof for their faults; and he blessed God for giving him so many opportunities to exercise patience. True, there were occasional mentions of his trials in notes to his missionaries, but these were confined to a few lines that were invariably edifying. "You can form no idea," he wrote to Xifré, "of how hell launches itself against me in the most atrocious lies, spoken and written, and threats of death (Fernández writes that he was once sent a coffin containing a cadaver and the note: "As you will soon be seen."); but with God's aid, I ignore them." [2] To the same fiercely loyal brother he had long since summed up the consolation such wrongs deposited in his heart: "I see what they say of me. I can only comment that it is a reminder of the patrimony left us by *Jesucristo*. This is the pay the world accords us. We do well to recall the words of Isaias: '*In silentio et spe erit fortitudo vestra.*'" [3] The only words his tormentors could elicit from him were said not to, but for, them: "Blessed be Thou, my God. Give Thy holy benediction to all who persecute and calumniate me; give them, Lord, prosperity—spiritual, corporal, temporal, eternal. And to me give humility, gentleness, patience and conformability to Thy most holy Will, that I may suffer in silence and love the pain, persecution and calumny Thou dost permit to descend upon me." [4]

II

The seasons followed one upon another until the summer of 1868, and still the long-threatened revolution held off or, better said, was held off, for Madrid had indeed seen sporadic mob violence, abortive attempts to set the blaze by which the old order might be consumed. So far they had been smothered by the banishment of certain military figures, among them the obstreperous General Prim. But such men knew how to plot from exile and, to Claret, it was a source of ceaseless amazement that Isabel and Francisco could not seem to credit the proximity of catastrophe. As early as 1863 he had reported his privileged preview of Spain's approaching tragedy: "The Lord is angry with this nation. He has told me that a great revolution will fall upon her, the queen will be dethroned, a republic declared, Protestantism introduced, and excesses of Communism suffered here." [5] Very well, this was the truth direct from Heaven, though perhaps to those with, at best, slight comprehension of Heaven's ways, the selection of this servant as God's mouthpiece *must* seem incredible. Nonetheless, what with a substantial sector of the press daily offering its rulers brazen insults, with bullets periodically whizzing through the streets of their capital, wherein, he marveled, lay the logic of their optimism? However, he had grown unutterably weary of his own warnings.

August found the royal family and entourage en route to Lequeitio, where Isabel proposed taking the baths. As usual, she had insisted that her confessor accompany them for the consolation (not, presumably, for advice) he alone could provide. Since he would minister wherever he found himself, the trip would impose no alteration in his labors.

The tranquillity of the outlands and the homage of its loyal population were gratefully soothing to the queen if a poor preparation for the cataclysm. A resurging sense of security soon had her so disarmed that, when her man-of-war, *Zaragoza*, unexpectedly put into Lequeitio Bay, she fondly paid it a visit; and it was a blow to learn, immediately afterward, that the *Zaragoza's* appearance had been instigated by a plot for her abduction! According to orders, once the fatuous family was safely aboard, the ship should have weighed anchor and sailed away to deposit a charming, but superfluous and embarrassing, monarch in some "suitable" foreign port. At the last moment, the crew quailed before the thought of visiting such an indignity upon her, a telling sidelight on the gallantry and affection Isabel inspired in her subjects.

As the shock of this revelation abated, perhaps the deference for her it proved actually served to bolster her confidence, because, although pressed by her confessor, they now started back to Madrid, the attractions of San Sebastián made her majesty forget her hurry. Why *not* indulge the pretty pleas of her ladies by tarrying in the famed resort? After all, her anxious prelate was always experiencing distressing "intuitions." That they were inspired by concern for her and her subjects heightened her fondness but, as so often, she persuaded herself that *this time* his fears (that her absence from the capital was most untimely) were groundless. So when he urged: "Señora, we *must* get on to Madrid at once. I tell you we are on the brink of revolution!" she resorted to gay irrelevance.

"But I haven't finished my baths."

"Forget the baths. The time has come to place first things first," he pleaded. Then seeing she was mentally formulating additional excuses, he declared grimly, "If your majesty were only a doll! I'd drop you into a suitcase, run to Madrid, and save Spain from the revolution." [6] But as Isabel was not a doll and, moreover, precisely "her majesty," he could neither drop her into a suitcase, nor, most pitifully, prevail to alter the royal whim, which was the reason that the dire news surprised her in the baths!

During the dalliance in San Sebastián the exiled generals had been converging upon Spain to join Prim (already standing offshore with disaffected naval elements) in a concerted action against the crown. The uprising was slated for the thirtieth, by which date those en route from the Canaries should have arrived. But certain loyal warcraft maneuvers aroused Prim's suspicion that his plan had leaked, and, determined that the queen should not be afforded time to reach Madrid, he struck on the eighteenth. Within three days he had won over the whole navy, whereupon the "gallant and sentimental" crew of the *Zaragoza* cannonaded the dethronement of Isabel II!

Receipt of this appalling news shocked her into something approximating a proper appreciation of the danger and she prepared to return to the capital. Her presence must certainly inspire her defending land forces. These were her people! They had seen her through crises almost as threatening as this. She could rely on the old magic to work this one more time . . . couldn't she? Nervously she reminded herself of how, without forewarning, she had dominated the *Zaragoza* merely by confronting it. Its present defection could never have occurred in her presence. Hadn't her wise confessor been saying all along that she could stem the tide?

But even as she reasoned herself into hope, her garrisons were falling, one after another, and, from morning to evening, the increasingly lugubrious dispatches increased her confusion. Now, too, Anthony Claret was conspicuously silent. No reproaches! This din in her ears was but the futile chatter of her frightened entourage. "The queen really must *do* something," but a precious week slipped by, and still the confessor, saying nothing, stood apart. Finally, on the twenty-ninth, Isabel entrained for Madrid, only to hear, before the departure, that her palace was already empty. So soon, none would risk being found there. There was no longer anyone to whom to return! Descending from the coach, she passed an agonized night in the station.

Morning brought the finale. "By courtesy of" the wily Napoleon III, Isabel, Francisco, their children, the royal committee (Marquesa de Novaliches, Count of Ezpeleta, Duke of Moctezuma, Marqués de Villamanga, Marquesas de Peñaflorida y de los Remedios, D. Julio Soca, D. Atanasio Oñate), the infantas' governesses, three generals and, of course, the long-suffering confessor, were escorted across the nearby frontier by the Marqués de Santiago's corps of sympathetic but realistic military. And at 2:45 P.M. their train pulled into ~France~ Bayonne station and the long exile that, for Anthony Claret, would only terminate with death!

No one had heeded his warnings while acting upon them ~Fatima~ might still have saved Spain. His prophecies had been too painful for acceptance. Now, however, there was no eluding the fulfillment; nothing to distract the royal refugees' attention from the ruin that was engulfing their loved and lost *patria!* From afar they sorrowed over each day's quota of

tragedy. The Jesuits had been savagely ejected from Spain—
again; and then the other orders. This prepared the exiles for
the dissolution of Claret's congregation, but certainly not for
the martyrdom of one of the missionaries at the Selva de
Campo house! (The founder's prediction of the blood-letting
to precede their glorious future had been made long prior to
his days at court and, though it could never have been out
of his mind, it was one impending disaster he had spared the
rulers.) The abolition of the St. Vincent de Paul Society was
the next shock. It was inconceivable that even the most ob-
tuse governors might fail to appreciate the value of its magnificent work for the poor to any regime! Let not those who
could, then, take the platform for mouthings anent the "welfare of the proletariat"! Ah, but it was too late for regal admonitions, or for logic; too late to prevent the demolition of
temples, the pauperization of the secular clergy; the vandali-
zation inherent in the demand for inventories of all church
and monastery art. Despoliation and, of course, the Reds'
ever more rabid attacks upon religion were no longer news;
nor that the invading Protestant sects were being welcomed
with significant jubilance by the *atheistic* press! The policy:
"divide and rule" is as old as history.

In Madrid the prime targets for journalistic reprobation
were: the venerated, the traditional, the characteristically
Spanish, and—Anthony Claret. No Church or court figure
was so resoundingly vilified as the prophet who had forecast
it all. Because he had been too impressive to escape into ob-
livion with lesser men? Because he was still *el santo* to millions of the stricken? Whatever the reason, all the old lies, the
exploded lies, were dragged out for lurid reaffirmation; and a
thousand new ones added. The inventories, the Madrid head-
lines proclaimed, "proved" that the archbishop of Trajanópolis, this former "dictator" of the nation, was a common thief!
As protector of the Escorial, he had "looted" its glorious art

treasure! He was public enemy number one who had well merited the seizure of his mail—a measure that now cut him off from his friends and missionaries remaining in Spain, men who understood that, unless prepared to face reprisals, they must even avoid mentioning his name in letters between themselves.

"In view of the predicament in which he finds himself, the *other* hasn't written . . ." was the phrasing resorted to by Padre González (to his brother). "Perhaps it would be well for you to write the *other* about the deposit . . ." [7] Don Dionisio was alluding to the Escorial scandal. During a revolution that predated Claret's time, three items of the Escorial collection had been preserved from the greedy fingers of another set of impious despoilers by the monks' precaution in hiding them above the false ceiling of the prior's cell. And when the protector was shown the two monstrances and image of the Virgin, dust-dulled but safe in their snug niche, one of his "intuitions" decreed that they be left undisturbed. Lost to sight for years, they had been forgotten by the public, but now a search of the old inventories had disclosed their existence. "Naturally" there could be but one explanation of the absence of these jewels (suddenly "discovered" to be of "fabulous value"). They had been "stolen" by the "unspeakable Claret"!

Loath to see the long-guarded objects lost to a conceivably happier future day, the men still lingering on at the Escorial had charged Director González' brother Ildefonso to remove them for reconcealment in a location of which they could truthfully declare themselves ignorant. But this precaution had boomeranged into the biggest "break" yet for the archbishop's foes, who knew exactly how to employ such ammunition! Having already denied knowledge of the missing items' whereabouts, the Escorial officials were greatly discomfited to hear that they were simply "covering up" for a vulgar thief, their sometime protector!

The tempest now whipped up against the innocent and absent prelate by the press outdid its previous worst. "While the newsmen editorially addressed demands to the government that it move for his extradition from France . . . and the gazettes printed nauseating verses and every manner of evil about him, Padre Claret was drawn by the cartoonists in the act of fleeing Spain weighted down with monstrances," wrote his contemporary, Bishop Aguilar.[8]

In distant Paris and deprived of authentic information, the victim could make small sense of the venomous dispatches. Isabel and Francisco, troubled by this latest injustice to both religion and their confessor, persuaded him to chance writing González to urge a public clarification of whatever the Escorial difficulty might be. Indeed, if the prelate were to be cleared of the charges already lodged against him in the Spanish courts, this was imperative. When he received this letter Don Dionisio immediately ordered the missing objects produced and, by gallantly assuming full responsibility for their sequestration, achieved the official, if briefly and most reluctantly reported, exoneration of his former superior.

III

Anthony Claret, who had once sternly "walked out on" the queen when convinced that his counsel was wasted upon her, who had returned to her side only under holy obedience, who had ceaselessly warned her of the inevitable outcome of her complacence, had not even considered deserting her in the bitterness of the final debacle. Meanwhile, he was perfectly aware that accompanying the royal family into exile was equivalent to renouncing his career. A brief train ride and his missionary work—forty years of it—was done! This sacrifice, seemingly of the greater usefulness to the lesser, was not made from his compassion for Isabel—though that was great. It was that God had twice fixed this burden upon him and, until such time as He saw fit to lift it, His servant must bear it on along however crazily narrowing a path. Without a complaint he must also carry the acute loneliness and mourning imposed by this futureless path away from his own, the beloved people and establishments that, ever farther behind, were being slaughtered and razed by his enemies, the boasted enemies of his Lord. They had dispersed his congregation; nullified his labors for the Escorial; ejected his nursing sisters from Montserrat. How long before that other fruit of a sleepless lifetime, the books, would be suppressed? And who would restore these ruins?

Not he, certainly. That he was not really old signified nothing. Into his sixty-one years he had packed a century's human activity. Never adequately supplied with the material, he had always punished his body cruelly to raise the ambitious monuments with which he had lined the route of his uncompromising march ahead over highways roughened by insults, false accusations and hatred; menaced by a ridiculously numerous gang of assassins. Even his devoted spiritual daughter Isabel had seemingly made a program of outmaneuvering his advance which should certainly have been to her best interest! Little wonder that he had arrived in France exhausted and far from well. Great wonder that his heart was yet overflowing with gratitude! "This world's pains are spurs to hasten our steps heavenward. As the deluge's swelling waters but lifted Noah's ark the higher, pain raises our hearts and souls. . . ." [9]

In Paris the royal refugees had taken up residence in the Hotel Rohán; the confessor in St. Joseph's convent school. "The Sisters and children are all very good. . . . Each morning I say the seven o'clock Mass and give Communion to the community . . . On Sundays Their Majesties . . . send the coach for me and we attend the 10:30 Mass at San Germán together . . . I also go to them each Monday and Thursday to instruct the Prince and the Infantas. Otherwise, as in Madrid, I am occupied by my ministries. . . .

"I should have mentioned that, less harassed since leaving Spain, her majesty receives the Sacraments more frequently. Yesterday, the Immaculate Conception, she came to the convent chapel to confess and receive Communion. She took breakfast with me and then, after the arrival of her family at ten o'clock, heard a second Mass, Don Lorenzo's. Edified by her piety, the people are amazed to hear her calumniated by some of her subjects. They say: 'The Spaniards are treating their queen as the French treated Antoinette.' " [10]

Conceded all his faculties by the archbishop of Paris, he confirmed and engaged in his other accustomed ministries. Occasionally he preached to the Parisians, using an interpreter to overcome the language handicap. Disapproving the trends he observed in the capital he dubbed "the modern Babylon," he embraced every opportunity to offset its iniquitous influence upon the Spanish and Latin American residents who, "lacking spiritual aid, may despair here, even commit suicide. I was horrified to read that Paris has 1,200 suicides every year." [11]

He constantly sought and found compensations for which to return thanks: "My health has improved. The last year in Madrid I was twice at death's door, whereas this year I am quite well. So perhaps it was to prolong my life that Our Lord brought me here. This is not said because I desire long life, merely to witness the Providence of God. How good, wise, and powerful is He Who can always work benefits from evil! I am well lodged, lack nothing; I don't even have to leave the house to celebrate. All is easier for me than it was in Spain." [12]

At the same time, such tranquillity, convenience and respect occasioned a sort of holy embarrassment, and a sadness: "Ever since leaving Spain my most constant contemplation has been the Holy Family's Egyptian exile. I ponder the distress they endured traveling that long road which offered nothing but privations and hardship, and contrast this with our comfort. They knew not where, upon their arrival, they might rest their heads, and we had a house all prepared for us where the sisters waited, eager to offer us every service. Ah, María! [13] This is what confounds me and [even as I write] fills my eyes with tears: to contemplate Jesús, Holy María and San José in such trouble and want while we three, Don Lorenzo, Brother José and this prelate, enjoy such ease, so many attentions. For it afflicts me to see myself unworthy to suffer something for love of Him."

Once recovered from their first depression, the royalists were again turning longing eyes toward Spain. Perhaps Isabel should abdicate in favor of her son. This plan, it was urged, would be welcomed by the Spanish majority, which was already pronouncing the republic a fiasco. But the *Carlistas*, too, were viewing the unpopularity of the revolutionary regime as opportunity—to revive the old cause of the pretender! If all this presaged more political ferment, Anthony Claret wished to be excused!

At home, after Isabel had made her Easter duty each year, he had always retired to the Escorial for a few weeks. This year he would go, instead, to Rome. His determination to avoid even an appearance of political interest had held him aloof from the Spanish delegations that were continuously waiting upon the queen, but he was naturally anxious for news of Spain. He needed enlightenment on everything which might affect the future of his congregation, presently centered at Prades, in the French Pyrenees. Better than any other the Holy City could supply this information, as well as the broadest perspective from which to judge all the circumstances. Rome held forth other attractions. The one he chose to give out as his motive in making the journey was the papal jubilee, April 11.

That he refrained from mentioning his decision that he would not be returning to Paris was to save both her majesty and himself the wear and tear of her inevitable emotional protests that she couldn't carry on, or even live, bereft of his spiritual direction. For, from his knowledge of her capacity for adjustment, he knew better. (It is likely he also knew she was to survive him by many years.) And if, as appeared increasingly certain, the abdication was imminent, his withdrawal was, at last, justified. His obligation had been ministry to the queen of Spain, not to the progenitor of Alfonso XII!

More heart-free than in many years, he attended the jubilee, rejoiced in new interviews with the great Pope who had shown him so much affection, always so thoroughly comprehended his trials, objectives and zeal for the faith. Lodged in the modest Mercedarian Monastery, he confessed the novices, conducted conferences, prayed for "my poor Spain," and wrote new books.[14] He had no money and wanted none. Funds long owing from Cuba had not been remitted; and he really had forgotten to mention to Isabel that no one had tendered the emolument she had allocated for the services she "couldn't live without." As, lacking transportation, he walked from one appointment to another, no such mishaps intruded upon his joy. He was free! And in Rome, the heart of Christendom! He was an apostle forever, a prelate only secondarily, and by no wish of his own. In these circumstances there was no anomaly in being a poverty-stricken prelate, while the very idea of a comfortably situated apostle was distasteful. His small unavoidable expenses were covered by token gifts which arrived now and then from here or there. He hardly noticed.

And now, something very wonderful happened: the opportunity to make a truly important contribution. In June, a papal bull announced the convocation, on December 8, of the Vatican Council. To it would be submitted for resolution questions of enormous import to the future of the Church. Their preparation would involve prodigious labors of research. And, to Our Lord's servant, Anthony Claret from Catalonia, was confided a substantial portion of this research. "I've been very busy collecting the documentation. Many anticipate great material benefits from the Council, much as the worldly Jews expected such from the *Mesias*. All *my* hope is in the spiritual good to be derived. May the Council prove the portal to shelter in the midst of the tempest which, already upon us, is increasing . . . [otherwise] woe to earth!" [15] exclaimed he who had been divinely instructed on the subject of apocalyptic "woe."

Nevertheless, as he pressed ahead with his research, drawing upon his knowledge of many places and peoples for the illumination of his notes, he was intensely happy. It was a vital and most fascinating work to which he referred enthusiastically: "Now it may be said that Our Lord's designs for me are being fulfilled. Blessed be God. How I hope that what I am doing will find favor with Him!" [16]

"I expect to remain in Rome until the conclusion of the Council, after which we shall see what He asks of me," he commented, perhaps a bit obliquely,[17] since he had already taken cognizance of his progressive physical deterioration. That he knew this task to be his final earthly assignment, however, only enhanced its sweetness. The important thing was that he would live to participate in the Council's glorious furtherance of God's kingdom here below! Could a lifetime of apostolic labor culminate in a more blessed climax?

In December, as he walked the Vatican's vast corridors and plazas among the brilliant press of 700 prelates and princes of the Church assembled from every corner of the globe, his hope for the good of men surpassed any he had ever experienced. And what but joy was this reunion, after so much time, with some of his most cherished coworkers in the Vineyard of the Lord? Here were: Caixal, sharer of his dreams and struggles for a great Catholic press; Blanco, of Avila, his friend and imitator; Cuenca's Payá y Rico, his consistent supporter; his admiring aide, Martínez of Havana —and many more, whose comprehension and appreciation (amounting to veneration) dissolved every twinge of remembered pain inflicted by years of persecution. At long last he could work closely with a company of such men: to shore up the defenses of the Church against the fury without; to close the insidious, creeping cracks within. Supported by their combined vision and energy, he would fight—and win— his predilect causes: clergy reform; a uniform children's catechism. Most important of all, they would stand shoulder-to-shoulder for the definition of papal infallibility against those others who—how sadly!—seduced by pride, had been lured into the error of Gallicanism. (How his heart swelled to see that beloved Spain, despite her rebellions and assorted upheavals, had not produced even one of these mistaken "theologians"! And now at the Council the Spanish hierarchy presented a sturdy bastion against the attacks upon infallibility launched by the cardinal archbishop of Vienna, the bishop of Rottenburg, etc.)

Listening to these personages' devious arguments caused him a chagrin so intense that it produced excruciating headaches. And during one fateful session ". . . the nonsense, and even the blasphemies and heresies they uttered roused my indignation and zeal to such a pitch that the blood rushed to my head in a cerebral attack. My mouth couldn't contain the saliva. It was emitted to one side, singularly, that scarred by the wound I received in Cuba. My tongue was entirely numb." [18]

He had suffered a stroke. However, insisting that he had been restored by the baths his physicians prescribed, he refused to consider his friends' urgings that he retire from the proceedings for complete rest; hurried back to the Council to hear out the fifty-two erudite dissertations on this preeminent question. The arguments favoring the definition had covered all the pertinent points, theological and historical, and, in any case, he knew himself physically unequal to a full exposition. Still, it was unthinkable that he fail to register his affirmation; or that either side might misconstrue his silence as indecision or indifference.

Therefore, on May 31, 1870, a diminutive but majestic figure claimed the rostrum and, turning upon this distinguished assembly the worn countenance of an aging, already stricken warrior of Christ, marvelously *beautified* by the signature of an assassin, addressed it briefly in concise and vivid Latin. He was not lifting his voice to propound obscurely based syllogisms, to pose theoretical fine points, but to give in condensed form just such a sermon as he might make to a crowd of Catalonian rustics, which is to say, a simple confession of faith. ". . . I am here to say that, from long study of Holy Scripture, of a tradition never once ruptured, of the words of the fathers of the Church and the Sacred Councils, from deep meditation upon the reasoning of the theologians which, for the sake of brevity, I shall not cite, I can with full conviction assure you that, in everything touching the sense and forms of the Apostolic Roman Catholic Church, the Supreme Roman Pontiff *is* infallible . . ." And he closed: "The truth of papal infallibility would be clear to all men *if* Scripture were understood. And why is it not? For three reasons. The first, as Jesus told Santa Teresa, is that men do not really *love* God.

The second, that they lack humility. It is written: 'I confess Thee Father Lord of Heaven and earth, because Thou has hidden these truths from the wise and those prudent according to the world, and revealed them to the humble.' Third and finally, there are some who do not *wish* to understand Scripture—simply because they do not wish the good. Now, with David, I pray: 'May the Lord have mercy upon us, bless us, let His Holy Face shine upon us.' I have spoken." [19]

The much-persecuted little archbishop of Trajanópolis, the faithful servant already on his way home to his Master, had indeed "spoken." He had put his sure finger on the hidden sores festering at the heart of the opposition to papal infallibility. In a few homely lines he had shown this high company that it was not entirely clean of men capable of refusing God the love He would have, who were strangers to humility, who, from resistance to good, elected to misread Scripture! It had taken the poorest and least assuming of their number, but ah! a prophet and a saint, to reduce this enormously agitating issue to its essence by the same uncomplicated method he would apply in dealing with any other spiritual problem. What say the Scriptures? *"Thou art Peter. On this Rock, I build My Church."*

The vote was cast, July 13, 1870, by 601 prelates. Of these, 451 responded: *Placet;* 88, *Non placet;* 62, *Placet juxta modum.* Scriptural truth had prevailed.

His soul flooded with joy, his heart at rest, his body racked by pain and close to collapse from the debility that now assailed it, a very happy little old man, Antonio María Claret, dragged himself through the Roman streets, back to the humble cell at St. Adrian's. It had not been in vain, their appeal—his *final* appeal—to that mysterious, trying mixture of good and evil which is the composite heart of God's earthbound children! Everything considered, everything judged by holy charity, *nothing had ever been in vain!* How well, how very well, indeed, it had all ended—the great Council, the lifetime of labor and suffering dedicated to one's fellow men, to their salvation . . . *"para siempre."* How wonderful, too, that they had terminated together! How good was God! And what a blessed gift, that all the days remaining could be reserved for praise of Him!

XIX

THE UNSPARED

WORD OF HIS PHYSICAL FAILURE reached Prades during the closing days of the Council and sent the Claretian superior speeding to Rome. Prepared to find the founder debilitated, perhaps emaciated, Xifré was nevertheless startled by the drastic changes wrought by the illness. "I'm taking your excellency back to Prades," he stated decisively, ". . . and regardless of what the French authorities may have to say."

"But why should they object? I've never involved myself in politics," sighed the deathly tired old exile.

"Everyone knows *that*, but . . . Anyway we shall go! What we all most wish is to have you with us."

"All together again! Yes, that is the *good* I also long for . . ." Prades was not Spain but, because his sons were there, it was home! Like any other father, why should he *not* go home to die among his own?

Shortly before midnight on July 23, just ten days after the great vote, the "man who was born to command" led Anthony Claret into their house and family. The congregation's joy in this homecoming was naturally shadowed by his ominously altered appearance. Padre Clotet's description of his own emotions reflected the general reaction: "Despite the ineffable consolation of having him with us, I was deeply pained to see him so weak. He could hardly stand! The change in his features was shocking and he could scarcely speak. 'My God!' I said to myself, 'can this be *el Señor Arzobispo?*' He took a little food and went directly to bed. All the community and students had been anxious to greet him and pay their respects individually but, in view of the hour and his immense fatigue, we couldn't permit it. The reception was therefore postponed until the following day.

"In our lovely orchard under the windows of the house a luxuriant grapevine forms a long green canopy. There it was that the *Señor Arzobispo* received the padres, students and brothers since, in this house, we had no large halls like those from which the revolution had driven us. Never shall I forget this solemn reunion of such a *good* father with his sons! Every face, commencing with the father superior's, glowed with happiness as, one by one, we approached to kiss his ring. Father superior and I stood beside him to announce the bishoprics and provinces of the members he didn't know. This concluded, he gave us a few kind words—and the function terminated. It was Sunday and the hour when the sun begins to gild the arbor's green leaves, an effect which lent the fiesta a lustrous splendor.

"As he was too weak to preach that day we begged him not to read either, or give a thought to anything but the reestablishment of his health. 'Don't worry about my reading,' he told us, 'for even if I wished, I couldn't.' But when urged to go back to bed, he objected, 'When I remain in bed longer than usual, I only grow iller.' We had the house doctor prescribe for him." [1]

These attentions apparently alleviated his condition and he began to participate in the devotional activities of the community, to get acquainted with the students. He was so proud of them! In them God had granted the sturdy foundations from which the great Claretian edifice would now quickly rise. And they were doubly proud: of their saintly founder; of his moving love for them.

"We're all out of our minds with joy to have him with us," wrote Leandro González, one of the seminarians. "In the orchard when we run up to kiss his ring, he murmurs: 'God bless you, God bless you,' with such tender paternal affection! He always accompanies us novices and students to the spiritual reading and examination, but whether from his love for youth or because these acts are held in the chapel before the Blessed Sacrament, I couldn't say. Perhaps the two motives are mixed. In any case, he will always leave the padres to go with us.

"I never cease to marvel at the fervor and recollection in which, after celebrating, our beloved padre leaves the altar! His arms, crossed before his breast as though to embrace Jesús, remain thus all the long time he kneels motionless on his prie-dieu.

"I also revere the tenderness with which he pronounces the name of Mary. Whenever someone accuses himself in the refectory and the reverend father general indicates that [Padre Claret] impose the penance, he says: 'Pray an Avemaría (or three) to the *Most* Holy Virgin,' with such affection we can't help knowing how very greatly he loves Our Blessed Mother.

"We were also much edified by a special proof of his simplicity and abnegation. Since he never eats meat or drinks wine, his glass contained only water at dinner on the day of his arrival. However, the reverend father superior signed the servant to bring another which he filled with wine and placed before the prelate. And, without offering the least resistance,

our dearest padre, as though he were a child, drank it out of
obedience and respect." [2]

The seeming improvement in his health amid such felicity
deceived everyone but the patient and, perhaps, those who
had heard his prediction that he was to go during 1870. But
now he had some special instructions for Clotet: "This little
book I'm working on is the last," he said gently. "I want you
to see to its publication, inasmuch as I shall die before long."

"You may be sure of my compliance, but oh! most excellent señor, *must* we lose you so soon? Surely Our Lord
wishes *you* to ordain the students who are now ready!"

"That could be," mused the founder. To see his splendid
and splendidly prepared younger sons firmly set upon the
apostles' road, to pass from their loving last attentions into
the Very Presence of the One he had adored and served for
so many years—that would indeed be a glorious thing! "It
could be . . ."

But it was not to be quite like that. For, though Anthony
Claret had not been conceded martyrdom by enemy knives,
he was to be spared nothing else that the mania of his persecutors could contrive. And now, in a final, totally senseless
exhibition of hostility, they would drive a dying man out of
the house that owed him its being, the company which loved
him as father, venerated him a saint but could do nothing to
prevent this shameful injury!

II

In spite of Padre Xifré's premonition that the arm of vengeance might prove long enough to reach from the Madrid of
the revolutionists across to the French slopes of the Pyrenees,
all had thus far gone off so calmly that there seemed no reason to conceal the archbishop's presence at Prades. So, when
he was invited to attend graduation exercises at a small

neighboring seminary, he did so. Pressed by the school's admiring faculty, he even made a brief talk to the class—in his native Catalán that is so similar to French. It was a mistake. Less than a week later: ". . . we received the saddest possible news. A true friend wrote to inform us that the Spanish consul at Perpignan had notified his ambassador in Paris that Padre Claret had been located at Prades, and solicited authorization for his arrest! Our correspondent who had all this from an official source urged father superior to come to Perpignan without delay." [3]

Xifré's anxiety sped him to the nearby city, where he conferred with their friend and then the bishop. It was agreed he should interview the prefect. Although the officer received him courteously and, after hearing the story, concurred that imprisoning the innocent and infirm prelate would be a colossal injustice, he pointed out, "Nevertheless, we are merely agents of the government with no choice but to obey its orders. Why don't you carry this matter to the empress?"

But what might be hoped from this? Paris was far, in both distance and spirit, from the rustic, politically unimportant Pyrenees and a war was in progress! Would the empress who had defied Rome protect a Catalonian churchman and former critic of Napoleon? Father Xifré returned to Prades to take counsel with the dismayed brothers. It was certainly no help that the Spanish ambassador was Olózaga, reputed to be "Señor O," perpetrator of the outlandishly spiteful Claret "biography." At all events, he was on record as their prelate's antagonist. Deeply depressed, they discussed the merits of disturbing the founder's contentment by apprizing him of the situation which threatened it.

"Imprisonment will kill him," mourned Xifré, "and unwarned, the shock alone will be horrible. Therefore, though we cause him new grief, it is doubtless better to prepare him."

They tried to soften the bad news by saying there was, as

yet, no reason to view the situation as hopeless. But Anthony Claret was not one to be deceived by wishful thinking. Always a realist and, from bitter experience, only too familiar with the caliber of these "new Spaniards," he said, "While Olózaga remains in Paris, I'll never be left in peace."

How right he was became clear on August fifth when it was learned that the arrest order had been signed! If his seizure was to be prevented, he must go into hiding at once.

"But where can I take him?" exclaimed the distracted Padre Xifré.

His answer came from the superior of the small seminary whose graduates had been favored by the prelate's talk. "To the Monastery of Fontfroide. I've already sent a message to its abbot asking that a room be prepared for him."

The Cistercians of the Immaculate Conception (founded at Senanque just a year prior to the definition of the Dogma of the Immaculate Conception) had, in 1858, acquired the dismantled ruins of an eleventh century monastery near Narbona where, with no material assets beyond a bag of potatoes, a pot to cook them in, and 126 francs of alms, a little company of twelve monks immediately established themselves and commenced a colossal labor of reconstruction. Now, not quite thirteen years later, a thriving community occupied the enormous plant it had already half-restored to its pristine beauty. Set against a vast wilderness of mountains in a steeply ascending canyon, accessible only over twelve miles of rough wagon track, Fontfroide certainly seemed an ideal refuge for a hunted missionary.

Fortunately, the bishop of Perpignan was in Prades on August fifth. He approved the plan for Claret's removal, which was put into effect at daybreak the following morning. Then, without the time, and maybe the heart, to bid his beloved novices a final "*adiós*," the founder, accompanied by

Xifré, left his only earthly home to undertake the last of his
many earthly journeys!

The promptitude of their departure was most fortunate.
A few hours later the police were knocking on the Claretians' door. "Where is *Monseñor?*" demanded the commissioner of the acting superior.

"Out."

"Out where?"

"We don't know," came the quite truthful reply, for no
one likely to be encountered by outsiders had been informed
of the fugitive's destination, or even his means of transportation. "He went off somewhere with the superior, but we
don't know where."

"At what time? Did they go by carriage?"

"Those things I don't know either."

III

On the stagecoach the Claretians might have been any pair
of shabby clerics. Before setting out the founder had re-
moved every mark that identified him as a prelate and donned
a regulation soutane. Now, a less likely subject of an international manhunt could hardly be imagined. Descending
from the coach one station before Narbona, they were met
by the Cistercians' Padre Antonio.

The little road over which they were soon jouncing on
and up to the abbey afforded breath-catching panoramas of
peaks and precipices climaxing in the superb effect produced
by Fontfroide's massive masonry sketched on an infinity of
grandeur, a scene to dwarf any ever encountered by the
widely traveled missionary. Everything would be all right!
Almighty God was to be seen in everything here!

As Padre Antonio led them to the sanctuary, to the Blessed
Sacrament Anthony Claret desired to visit before seeing any-

one at Fontfroide, he unobtrusively slipped on his pastoral ring. . . .

Prior Juan Javier and his monks wished to offer the archbishop of Trajanópolis every honor and service owing his high dignity. He would not have it! He had come to them for refuge, a tired old apostle, broken in health, a prelate without a diocese or a possession and, fantastic as it seemed, a fugitive from the "law." He was grateful to be here, grateful to know these fine men more than willing to bear the burden of his last illness and death. Until these were upon him, however, he would accept no more than the privilege of sharing their monastic austerity. No, he wouldn't even occupy the priorial seat or don his episcopal insignia for the conventual Masses, but take a place among the choristers. Well then—on Sundays he might relent. It was quite useless for them to expect any further concession.

Padre Javier was a man who practiced the same simplicity and humility which distinguished his guest. Now, for their mutual consolation, he called on Padre Claret daily, frequently conducted his easy strolls through the surrounding beauty—which was almost a preview of the Ultimate Beauty. The visitor greatly appreciated this kindly attention, but he couldn't feel justified in accepting so much of the prior's time. "*Padre mío*," he demurred, "all my life I've looked forward to ending my days in a monastery, so it really isn't needful that you give me these special consolations."

"What I most admired in him," declared the prior, "was his total faith, his extreme charity for his pursuers, the simplicity and humility he manifested in his frugal regimen and in opposing all the honors we would have wished to pay him in tribute to his character, as well as to the elevated position he had held in the world." [4]

The monks found much that was marvelous in his quiet observations. One day he broke off a preoccupied floor-pacing to tell them: "Something most extraordinary is taking place in this country." And forty-eight hours later the isolation of their lofty retreat was penetrated by the paralyzing news of the Sedan disaster! Napoleon III, master of France, master of international meddling, was finished, justifying his premonition and, moreover, the five-year-older prophecy to his Merced missionaries—when the emperor had been at the apex of his *very* earthly glory!

They were happy together at Fontfroide—Anthony Claret and the industrious Cistercians. And at Prades his affectionate followers were also happy in the assurance that their spiritual father was so and, at last, safe. On October 5, however, they were thrown into consternation by a letter from Padre Puig, his chaplain, which stated that his excellency had suffered several alarming attacks. They had left him too weak to eat or even arise from bed, in his case a decidedly formidable symptom! To combat what seemed to be a progressing paralysis the doctor had prescribed energetic massage.

Puig's reports sent on each of the two succeeding days wavered between hope and despair—and, on the seventh, Xifré once more set out for Fontfroide, where he arrived at dawn on the eighth to find the invalid now prostrated indeed, with all the physicians of Narbona's vicinity in consultation over his unconscious form! He had suffered a severe apoplectic stroke.

They were good doctors and soon had him restored to consciousness. It was their duty to the patient, the anxious religious, their own high calling to do everything in their power to prolong his life. But it might appear to have been a debatable favor. Indeed he intimated as much, once his improvement permitted articulation. Though he was never to utter a complaint, he responded to their encouraging prognostications: "But, my sons, death is what I ardently desire."

"It is a sin to wish for death," chided Dr. Tarroni.

Lapsing into Latin, the sufferer quoted calmly, "*Cupio dissolvi et esse cum Christo.*" I wish death and to be with Christ

"Our hope to reanimate him faded before this reply," [5] Tarroni later reported. And, in any case, their science certainly supported his still surer knowledge that time was running out. He received the Last Sacraments fervently from Padre Xifré—in whose firm hands he could confidently leave his Claretian family, and the ordination of "the little ones." There were *so* many blessings to praise! He could even go *now* with the assurance of Rome's approval of the congregation's constitutions. The glory of its future would be one more to enjoy in Heaven! That night his faithful watchers believed him already there. But, in the early hours of the ninth, he returned to them and by ten o'clock the amazed doctors were of the opinion that the crisis had been passed, that he now had a good chance of survival.

lasting good
he sought

It had not been the crisis. Two more days and he was again so low that Xifré telegraphed: *Jaime Clotet, Missioner, Prades: The founder is dying; his vestments and episcopal insignia required for interment. Stagecoach to Narbona; Hotel Dorado, Fontfroide, October 11, 1870.*

This message interrupted the community's dinner. Everyone hurried to the chapel to say the prescribed prayers for the dying. Then they packed the archbishop's effects and saw Padre Clotet off.

On the coach ". . . I had hardly a thought for anything but our beloved *Arzobispo*. 'Perhaps I shall be too late,' I told myself. 'But even so, at least I'll be able to see him and kiss his ring.' The instant I arrived I asked the porter: 'Monseñor still lives?'

" 'He does. I'll show you to his room.'

"We climbed a stone staircase to a second-floor terrace. On a big door with a window was posted a note reading:

'Servants: close this door.' We entered by it and crossed a vestibule to another door and sign: 'Entering the sickroom prohibited without doctor's permission. Make no noise in vestibule.'

"As I paused on the threshold two religious met me and invited me in. 'Is my father superior here?' I whispered.

" 'He's in his quarters.'

" 'Then I'll see him first,' I told them.

"They took me to his cell where I found the reverend father superior of Fontfroide with him. After the greetings and my inquiry about the ill one's condition, Padre Xifré told me how serious it was. Then, when I had reported on the congregation and all that had occurred during his absence, he said: 'I must go back' and, turning to the head of the monastery: 'Padre Clotet is the subdirector of our congregation. I am leaving him here with the *Señor Arzobispo*. God willing I shall return, but whatever occurs, I shall approve your resolutions.' He bid us good-by and I went to visit our sick man.

"He was delirious, but I said to him, 'Most excellent señor, here I am with you.'

" 'Who are you?'

" 'Padre Clotet.'

" 'Padre Clotet?'

" '*Sí*, your excellency.'

" 'Well listen, Padre Clotet. I think we should go to Gerona. Its bishop has a great affection for me, and besides, D.N. is there.'

" 'Very well, your excellency, only not right now. The weather is very poor for travel, and especially for one in your excellency's present condition.' This seemed to tranquilize him." [6]

He was not habitually delirious. Long hours together he lay motionless in prayer, clasping his crucifix, weakening steadily under the compassionate eyes of his devoted son, the physicians, the prior and his monks. He had spoken truly when he said "lying in bed only makes me iller."

"I told him that when he reached Heaven he must beg God to make me a saint," wrote Clotet. " 'I shall do that,' he said," [7] and resumed his more or less constant murmuring of pious ejaculations.

Several of his attendants were Italian monks, whom he always addressed in their tongue—perfected in Rome by his rule to speak nothing else at St. Adrian's. In fact, though so far gone in illness and frequently quietly delirious, he invariably replied to questions in whatever language they were put. (Spanish and Catalán, besides French and Italian, were used in the house.) At times he whispered softly in Latin: *"Adoramus Te Christe et benedicimus tibi."* Or again: *"Quoniam bonus, quoniam in saeculum misericordia ejus."* This when Padre Clotet, who believed him unable to see, guided his semiparalyzed arm in raising his crucifix to his lips.

And still he lingered, meekly accepting whatever medicines or broths were tendered, whispering of obedience, his desire to defer to their wills, as consistently in delirium as when his head was clear. There was no corner of his subconscious which had not been imbued with holiness. Night after night the religious reciting the prayers for the dying in his cell waited breathlessly for the end. Night after night there were hourly changes but—not *the* change. What was keeping him alive? Not his sturdy constitution—for that he had abused cruelly, depriving it of rest, sleep, food for forty-two overworked years. Here was a man prepared for death, longing for death, by day and by night fiercely assaulted by excruciating attacks, any one of which should have killed him, and—unable to die. Was this not martyrdom?

On October 12 the doctors doubted his survival until midnight. By nightfall of the thirteenth their warnings had undergone modification. They could not yet vouch for a *complete cure!* On the fourteenth: "His excellency is doing well. Right now he is sleeping easily. Barring an unforeseen complication, it would appear that he will make a full recovery," Clotet wrote Prades. "The father physician says: 'Monseñor had me fooled!' " [8]

But that evening there were other worries. The prior had been notified the house was to be searched by the republicans the following morning. Somehow it had become known that Anthony Claret was at Fontfroide—where, according to Narbona's republican press, he was busily collecting arms for the *Carlistas!* "The rabble will be barred from the sickroom, of that I can assure you!" affirmed the priest-physician to Clotet and Puig. "I am responsible for the patient's life and I won't have him disturbed!"

"How do you propose to resist a mob?" asked Clotet.

"I tell you it won't get into that room while I live!"

Padre Clotet made a silent vow that he would be the shield not only of his beloved prelate but for the loyal doctor as well. Morning found him quite prepared to die in their defense, but the prior reassured him, "I somehow don't believe they will come. If the commissioner does, however, I shall be pleased, because he will see how false the whole story is." In any event, Clotet, who knew that Prades' subprefect had been importuning the congregation for his excellency's address, spent a nervous day.

Neither mob *nor* commissioner appeared on the fifteenth, but the sick man took a turn for the worse. The daily bulletin to Prades closed: "Once again it is feared that our venerable founder is approaching the end. He is supremely tranquil, never loosens his clasp on his crucifix, kisses it frequently. The paralysis appears to be affecting his tongue." [9]

The tension achieved its tautest on the sixteenth. Even if

he survived the day—and this would be beyond the natural order—he could not pull through the night, agreed the physicians. Strangely, he was perfectly lucid again; and his tongue greatly improved—or how might he have made one of the padres a full exposition on the Passion of Christ? "When asked what pains him, he says: *'niente'* or *'nada'* (nothing); how he feels; *'benissimo'* or *'muy bien'* (very well). . . . He is more bothered by thirst than anything, but we give him something to drink every few minutes. . . ." [10]

But as night came on, he fell into a stupor, followed by a fearsome attack. Appearances to the contrary, the doctors had known. With the approach of midnight, they spoke again—to suggest the lighting of the candles before the Virgin's image. All assembled to render their final service to the *living* prelate. Then: "Hardly had we commenced the psalm when his voice was leading ours! If we began a *Salve,* he finished it, and thus with all the rest of the prayers! Moreover, these terminated, he declared that he was hungry! Might he not have a bit of bread? Padre Francisco, with his characteristic gentleness, told him in Italian that bread wouldn't be good for him . . . that it were better just to keep thinking of Jesus Christ, the Heavenly Bread. To which his excellency replied: *'Benissimo. . . .* What else is there to say? *Che più?* What else?' Fearful that he was overexerting himself, I said:

" 'Monseñor, I am very tired. Don't you think you could rest a while now?'

" 'Fine,' he concurred.

" 'Good. Then we can both rest.'

"But he soon forgot *our* fatigue and commenced again, 'What more . . . ?' This morning the reverend father superior took advantage of his improvement again to administer the Most Holy Viaticum, in the presence of all the community."

On the eighteenth: "My invalid passed a most peaceful night, with no molestation but hiccoughs. . . . Contemplation of his state moves me deeply. We who knew the man active as fire now see him as the prone tree trunk, paralyzed. Memory, comprehension of the world are both gone; he has no remnant of interest for earth, or its inhabitants. . . . He hardly recognizes another phraseology than Heaven's: the psalms, Biblical expressions . . . and nevertheless, this man is *still* hated, still pursued. . . .

"*El Arzobispo* is a lamp gradually burning down; but God could refill this lamp. To me, his voice that used to be that of a prophet, seems, when he isn't in the throes of the fever, to be an angel's. . . . The doctor is trying to get him to eat, because he definitely is better." [11]

And so it went. The night of this "definitely better" day when they would have had him eat, the situation suddenly became acute. His agony was so intense and prolonged that the religious about him found it almost unbearable. And this time the doctors, having verified the beginning of internal decomposition, affirmed that death was a matter of minutes.

Hoping to ease him, they changed his bed linen and heard him say: "I am very sick." Belying the statement, he brightened and demanded energetically that Clotet and Puig join him in saying ejaculations. This went on so long that the former began to reel dizzily. Again he pleaded for rest, and this time really on his own behalf. Refreshed by a nap, he returned to the sufferer, noticed that now his hearing was so keen that "he mistook our lightest whispers between ourselves as addresses to him. 'Eh? What did you say?' . . . '*Merci*,' he said clearly when I gave him his water; and I replied, '*Monseigneur, a votre service.*'

By one A.M., however, his voice was again so thin we could scarcely hear it; and the fever seemed to be rising. . . . I gave him his crucifix, saying, '*Mi señor*, I have the pleasure to present the image of Jesús to your excellency's lips, for kissing.'

" *'Benissimo, benissimo. Adoramus Te Christe,'* he breathed.

. . . With this I thought inexorable death had finally fallen across his senses, but—the doctor took his pulse and said, 'He's better!'

"A few minutes after the bed had been changed again before noon, he asked if we had remembered to change his nightshirt.

" 'Everything, your excellency. Everything was changed.'

" *'Benissimo . . . benissimo,'* he responded. The poor little one!" [12]

The hours dragged on and on, long peaceful periods of prayer and ejaculations, broken every day or so by the attacks. He began to mix his languages indiscriminately without consciousness of doing so. What was the difference? He had preached in them all—such long sermons! In a strong, sonorous voice! The voice was gone, but not the languages, not the things his mind and heart and soul had mastered. . . .

During Padre Clotet's long night watch on the nineteenth he was startled by the patient's abrupt question, "And shall you go to the United States, then?"

Confused by the matter-of-fact manner in which the prelate put so seemingly incongruous a question, Clotet hesitated a moment before replying evasively, "On that I shall confer with the superior."

"*Benissimo* . . ." sighed the old one contentedly.

A bit later he raised his index finger and pointed toward the foot of the bed. The gesture was so deliberate and controlled that the watcher automatically turned to see who might have entered. But *he* saw nothing. Could this be related in some way to the surprising query? Impossible to know.

The twentieth passed without incident—no pain, delirium or agitation. An aged monk who, for days, had been offering his life for Anthony Claret's, was convinced and had half-persuaded several others that Our Lord had accepted this plan. Even the doctor again believed there was a chance for his life. And then when Clotet took over the midnight watch he heard about the latest fluctuation. The man he relieved told him the archbishop had suffered an hour of delirium during which he asked for his Missal and then—proceeded to celebrate Mass! Right now, however, he was sleeping naturally.

"At two o'clock he awakened and told me in Spanish that he thought a little chicken soup might do him good.

" 'Your excellency, it's the middle of the night, but as soon as Padre Amadeo gets up you shall have it.'

" '*Benissimo*. Let me sleep until then—that is the most important.' " [13]

A few hours later, after he had his broth, the prior asked Padre Clotet to relay a message to Xifré for him: "It would be wrong to abandon hope for the archbishop's life, even though we can't affirm that we shall save it." To this, the writer attached his own postscript: "At the moment his excellency is doing well. I forgot to say before that he had recovered movement of the left leg, and since then, the same is true of a part of the arm, that is, from elbow to shoulder." [14]

Of Xifré, who visited him for a third time on the twenty-first, one of the quiet days, the founder asked, "What are they doing at Prades?"

"At Prades, your excellency, they are offering prayers, many prayers that God may restore you to health, if it be His will."

What more did he need to know? His house was safe—unified in prayer, the all-important thing! From this moment the gradual sinking began. There would be no more little flare-ups of energy, no more petitions for a bit of bread or broth.

But even when a new, the final, stiffening had assailed his tongue, he continued to mutter ejaculations automatically.

"Your excellency has wished to die with Christ and you shall die with Him," encouraged the faithful Clotet.

The dull mumble from the bed lifted, cleared, became articulate: "Say it *again!*"

"You *shall* die with Him."

The agony had commenced, but Anthony Claret only grew calmer. Nineteen days of terrifying torture had not evoked a complaint, not a single outcry. Anything was endurable now and, in the ensuing three, he endured everything: the most excruciating, uninterrupted pain any of his attendants had ever witnessed or imagined. No instant of relief now in unconsciousness. No delirium. None doubted his mental clarity. Oh yes, he was truly the *unspared!* Why? The priest-physician would answer that for the anguished Clotet. "His excellency passed his purgatory *here.*"

On the twenty-third, he emitted an urgent, but unintelligible, sound. Clotet bent to him encouraging him to try again. What was it he wished? The wooden form whose stentorian breathing had been its only stirring in hours now awesomely elevated a hand, extended it, made the sign of benediction. His lips labored over three syllables.

"*Ay!* I understood! 'You wish absolution, *mi señor?*'

" '*Sí'*—on a hoarse exhalation.

" '*Muy bien,* your excellency. I shall give it this instant.' " [15]

When Padre Clotet had absolved him, there came a resurge of power on which he recommenced the ejaculations. He made the sign of the Cross. He gave his breast several blows of contrition. He kissed the crucifix they raised to his lips.

Through tears, not dimming but dazzling with reflected candle rays, the religious hovering about his bed saw this emptying of body, brain and heart in praise of his Lord. A terrible, a gloriously terrible night! The hours wore on. . . .

At four, Padre Clotet had to withdraw to say his Mass. When he returned he heard the monks' soft intoning as an angelic choir. Once, Anthony Claret gazed directly, deeply, into his eyes, and he was shaken by a conviction of recognition, of a final communication.

Now the bed was unnaturally still; from the one lingering upon it, from the *man* Claret there was nothing more to expect. Jaime Clotet, then, would say it for him—"Jesús . . ." he commenced.

". . . *Jesús, María y José, into thy hands I commend my spirit,*" it came, God be praised! in the full, round tones which rose—together with that spirit—at 8:45 on this morning of October 24, 1870.

Raphael

XX

THE SAINT

"WHAT MORE . . . ?" he had asked, over and over, while dying, as he had lived, with Christ.

"What more . . . ?" echoed the grieving Claretians when the French republicans denied their founder's burial with due episcopal honors in the monastery church! Would nothing less than posthumous persecution satisfy the picayune jealousy and malice of those now ruling the trio of European nations he had served so prodigiously? Still, it was inestimable consolation, the holy paradox whereby they could all— the Spain of his birth and heart; the Italy he had looked to for the authority he had so forcefully affirmed; the France to which he had twice fled in trust (now betrayed!)—be represented at his Funeral Mass. Frenchmen, Italians and Spaniards typifying the best of each would stand before his modest churchyard tomb. And they would be venerating him as a saint!

The prayer, tears and homage of such men had first transformed the death chamber into a chapel. Then, on the morning of October 26, they had borne his body, in solemn procession, to the church. Now it lay, serenely beautiful, upon its catafalque, every vestige of the protracted agony, of the emaciation that had fallen upon him at the Council, magically obliterated. "In all the twenty-one years I had known him, I never saw him look so well," noted Padre Clotet. "At death, his color had been ghastly, but it freshened at once and, before the interment, took on a living tint, a little dark as he had been in health." Moreover, the body had remained perfectly flexible for, at the end, it did escape one physical castigation—rigor mortis.

On the nights of the twenty-fourth and twenty-fifth there had been, for this southern mountain country, an exceptional celestial manifestation. The heavens had been brilliantly illuminated by the aurora borealis. Those who had loved Anthony Claret could not be dissuaded from their fancy that a radiantly smiling Heaven was celebrating his reception into glory!

During the Requiem Mass on the twenty-seventh, Clotet's description continues, "My attention was attracted by a little bird which had somehow gotten into the church and was leading, most harmoniously, the singing of the monks. . . . More unusual still, it kept silence while the celebrant or ministers sang. Padre Puig also heard it. I saw it flying about beneath the temple's Gothic arches all through the Mass, but this terminated, it disappeared . . . I wouldn't care to call this a miracle; but it was a thing that touched my heart." [1]

That day his vault in the cemetery wall was sealed with the plainest of slabs marked merely: "*A. M. C.*" (Later replaced by a marble piece inscribed: "Here rests the Most Illustrious and Most Reverend D. Antonio María Claret y Clará, Archbishop of Trajanópolis in infidel lands, native of Spain. Died at the Monastery of Fontfroide, France, October 24, 1870, at age sixty-two. '*I loved justice and loathed iniquity; for this, I died in exile.*' ")

To him alone had Spain refused the amnesty already applied to all its political dissenters, even those who had borne arms against the revolutionists; while their French counterparts would have snatched him from his death bed! But now a strange thing took place. Suddenly, for this poor man who had died in an isolated hiding place, separated from his congregation, deprived of the attendance of lifetime friends, the honors owing his high station, such an immense wave of veneration broke across precisely the countries which had rejected him and hunted him that, to some, it must have been decidedly terrifying. Elaborate processions, Masses, pomp, floral arches—in brief, splendor—was everywhere offered *"el apóstol de las Españas,"* as he was hailed on their streaming banners. Had these been followed only by the anathematized clergy and religious, they could have been suppressed. But the multitudes—the whole peoples—were also marching and praying, weeping and praising beneath them, in an ominous disregard for such thinking as characterized the Olózagas of their day. Alive, Anthony Claret had been the *políticos'* "game." Dead, he was altogether too formidable to handle!

A much greater phenomenon became known. In Gerona the officiating priest at his huge Funeral Mass had been rendered powerless to sing the passage: *"A porta inferi"* leading into the response: *"Erue, Domine, animam ejus."* ("From the gates of hell"—"Free, Lord, the soul of Thy Servant.") All recognized the significance of the impediment to prayer for Anthony Claret's soul, which was also encountered by many ecclesiastics including Cardinal Barili and Padre Clotet and even laymen. A lady noted for her goodness and piety was insisting that he had appeared to her to say: "Don't pray for me, my daughter. I am in Heaven and there is no need for it."

So thousands had soon redirected their prayers for him— *to* him! And already prelates, priests, the faithful of all classes were making their way to his humble tomb there to implore—and receive—the protection, benefits, or spiritual fortification they might most require.

Appropriately, the men of Fontfroide who had received him so warmly, nursed him so tenderly and, finally, buried him so reverently, were among the first to be granted his sign and promise. In 1875, France was overwhelmed by fearsome floods. With the abatement of the devastating torrent that had boiled down their canyon to wash out their cemetery, they were awed and rejoiced to see the wall enclosing Anthony Claret's crypt uniquely spared. There it rose in affecting solitude, all that remained of the ages old burying grounds. The monks accepted it as a pledge. They who had stood guard over his death could rely on his love to stand guard over their living. It proved, indeed, so, for, in 1886 when France's secular government ejected all the other religious communities, the forty of Fontfroide were, otherwise inexplicably, left quite undisturbed in their lofty retreat!

II

The justification that had surged from his death grew and flourished with startling rapidity. Within a year Bishop Francisco de Asís Aguilar had published his serene but devastating biographical vindication of his persecuted friend, a work which literally "took apart" the Olózagas, Funes, Lustonós, and other calumniators. Once and for all the politicians and the antagonistic elements of the Spanish press were silenced by the candor of this book. Padre Clotet's famed *Resumen* of the founder's career was also produced and fervently read by the public. Following the main text, this volume carried a series of testimonials headed by a letter from Pius IX, that were signed by: all the Spanish prelates, all parish priests of the dioceses of Tarragona, Segorbe and the Canary Islands, the majority of the pastors in whose

churches the missionary had preached. Soon Spain's highest
civil authorities were conceding that a "gesture of reparation
for the revolution's great injustice to Sr. Claret" was owing.

The Claretians, back in Spain again and already justifying
his predictions of their great expansion, most certainly concurred in this opinion! In 1887 they had launched the preliminary labors in the cause for Claret's beatification; and the
first *Información* [2] was carried to Rome by Xifré in December, 1890. The seals were broken on January 4, 1891, and
the colossal work of study, investigation and verification was
under way! The Supreme Pontiff, now Leo XIII, was hardly
surprised by the superlatives employed by Cardinal Ledo-
chowski and other Vatican dignitaries in referring to Claret's
record. His Holiness had been one of those who had heard
the unpretentious but most affecting "sermonette" delivered
by the feeble, brutally scarred little prelate before the Vatican Council.

Fontfroide grieved to relinquish the remains there cherished for twenty-seven years, but they belonged to the congregation and, yes, in spite of everything, to Spain—now raising an immense clamor for their return. On June 11, 1897,
his tomb was opened and the caskets extracted. The outer,
of timber, was in an advanced stage of decay, result of the
water which as evidenced by the sediment it contained, had,
in submerging the cemetery, invaded the crypt. Even the
zinc inner casket was badly perforated. This indicated there
could be small hope that the remains might be found in recognizable condition. Nevertheless—they were. ". . . the body
and facial features were perfectly preserved, the latter, however, a little wasted. The two Narbona doctors who examined the corpse verified the muscular intactment and, in the
abdomen, the tension or resistance that indicated the incor-
rupt state of the internal organs. All who witnessed the ex-

humation certified that the body gave off no noxious or disagreeable odor." ³

The precious remains of him who, as plain Padre Claret,
an itinerant preacher, had established his tiny congregation
at Vich forty-eight years before, were going home again—
over the frontier into Catalonia, on to Vich, to Merced, the
very first Claretian house—this time to stay. Some of those
forming the escort were second-generation Sons of the Immaculate Heart of Mary already at the height of their maturity! Others were the abbot of Fontfroide, a group of his
monks, and Perpignan's vicar general. The hearts of all of
them rejoiced in equal measure at the crowds which, along
the route, turned out to honor this triumphant homecoming.
At Gerona they saw the bishop, surrounded by the council
and a throng of the faithful, kneeling on the station platform
intoning the prayers for the dead. The parish priest and population of Granollers were doing the same. All the dignitaries
of Centellas and Baleña were on hand to honor the passage
of "the apostle of Catalonia."

The welcome of the populace of Vich was tremendous!
The levitical city he had loved so well, where he had studied
so hard, prayed so incessantly, been ordained a priest of
Christ and then consecrated His prelate, and where, yes, his
persecution had also commenced, had never been so mag-
nificently embellished as on this great evening (June 13,
1897). As the procession, headed by the bishops of Vich and
Segorbe and the abbot of Fontfroide in full episcopal regalia,
moved toward the cathedral, it passed between uninterrupted
lines of lavishly decorated balconies, beneath flamboyant
Arcos de Triunfo and the profusion of newly installed lan-
terns that made this night more brilliant than day. Every site
with which Anthony Claret had been identified in life had
been especially beautified.

The coffin was mounted on a majestic catafalque in the

center of the cathedral. The responses were sung to full orchestra accompaniment. Later, the catafalque was guarded all night in the lovely San Bernardo Calvó Chapel where great waves of humanity honored him until two A.M., cathedral closing time. The brilliant Requiem was sung by Bishop Aguilar at ten, followed by Bishop Morgades' stirring sermon on the glories of their humble brother prelate, and three consecutive Responses presided over by these two and the reverend abbot of Fontfroide, respectively. And then, at last, his congregation received Anthony Claret's earthly remains—at Merced!

III

The abundant first *Información* imposed a colossal labor which consumed nine years. Its study by the Congregation of Rites was commenced November 28, 1899; the approval ratified by Leo XIII, December 4 of the same year. The *Non Cultus* was confirmed the following July 8. The way was now clear for Postulator Jerónimo Batlló to advance with the apostolic processes. Without discussion the first, concerning the fame of sanctity and virtue, was unanimously approved by the Sacred Congregation, May 17, 1904. The second, proof of virtue in heroic degree, was confirmed by Pius XI, January 6, 1926. Now nothing remained to be verified excepting the miracles, and this was comparatively simple. Throughout a lifetime that had been one continuous prodigy his days had abounded in individual miracles, and ever since his death he had been showering them from Heaven upon the poor children of earth. Two of the first three submitted were accepted—and sufficed.

One had been worked in favor of Javiera Mestre Cornadó, a fifteen-year-old victim of smallpox, contracted at the end of May, 1897. On the seventh day of the affliction the girl was in wild delirium with a temperature registering 41° C.

and appeared to be doomed. Dr. Dionisio Soler Arrugaeta, who had been seeing her twice daily, advised the administration of the Sacraments. That night the young sufferer's mother and a friend, after praying fervently to Mary's Immaculate Heart, begged Anthony Claret's intercession as they applied his relic, a bit of silk, to various portions of Javiera's body. The girl was instantly restored to her senses. Within minutes the fever entirely abated and she fell into a natural sleep from which she did not awaken until nine the following morning. When Dr. Soler arrived for his first visit of the day he found that the eruptions which had been progressing toward fistulation the previous evening had completely disappeared! "This," he affirmed, "is not normal. What we have here is a miracle." It took place in the city of Lérida.

Sor Benigna Sibila Alsina's miracle is world known. The twenty-nine-year-old Philippine religious had fallen ill in November, 1926, of an exceedingly painful stomach ailment. She could eat or drink nothing that did not induce vomiting, and this soon caused acute anemia. When a succession of physicians failed to help her, she was sent to first one, then another of Spain's finest clinics for diagnoses and treatment by the country's outstanding specialists. The pyloric ulcer located by their X-rays resisted all dietary measures and medication. Her only relief from pitiable torture lay in morphine. The renowned Doctors García Die of Sarría and Pou Font of Palautordera concurred that the only hope lay in surgery. It was now May, 1930, and, after three and a half years of constantly increasing agony and discouragement, Sor Benigna was so exhausted and disillusioned that she not only refused to submit to the operation but, on May 11, even discarded her medicines. For her it must now be either a miracle or the mercy of death! The same day she commenced a Novena to Venerable Anthony Claret.

The little sister awakened the very next morning to realize

that her pain had vanished and had been replaced by an almost forgotten energy. Bedridden for months, she rose without difficulty and, from that day forward, ate her meals with relish and no ill effects whatsoever! Dr. García Die's next examination failed to detect *any* of her former chronic symptoms and the new X-rays verified the "definite and radical" disappearance of the ulcer!

Thus it was that, by the brief: *Tuto* (*de tuto procedi posse*—authorization is given to go ahead with everything) Antonio María Claret y Clará won his beatification, February 25, 1934. It was a magnificent ceremony attended by 50,000 of the world's Catholic faithful, including the ambassadors or ministers of fourteen European, six American, nations. Prince Jaime de Bourbon was there, claiming the privilege of his great-grandmother Isabel II: consolation from Anthony Claret's sanctity in a time of rejection. For once again Spain was in the midst of a republican era. Along with hundreds of devout men and women who, had things been otherwise, might one day have been his subjects, he rejoiced to witness the glorification of his ancestress'—and the nineteenth century's—greatest confessor.

On this great day, just before entering St. Peter's to kneel before Blessed Anthony Claret, His Holiness Pius XI told representatiives of the Missionary Sons of the Immaculate Heart of Mary: "We have a new *beato* . . . a figure truly great . . . an indefatigable apostle . . . and furthermore, a modern organizer. . . . He was *the* great precursor of today's Catholic action, particularly of the Catholic press whose immense value he had comprehended. In the cause of this splendid medium—the book, the periodical—he counted all his sacrifices very little. And moreover he was a most fecund writer. . . . His dedication to the diffusion of books, pamphlets and circulars was really extraordinary. . . . He desired to make the printed word available to one and all. . . ." [4]

Behind the Pontiff's fine tribute sang out the beautiful clamor of all the Vatican bells in honor of this latest of their founder's victories. Henceforth "one and all" could publicly pursue devotion to him, pray to him that this, and all his holy desires for men, might attain fulfillment!

IV

As they returned to their stations all across the world his Claretians may well have carried a premonition that they would soon be called upon to suffer the persecution Claret had known so well. His words should have partially prepared them. They could hardly have forgotten his "straight talk" on "the great wars and all their consequences," the Communism that would be the culmination of the "great judgments of God which are going to fall upon the world." Both these evils now certainly fell full force upon Spain. The frenzy of the Stalinist hordes, naïvely or cynically designated "the Spanish Loyalists" (whom some of *us* crossed the sea to help fight their Christian countrymen!) almost seemed to single out the Claretians for extinction. Hardly had they achieved the transference of the founder's remains from the Gospel side of Merced's main altar to the elegant new sepulcher above it when Spain's most recent civil war was upon them. There came the destruction of the temple, most of the congregation's records and relics, and, of course, the desecration of the wonderful new shrine. Blessedly, the fiendish attack did not accomplish the maximum injury it contemplated—the Reds' obliteration of the sacred remains—for, by some prevision granted his sons, their removal and concealment were attained just ahead of the hurricane. It was not the end. Came now the massacre of a substantial number of the brave missionaries, who were dropped into a common grave by Russian bullets! But was not the acquisition of so many ad-

vocates in Heaven compensation for the "irreparable loss"
sustained in "this catastrophe without precedent in our history"? [5] Now there were 275 Claretian martyrs [6] to the glory
of Mary, the Church of her Son, their *beato* and their nation; to fortify the inheritors who would forthwith send the
Claretian thunder prophesied in the *Apocalypse* reverberat-
ing around the earth!

They came to America in numbers, joining other Claretians who, since 1902, had been transferring to the United
States, these exiled sons of the blessed exile whose stiffening
lips had shaped the query so surprising to Padre Clotet: "And
shall you go to the United States?" In those last agonized moments something had "come" to him. Dates, eras, have no
meaning before eternity. And now, with the zeal for the
salvation of all men, with the industry and energy that characterized Anthony Claret and that, in a lesser degree, has
ever seemed to typify their race, the Spanish Claretians set
about their great works for the North American Catholics,
meanwhile opening their ranks to many of these. Like his,
too, was their charity for their persecutors, their faith that
their homeland would again be granted decent, God-revering
rulers. They refused to resent the ignorance that had impelled certain Americans to invoke the name of their own
great liberator in the cause of Spanish Communism. Knowing
too well that wrong has always been unleashed in the name,
and in the name only, of "liberty," they overlooked that
wrought by the "Abraham Lincoln Brigade." They were
missionaries; had come to renew Spain's first, incalculably
precious gift to this continent: the faith of Christ. And simultaneously, they labored with diligence for the final triumph
of the founder—canonization. . . .

How well they worked, in concert with their 4,000 brothers living in 240 religious houses in twenty-four countries,
searching out, investigating, documenting the prodigies

worked through Anthony Claret's intercession since his beatification, how well they prayed, is seen in the following communication which, from its opening month, made Holy Year, 1950, doubly glorious for all the Missionary Sons, for all the millions of *el beato's* devotees throughout the world:

Apostolic Delegation:

The Supreme Pontiff, Pius XII, has today, just sixteen years after beatification, decreed the glory of the saints for the great apostle of the nineteenth century, Anthony Claret. In that glory the new saint shines forth as a confessor and bishop, missionary and teacher, religious founder and beneficent leader in social work, first in Catalonia and the Canary Islands, then at Santiago in Cuba and in all of Spain, and through his religious children, the Missionary Sons of the Immaculate Heart of Mary and the Teaching Sisters of the Immaculate Conception, in the greater part of the world. These religious congregations are the fruit of his zeal for the salvation of souls, a zeal that was a fire of burning charity and that was transformed into a light illuminating minds and leading thousands upon thousands of erring souls back to Jesus Christ.

Characteristic of this saint was a mysterious supernatural light. This light is revealed abundantly in his one hundred and forty-four volumes written solely for the glory of God and love of neighbor, and also in his twenty-five thousand discourses extolling Christian virtues and the supreme truths of faith. Even during the celebration of Holy Mass that light often appeared visibly, as if it were a halo for the Lord Whom Anthony Claret carried and guarded in the tabernacle of his soul. It was his ardent wish to convert the entire world, and he was able to infuse the same thirst of charity for souls into his sons who today, numbering about four thousand, fruitfully toil in the apostolic ministry, in religious teaching and in the supervision of diocesan seminaries.

His Holiness, Pope Pius XII, in granting the honors of the altar to Claret, called him "one of the best fruits of the Divine Redemption," and Anthony Mary Claret was truly great as a missionary, catechist, educator and social benefactor, and above all else as a shining star of sanctity. The opposition and sufferings which he silently bore with heroic courage have made him even greater.

From this moment may our fervent prayers rise to Saint Anthony Mary Claret. Let us join in the prayerful auguries of Our Holy Father, Pope Pius XII, who in giving us this new saint, earnestly desires that he may continue from Heaven and through his children and devotees his magnificent work for the spiritual and social welfare of nations.

Finally on this occasion I am happy to express my felicitations to my many friends among the Missionary Sons of the Immaculate Heart of Mary, and to the members of the Claretian American Province, with cordial good wishes for their priestly ministry and for their works of religion and charity.

Amleto Giovanni Cicognani
Apostolic delegate to the
United States.

The great day was the seventh of May, month of Mary, of the Holy Year, 1950. It found St. Peter's crowded to its tremendous capacities by the tens of thousands privileged to combine the Holy Year pilgrimage to Rome and the exceptional blessing of attending the canonization ceremonies for the modest missionary who would henceforth be: *Saint Anthony Claret*. Among the great delegations from all parts of the world who poured into St. Peter's that day, how especially proud, happy, how supremely grateful must have been the one from his again Christian Spain! And among the thousands of princes, prelates, ecclesiastics and religious of the Church there assembled to honor him, how indescribably joyous, reinspired, and humbly grateful for their holy triumph the Claretians most surely were!

In the seven years since then the devotion to Saint Anthony Claret has enjoyed a huge expansion. This is not surprising. The saint who was and will ever be a corporal, as well as a spiritual, physician is now our patron against one of humanity's ugliest bodily afflictions: cancer. He is also, and eternally, our protector against those much more frightful ills: communistic godlessness and sin. For the greatly agitated, dreadful time in which we live—and shall die—the twentieth century, he is therefore the Saint of *Hope!*

Atheistic Communism

ST. Jude
please
help us to trust

NOTES

The quotations from Saint Anthony Claret found in the text but not listed in these notes are from his *Autobiography* (Claretian Major Seminary, Compton, California, 1945) unless otherwise identified.

CHAPTER III

1. Cristóbal Fernández, C.M.F., *El Beato Padre Antonio María Claret*, Editorial Coculsa, Madrid, 1941, Vol. I, p. 54.
2. Fernández, ibid. p. 64.

CHAPTER IV

1. In November, 1836, according to Fernández, *El Beato Padre Antonio María Claret* (p. 100), in refutation of claims that the assistant pastorship dated from his return to Sallent.
2. Both reproduced by Fernández, ibid. pp. 98-99.
3. Fernández, ibid. p. 98.
4. Later to become a Mercedarian.

CHAPTER V

1. My italics.
2. *Proceso informativo de Vich*, Section 80; *Proceso Apostólico de Vich*, Section 18.

CHAPTER VI

1. *Vida del Don Antonio María Claret*, Imprenta de Pascual Conesa, Madrid, Spain, 1872.
2. Ibid. pp. 62-63.

3. *Proceso Apostólico de Vich*, Sessions 127 and 140; *Proceso informativo de Vich*, Session 90; *Proceso Apostólico de Tarragona*, Session 33; *Proceso informativo de Tarragona*, Session 15; *Proceso informativo de Vich*, Session 26.

4. *Archivo Claretiano de Vich*, No. 409; *Proceso informativo de Barcelona*, Session 15. (P. Ventalló of the *Seminario Conciliar* and Claret's Latin teacher, Más y Artigas, were other witnesses.)

5. Letter, Soler to Masmitjá, Aug. 12, 1844, quoted by Fernández, pp. 194-195.

6. Ibid. p. 195.

CHAPTER VII

1. In Catalán: *Cami dret y segur por arribar al Cel;* in Spanish: *Camino Recto y Seguro para llegar al Cielo,* or *Camino Recto.*

2. Fernández, *El Beato Padre Antonio María Claret,* p. 170.

3. Quoted by Fernández, p. 206.

4. Ibid. p. 207.

5. Ibid. p. 298.

6. *Archivo Claretiano de Vich*, No. 663.

7. Fernández, ibid. pp. 208-209, based on: *Archivo Claretiano de Vich*, No. 2, 164, IX, 35; *Proceso informativo de Vich*, Sessions 52, 45, 89; *Proceso Apostólico de Tarragona*, Session 14; *Proceso Apostólico de Vich*, Session 13.

8. *Archivo Claretiano de Vich*, No. 410 and No. 2, 164, VIII, 74.

9. *Archivo Claretiano de Vich*, No. 2, 164, IV, 14.

10. Fernández, ibid. p. 249.

11. Opúsculos, I, 105.

12. *The Modern Apostle, Blessed Anthony M. Claret,* Claretian Missionaries, Dominguez Seminary, Compton, California, 1934, p. 4.

CHAPTER VIII

1. Quoted by Fernández, ibid. Bk. I, pp. 218-219, from Bertrans' *Petjades apostoliques del B. Claret en el bisbat de Solsone.*

2. Ibid. pp. 219-220.

3. *Proceso informativo de Vich*, Sessions 75, 76; *Proceso Apostólico de Vich*, Session 8; *Proceso informativo de Barcelona*, Session 10.

4. *Proceso informativo de Barcelona,* Session 10; *Proceso informativo de Vich,* Sessions 66, 67.

5. *Archivo Claretiano de Vich,* No. 694.

6. Later bishop of Seo de Urgel.

7. *Archivo Claretiano de Vich,* No. 650.

8. *Archivo Claretiano de Vich,* No. 497.

9. *Opúsculos,* I, 105.

CHAPTER IX

1. *Archivo Claretiano de Vich,* No. 685.

2. Quoted by Fernández, p. 449, who credits *El Católico,* August 11, 1848.

3. Ibid. p. 450, crediting *Iris de Paz,* 1925, p. 386.

4. *Proceso Apostólico de Vich,* Session 119; *Archivo Claretiano de Vich,* No. 692.

5. *Archivo Claretiano de Vich,* No. 566.

6. Editor of *Revista Católica,* later to become bishop of Barcelona.

CHAPTER X

1. Popularly known today as: The Claretian Missionaries.

2. Fernández, ibid. p. 532.

3. Whose fame for heroic virtue is being studied by the Church (Fernández, ibid. p. 537).

4. Ibid. p. 540.

5. Quoted by Fernández, ibid. p. 542.

6. Later to be bishop of Barcelona.

7. Claretian Missionaries, *The Modern Apostle, Blessed Anthony M. Claret,* p. 24.

8. Quoted by Fernández, ibid. pp. 561-562.

9. Quoted by Fernández, ibid. p. 564-565.

10. The Revolution of 1868.

11. *Proceso informativo de Barcelona,* Session 8; *Proceso informativo de Vich,* Sessions 65, 80; *Proceso Apostólico de Vich,* Sessions 31, 32, 142.

CHAPTER XI

1. Page 6; 925; 1850.
2. *Archivo Claretiano de Vich,* No. 1, 594.
3. Fernández, ibid. p. 610.
4. *Archivo Claretiano de Vich,* No. 2, 596.
5. Letter dated March 25, 1851. Quoted by Fernández, ibid. p. 623.
6. Fernández, ibid. p. 647.
7. Known today as Camagüey.

CHAPTER XII

1. January 6 (Epiphany).
2. Vilaró, quoted by Fernández, ibid. pp. 663-664.
3. Fernández' use of this term likely meant "separation" since Spain did not countenance legal divorce. (F.R.)
4. Which occurred the following September 27.
5. Quoted by Fernández, ibid. p. 675.
6. Ibid. p. 676.
7. Ibid. p. 711.
8. Ibid.
9. Letter to Padre Bres, September 3, 1862, quoted by Fernández, ibid. p. 715.
10. Ibid. Paraphrased from the *Autobiography.*
11. *Proceso informativo de Vich,* Session 35; *Proceso Apostólico de Tarragona,* Session 14.
12. Ibid.
13. Ibid.
14. Letter of December 23, 1852.
15. Letter to Padre Sala, November 4, 1852, quoted by Fernández, ibid. p. 723.

CHAPTER XIII

1. *Proceso Apostólico de Tarragona,* Session 12.
2. Francisco de Asís Aguilar, *Vida del Exmo. y Ilmo. Sr. Don Antonio María Claret,* p. 152.
3. *Proceso Apostólico de Vich,* Session 201.

4. Letter to Padre Barjáu, September 4, 1853.
5. Quoted by Fernández, ibid. pp. 826-827; by Aguilar, ibid. pp. 152-153.
6. August 18, 1851.
7. August 5, 1854.
8. Quoted by Fernández, ibid. pp. 838-839.
9. Circular of May 27, 1851.
10. To Padre Bres.
11. Quoted by Fernández, ibid. pp. 769-770.
12. Quoted by Fernández, ibid. p. 686.
13. Pius IX to Claret, December 27, 1854, quoted by Fernández, ibid. p. 689.

CHAPTER XIV

1. Related by De la Pezuela, *Archivo Claretiano de Vich*, No. 745.
2. *Proceso informativo de Vich*, Session 35.
3. *Delicias del Campo*, Claret, pp. 8-9.
4. Fernández, ibid. p. 735.
5. Fernández, ibid. p. 742.
6. August 17, 1856.
7. *Proceso informativo de Vich*, Session 32.
8. *Proceso Apostólico de Vich*, Session 24; *El Redactor*, November 9, 1856.
9. *Archivo Claretiano de Vich*, No. 379.
10. Ibid. No. 380.
11. *El Redactor*, February 10, 1856.
12. February 6, 1856.
13. *Proceso Apostólico de Tarragona*, Section VIII; *Autobiography*, p. 190.

CHAPTER XV

1. Fernández, ibid. p. 970.
2. The letter that was, however, dated May 8, 1856.
3. *El Redactor*, April 4, 1856.
4. Ibid. March 16, 1856.

5. Ibid.

6. Curríus, *Epistolaria,* Folio 61.

7. Full letter quoted by Fernández, ibid. pp. 985-987.

8. Aguilar, *Vida del Exmo. y Ilmo. Sr. D. Antonia María Claret,* p. 240.

9. Quoted in *Tesoro de Barriosuso,* No. 501.

10. By Claret, according to Bishop Aguilar, p. 242.

11. Thus, in a way, his recall had arisen from the death of Toledo's prelate, Isabel's previous confessor.

12. Quoted by Fernández, ibid. p. 1,033.

13. May 31, 1857.

14. *Archivo Claretiano de Vich,* unclassified.

15. *Tesoro de Barriosuso,* No. 202, III, p. 652.

16. Quoted by Fernández, ibid. p. 1,042.

17. St. Gregory the Great established the custom which continued to name successors to prelates dispossessed of their jurisdictions through pagan or heretical conquests, even though the titular bishops and archbishops could not assume practical rule of the dioceses to which they were elected. Trajanópolis was an ancient Thracian see.

18. Quoted by Aguilar, ibid. p. (erroneously numbered) 462, corresponding to 262, from *Revista Católica,* June, 1860.

CHAPTER XVI

1. San Lorenzo del Escorial (erected 1563-1584) comprised of a huge church, monastery, palace, and the royal mausoleum, rises on a plain twenty-seven miles northwest of Madrid.

2. Quoted by Aguilar, ibid. p. 266 (erroneously numbered 466).

3. Aguilar, ibid, p. 269 (erroneously numbered 469).

4. Ibid. p. 272 (erroneously numbered 472), and p. 273.

5. Founded in 1616 and largely supported by the Spanish prelates and universities.

6. Chap. VIII, v. 13.

7. Chap. X, vs. 1-3.

8. *Proceso informativo de Vich,* Session 126.

CHAPTER XVII

1. For the complete record, see: Fernández' *El Beato P. Antonio María Claret*, Editorial Coculsa, Madrid, 1941, Vol. I, 994 ff.
2. Ibid. Vol. II, pp. 71-84.
3. Quoted by Fernández, ibid. Vol. II, p. 624.
4. Quoted by Fernández, ibid. Vol. II, p. 631.
5. Quoted, ibid. p. 632.
6. Quoted, ibid. p. 633.

CHAPTER XVIII

1. Fernández, ibid. Vol. II, p. 658.
2. Ibid. p. 677.
3. Ibid. p. 678, quoted from letter of March 15, 1860.
4. Quoted, ibid. p. 680.
5. *Proceso informativo de Tarragona*, Session 8.
6. *Proceso Apostólico de Vich*, Session 205.
7. Quoted by Fernández, ibid. Vol. II, p. 781.
8. Aguilar, ibid. p. 388.
9. Letter to Jacoba Balzola, October 10, 1868. Quoted by Fernández, ibid. Vol. II, p. 798.
10. Letter to Curríus, December 9, 1868.
11. March 28, 1869. Quoted by Fernández, ibid. Vol. II, p. 801.
12. Letter to Padre Carmelo, November 18, 1868.
13. Letter to María Gascué Balzola, November 8, 1868.
14. *Triduo de María Santísima en desagravio* and a life of San Pedro Nolasco were written in Rome.
15. To Curríus, October, 1869.
16. Letter to Madre París, July 21, 1869.
17. Letter to Xifré, July 21, 1869.
18. In slightly varied wording to Curríus and Xifré, June 1, 1869, and July, 1869, respectively.
19. Quoted by Fernández, ibid. Vol. II, pp. 836-837.

CHAPTER XIX

1. *Archivo Claretiano de Vich*, No. 857.
2. *Archivo Claretiano de Vich*, No. 812.
3. *Archivo Claretiano de Vich*, No. 855.
4. *Proceso de Carcassonne*, Session 4.
5. *Proceso de Carcassonne*, Session 3.
6. *Archivo Claretiano de Vich*, No. 860.
7. Ibid. No. 826.
8. *Archivo Claretiano de Vich*, No. 827.
9. *Archivo Claretiano de Vich*, No. 829.
10. Ibid. No. 830.
11. Ibid. No. 832.
12. *Archivo Claretiano de Vich*, No. 834.
13. Ibid. No. 837.
14. Ibid.
15. Ibid. No. 880.

CHAPTER XX

1. *Archivo Claretiano de Vich*, No. 844.
2. Consisting of six sections executed in Tarragona, Madrid, Barcelona, Lérida, and Carcassonne (France) besides Vich, totaling 143 Sessions which filled two huge volumes (1,994 folios).
3. Aguilar, *Historia de la Congregación*, II, p. 264.
4. Quoted by Fernández, ibid. II, pp. 919-920.
5. Fernández, ibid. Vol. II, p. 895.
6. 1950.

SELECTED BIBLIOGRAPHY

Aguilar, Francisco de Asís. *Vida del Exmo. y Ilmo. Sr. D. Antonio María Claret.* Madrid; Imprenta de Pascual Conesa, 1872.

Aguilar, Mariano, C.M.F. *Vida del Padre Claret.* 2 Volumes. Madrid; Establecimiento Tipográfico de San Francisco de Sales, 1894.

Claret, Antonio María. *Autobiografía.* Madrid; Gráfica Unión, 1951.

———— English Translation (by Louis Joseph Moore, C.M.F.). Compton, California; Claretian Major Seminary, 1945.

Claretian Missionaries. *The Modern Apostle, Blessed Anthony M. Claret.* Compton, California; Dominguez Seminary, 1934.

Echevarría, Juan, C.M.F., Ph.D., *Reminiscences of Blessed Anthony Mary Claret, Archbishop and Founder.* Compton, California; Claretian Major Seminary, 1938.

Fernández, Cristóbal, C.M.F. *El Beato Padre Antonio María Claret.* 2 Volumes. Madrid; Editorial Coculsa, 1941.

Puigdessens, José, C.M.F. *Espíritu del Vble. Antonio María Claret.* Madrid; Editorial del Corazón de María. Printed by: Tipografía Claret, Barcelona, Spain, 1928.

Sargent, Daniel. *The Assignments of Antonio Claret.* New York; The Declan X. McMullen Company, 1948.

Sugranes, Eugene, C.M.F. *Venerable Anthony M. Claret.* San Antonio, Texas; Lodovic Press, 1921.

NOTE: Apostolic and Informative Process references follow the documentation of Cristóbal Fernández, C.M.F. (F.R.)

INDEX